The Jews Under Roman Rule

Rome's Conquest, Occupation and Wars in Israel and Judea; How it Changed the Jewish Temple and Law

By William Douglas Morrison

PANTIANOS
CLASSICS

Published by Pantianos Classics

ISBN-13: 978-1-78987-212-5

First published in 1890

The Golden Candlestick from Titus's Arch at Rome

Contents

List of Authorities

The following are the principal sources of this history. References to modern literature will be found in the notes:

Apocalypse of Baruch, The. See Ceriani, *Monumenta sacra et profana*, Milan, 1866; Fritzsche, "Libri apocryphi Vet. Test. grace," 1871; Lagarde, "Libri Vet. Test. apocryphi syriace," 1861.

Apocrypha, The. See "The Speaker's Commentary," and the Commentaries of Grimm, Fritzsche, Keil, and Reuss.

Appian. See "Appiani Romanorum historiarum quae super-stint," ed. Mendelssohn, 1879.

Assumption of Moses, The. See Ceriani, "Monumenta"; Hilgenfeld, "Novum Test. extra canonem receptum," 1876; "Messias Judaeorum," 1869.

"Corpus Inscriptionum Hebraicarum," Chwolson, Petersburg, 1882.

"Dio Cassius," ed. Dindorf, Leipzig, 1863.

"Diodorus Siculus," hook xxix., ed. Dindorf, Paris, 1855.

Enoch. Laurence, "The Book of Enoch," Oxford, 1821; "Libri Enoch versio Aethiopica," ed. Laurence, 1838; Dillmann, "Das Buch Henoch iibersetzt," Leipzig, 1853; Schodde, The Book of Enoch," Andover, 1882.

Ezra, The Fourth Book of. Hilgenfeld, Messias Judaorum"; Fritzsche, "Libri apocryphi Vet. Test.," Leipzig, 1871; Bensly, "The Missing Fragment," Cambridge, 1875.

Flavius Josephus," ed. Havercamp, 1726; Dindorf, 1845; Niese, 1885.

"Fragmenta Historicorum Graecorum," iii., C. Muller.

Jubilees, The Book of. Ceriani, "Monumenta sacra et profana," i. 1861.

Mischna, The. "Mischna sive totius Hebrmorum juris, rituum antiquitatum ac legum oralium systema cum clarissimorum Rabbinorum Maimonidis et Bartenorm commentariis integris," &c. G. Surenhusius, Amsterdam, 1698.

"Monumentum Ancyranum." Mommsen, "Res gestm divi Augusti," 1883.

Philo," ed. Mangey, London, 1742.

Plutarch's Lives."

Polybius, "Hist.," xxvi.-xl.

"Reliquiae Sacrae," Routh.

Sibylline Books, The. "Oracula Sibyllina" curarite, C. Alexandre, Paris, 1869; "Oracula Sibyllina," J. H. Friedlieb, Lipsiae, 1852.

Strabo, "Geography," xvi.

Suetonius, "Lives of the Caesars."

Tacitus, "Annals and Histories."

Targums, The. Etheridge, "The Targums of Onkelos and Jonathan," London, 1862.

Testament of the Twelve Patriarchs. Testamenta XI I. Patriarcharum," ed. Sinker, Cambridge, 1869; Appendix, 1879.

Preface

The epoch of which this volume professes to treat embraces a period of about three hundred years (B.C. 164 to A.D. 135), and has an intimate bearing on one of the most momentous turning-points in the history of the world. The first half of this period is almost co-incident with the formation of the great confederation of Mediterranean states under the supremacy of Rome—a confederation which constituted the most important external preparation for the success of Christianity; the second half is co-incident with the birth development and primitive organization of the Christian faith. These are events which gave a new direction to the history of humanity in the West; they are the starting-points of a fresh era in the life of the world; unlike some of the records of antiquity, an account of them is not merely a revelation of what has transpired in the past; at the present moment they are still exercising an immense influence on the deepest sentiments of mankind.

In the first part of this work I have given an account of the relations which existed between the Jews—the people to whom Christianity was primarily addressed, and the Romans the people who held together, under one common dominion, the various nationalities through which the Christian faith was destined to spread. In the execution of this task I have not carried the narrative beyond the final destruction of the remnants of the Jewish state under the Emperor Hadrian. After this date an entirely new chapter in Jewish life begins. Henceforth the Jews ceased to be a nation, and again became what they have since remained, simply a religious community. The hope of being able to gratify their national aspirations by force of arms was gradually relinquished. Withdrawing from the broad current of the world's political activities, they began the construction of another Sacred Book, and committed to writing the immense mass of oral laws and traditions that had been accumulating for centuries in the schools of the scribes. The gigantic results of these peaceful labours was the Talmud. This was a form of activity which did not bring the Jews into collision with the civil power, and accordingly the attitude of the Romans towards them, in the period subsequent to the reign of Hadrian, underwent comparatively little change, and calls for little comment.

The narrative part of this work opens with the first indications of Roman contact with the Jews. At this time Roman and Jewish policy was dictated by similar considerations. Both peoples were bent on crippling the power of Syria, and when the Jews, under the Maccabees, revolted against the enfeebled successors of Alexander, the Romans encouraged the insurgents and willingly accepted their alliance. For many years after the Jews had successfully asserted their claim to independence, the Romans continued to befriend them. But when the authority of the Senate was overthrown, and supreme power in the commonwealth fell into the hands of military chiefs, a change in Roman foreign policy was one of the first effects of this revolution. While the oligarchy in the Senate was supreme it was not a part of Roman policy to extend the frontiers of the republic so as to include the great Hellenic communities of Egypt and Western Asia. The senators dreaded the results of Greek influence on Roman life; but their successors, the military leaders, were hampered by no such fears. The era of conquest was renewed, and, under the auspices of Pompey, the western portion of the Syrian monarchy (of which Palestine formed a part) was brought within the jurisdiction of Rome. For several years after this event the policy of the Romans towards the Jews, consisted in administering the internal affairs of Palestine through the intermediary of vassal princes. But this method was gradually abandoned; it was not sufficiently favourable to the process of consolidating the empire, which was one of the chief objects of imperial solicitude. Accordingly, soon after Herod the Great's death, the two most important portions of the Holy Land—Judaea and Samaria were placed under the control of a Roman procurator.

With the exception of one short interval the rule of the procurators lasted till the destruction of the Jewish state. The manner in which these officials administered public affairs was sometimes highly exasperating, but, on the whole, the direct rule of Rome was less inimical to local liberty than any preceding system of government. The Roman method of collecting taxation was undoubtedly defective, and easily lent itself to purposes of extortion; still it is very questionable if the Syrian and Maccabaean methods, under which the Jews had previously lived, were one whit better. The Roman emperors freely recognized the evils which often disgraced the collection of the revenue, and the reason why such a system continued to exist was because a more enlightened one had not then been devised. The Jews were not the only sufferers from it; it was in operation in every province of the empire.

Roman rule, as we shall see, with all its imperfections conferred many inestimable advantages on the Jews. The factions into which Jewish society was divided when the Romans took possession of Palestine, had reduced the country to a deplorable state of anarchy; it was the strong hand of Rome which parted the embittered combatants and inaugurated a new epoch of order, security, and peace. The absorption of Jewish territory into the vast organism of the Roman Empire opened up more ample fields for Jewish enterprize, and enabled the Jewish trader to transport his wares in security over wider portions of the globe. The Caesars also granted the Jews many privileges and immunities which provincials in other parts of the empire did not enjoy; in fact, their position under Rome was, in many respects, more advantageous than it had been during any previous period of their history.

Unfortunately for the Jews the religious ideas, which had been fermenting in the race for centuries, began to assume a political form under Roman rule. While the Syrians were masters of Judaea the population had no religious scruples about the payment of tribute, or the pollution by heathen conquerors of the sacred soil of Palestine. But under Roman supremacy a new development took place in Jewish theology, and, at the commencement of the Christian era, almost the entire population of Judaea had come to believe that it was an act of impiety towards Israel's God to pay taxes to Rome. This belief took a practical form in the revolt of the Zealots. The revolt was suppressed, but the influence of this party, whose watchword was "No king but God," continued to increase till it culminated in the great uprising which ended in the destruction of Jerusalem. Even after this catastrophe the flame of Jewish fanaticism was only temporarily extinguished; it burst out afresh with uncontrollable fury both in Judaea and among the Dispersion; and the Emperors Trajan and Hadrian had to adopt the most sanguinary measures before it finally succumbed.

The first part of this volume is accordingly intended to show that the repeated efforts of the Jews to overthrow Roman rule did not arise so much from the oppressiveness of imperial administration as from the growing supremacy of a new order of religious ideas among the Jews.

The second part deals principally with the internal structure of Jewish society till the downfall of Jerusalem. The civil and religious functions of the Sanhedrin are set forth; as also the sacrificial system of worship at the Temple, the revenues and duties of the priesthood, the relations between the Temple and its unconscious rival the Synagogue. The synagogue introduces us to the scribes—a body of men whose influence on Jewish life at this period can hardly be over-estimated. The scribes were not only the interpreters of Law and Tradition, they were frequently its creators, and always its disseminators among the masses of the community. The Pharisees, as we shall see, were the disciples of the scribes; while their opponents, the Sadducees, will be shown to have been primarily and essentially a political party. The friction between these two parties was originally of a political character, and the line of division between them in Roman times, on certain points of law, ritual, and theology, was only the indistinct remains of the wide gulf which had separated them when Judaea was mistress of her own destinies. The Essenes, a peculiar outgrowth of Jewish life, present many points of contact with the Pharisees. In fact, the essence of their system consisted in pushing the principles of the Pharisees, concerning ceremonial purity, to their logical conclusions. In order effectually to avoid the risk of becoming unclean, the Essenes ultimately abandoned human society altogether and formed communities of their own. I have described their life, habits, practices, and beliefs, as well as the relation in which they stood to Judaism and Christianity.

Having sketched the nature and constitution of Jewish parties, I next proceed to give an account of the different races which composed the population of Palestine. I have pointed out that the people who inhabited this portion of the Roman Empire were not a nation, and were not held together by any of those ties of race, religion, or common traditions, which constitute the strongest bonds of nationality. They were merely an assortment of peoples settled together on the same soil; they had never amalgamated into a homogeneous whole; and Palestine, in Roman times, is nothing more than a geographical expression. In no part of Palestine, except Judaea, was the population purely Jewish; in Samaria, Galilee, and Peraea, as well as along the Mediterranean coast, there was a mixed population of Jews, Syrians, and Greeks; in some districts, and especially in several of the large cities, the Gentile element, distinctly preponderated over the Jewish. The Messianic hope was of course confined to Jewish circles; in the chapter devoted to the subject, I have pointed out the nature, scope, and influence of this momentous expectation.

In this work attention has also been called to the life of the Jews outside Palestine. The confined area of the Holy Land did not offer a large enough field for the energy and enterprise which animated the race. Some of the Jews were, it is true, on different occasions forcibly deported from their native home, but it is probable that the majority left of their own free choice. At the commencement of the Christian era the Jewish immigration, especially in the eastern provinces of the Roman Empire, had assumed such proportions that the communities of Jews abroad surpassed their co-religionists at home in numbers, influence, and wealth. I have described the position of these communities before the law of Rome, the privileges they enjoyed, the manner in which they were organized, and their relation to the parent community at Jerusalem. I have shown the power which Gentile ideas had upon these communities of the Dispersion; how Greek thought subverted many of the fundamental conceptions of Judaism; how the Jews succumbed before it by assuming that Hellenic wisdom had originally sprung from themselves; and how, finally, the original meaning of the Old Testament Scriptures was exploded by an allegorical method of interpretation which was intended to bring them into harmony with the prevailing principles of Greek philosophy. Such a state of things, strange to say, existed side by side with an ardent zeal for the propagation of Judaism. The manner in which this remarkable propaganda was conducted, consisted in placing Hebrew sentiments in the mouths of the heroes, sages, philosophers, and mythical personages of heathen antiquity. These efforts were attended with considerable success, and in the first century of the present era the Roman Empire contained a great number of converts to Judaism. But Judaism, even in its Hellenic form, still retained its national character—it never permitted the convert to stand exactly upon the same level as the born Jew—Judaism, in fact, was unable to satisfy the cravings of the human conscience for religious equality, and it will be shown that most of its converts, as well as many of the Hellenic Jews, ultimately found a refuge in the universalistic principles of Christianity.

The rise of Christianity falls within the period to which this volume is devoted. But as an adequate account of so momentous an event would transcend the limits assigned to the Series, I have deemed it better to confine myself to an historical description of the institutions in existence among the Jews at the period when Christianity arose. A work of this nature will serve the purpose of shedding more light upon the Christian documents handed down to us in the New Testament, and will also assist us in forming a more accurate estimate of primitive and apostolic Christianity. It is impossible to understand the historic and doctrinal contents of the New Testament writings, without some knowledge of the times in which these writings originated. These times have passed away with the downfall of ancient civilization; we are now living in another world; we are surrounded by a new order of ideas and institutions; the contents of the New Testament are a product of antiquity; to be fully comprehended they must be placed in their original historic framework, and looked at in the light of the age which called them forth. This indispensable framework the present volume endeavours to supply. It is the first English book, so far as I am aware, which is exclusively occupied with this period; the *Story of the Jews*, in the same Series, deals in general outline with the entire history of the race.

Besides making a study of the original sources in the preparation of the present work, I have also availed myself of the most recent investigations connected with this department of historical research. In the domain of Talmudic literature I must express my obligations to the works of Surenhusius, Lightfoot, Derenbourg, Weber, Wunsche, and Hamburger. Niese's new critical edition of Josephus, now in course of publication, is still too incomplete to be of much service for our period. In verifying references and revising the proofs, I have been much indebted to Mr. J. Morrison.

W. D. Morrison.
Wandsworth Common, *London* 1890

Roman Policy Before the Conquest - B.C. 164-65

The Romans first entered into political relations with the Jews in the course of the second century before Christ. At this period the Romans had risen to a position of undisputed supremacy among the nations of antiquity. The power of Carthage was shattered at the battle of Zama (BC. 201); the once formidable kingdom of Macedonia was on the eve of becoming a Roman province; and the Syrian monarchy, after the defeat of King Antiochus at Magnesia (B.C. 190), had to accept such hard conditions of peace as reduced this great monarchy to the rank of a vassal state. In political sagacity, as well as in warlike qualities, the Roman people at this epoch were without rivals, and Roman power extended far beyond Roman arms. From the Pillars of Hercules in the west to the banks of the Orontes in the east Roman influence was supreme and the word of Rome was law. The might and valour of the Romans, as well as their policy and patience, had become known among the Jews, and one Jewish writer speaks of them as a people who could make and unmake kings at their will.

Very different was the position occupied by the inhabitants of Palestine. The captives who sat and wept by the waters of Babylon did not become a free people when the more ardent among them were permitted to return to their native land. The little community of Jews which settled in Jerusalem and restored the temple of their fathers still continued under the dominion of the Persians, and on the overthrow of the Persian monarchy by Alexander the Great, the Jews of Palestine simply experienced a change of masters (B.C. 332). After Alexander's death his inheritance was divided between the two Greek lines of kings which arose in Egypt and Syria, and Judaea was sometimes in possession of the one line and sometimes of the other, according to the varying fortune of diplomacy and war. During the whole of this period the Jews had no thought of asserting their independence. They were perfectly contented to remain in a state of political vassalage so long as they were permitted to enjoy religious liberty. After the exile the Jews had ceased to be a nation, and had become a church. It was not a common country, but a common faith, which united them. Patriotism did not extend beyond the feeling that the soil of Palestine was holy ground, which ought only to be inhabited by the chosen people of God.

Sometime before the Romans actually came into contact with this religious community the principles of Roman policy profoundly affected the position of the Jews. In the second century before Christ Palestine, after many struggles, finally became a part of the Syrian monarchy. Now, it had become a settled purpose with the Romans to weaken and hamper this monarchy, and to prevent its recovery from the defeat which the Roman army had inflicted at Magnesia on the Syrian king (B.C. 190). A striking instance of this policy is seen in the attitude which the Romans took up towards Antiochus Epiphanes, king of Syria, when he was on the point of bringing an arduous campaign against Egypt to a successful close. The king was besieging Alexandria, when a Roman envoy appeared in his camp and bluntly ordered him to retreat. Antiochus hesitated, and asked for time to consider this peremptory demand. But the envoy immediately drew a circle in the sand around the king, and said, "Before you leave this circle the Senate must have an answer." To defy the imperious messenger was hopeless; Antiochus reluctantly abandoned his enterprise and returned home (B.C. 168). Before he could possibly meet the Romans on equal terms, the king saw that it was necessary to weld the different nationalities of which his empire was composed into a homogeneous people. The only way of accomplishing this object was to induce his subjects to adopt a common form of faith He accordingly issued an edict to that effect a step which immediately led him into collision with the Jews. Syrian emissaries were sent into Judaea to abolish Judaism and establish the worship of Olympian Zeus. The abomination of desolation was set up in the Temple; the Sacred Scriptures were burnt; the practice of circumcision was forbidden on pain of death, and all the horrors of a religious persecution descended on the land (B.C. 168).

Persecution did not produce the results which the despot had anticipated. For some time the people did not pass beyond the bounds of passive resistance. At length the spirit of the community began to rise against a state of things which was making life intolerable, and it ultimately found public expression in the daring conduct of an aged priest named Mattathias. This man belonged to a family of distinction, and occupied a prominent position in the town of Modein, situated westward of Jerusalem. One day he was called upon by a royal official to use his influence in favour of the establishment of heathenism in the town. But the old man had for some time beheld with growing indignation the persecution which was being inflicted on his co-religionists. He not only refused the Syrian officer all assistance, but slew him while he was making preparations for a heathen sacrifice.

The insurrection of the Jews had virtually begun (B.C. 167). Mattathias and his sons fled to the hill country of Judaea, and were soon joined by others who had caught the spirit of revolt. Mattathias died in the following year, but he left five heroic sons to carry on the contest. His third son Judas, who received the name of Maccabaeus, was selected by the insurgents to succeed his father (B.C. 166-161). Under Judas the revolt assumed larger proportions, and in a short time he was able to meet and defeat the Syrians in the open field. The situation which the Romans had created in Syria was favourable to the Jewish cause. In order to find money to pay the tribute imposed by Rome upon his house, Antiochus had to undertake an expedition into the Far East, which depleted Syria of a large number of troops. During the king's absence the government of the country was entrusted to a high functionary named Lysias. Lysias took a serious view of the rebellion in Judaea, and dispatched a force under the command of three generals to suppress it. But this army met with alarming reverses at the hands of Judas, and Lysias was obliged to go to Palestine in person to conduct the campaign. Meanwhile Antiochus had been apprised of the disasters which had befallen his captains, and was hastening homewards to assume the supreme direction of affairs, when death put a termination to his career (B.C. 164). The pressure of Roman policy upon Antiochus was the indirect cause of the Jewish revolt, and the immediate cause of the king's inability to suppress it.

After the death of Antiochus, the distracted state of Syria and the struggles of rival pretenders for the crown strengthened the position of the Jewish patriots. Antiochus V., son of the late king, was only nine years old when he began to reign (B.C. 164). His father had appointed a courtier named Philip regent during his son's minority. But this arrangement did not satisfy Lysias, who had the young king in his custody, and who was carrying on the campaign in Palestine when the news of his supersession by Philip arrived. Lysias immediately left off the contest with Judas, and devoted his energies to the task of resisting Philip's claims. At this juncture, if any historic value can be attached to a statement in the Second Book of the Maccabees, two Roman envoys, Quintus Memmius and Titus Manlius, who were probably on their way from Alexandria to Antioch, offered to take charge of Jewish interests at the Syrian capital. Peace is said to have been the outcome of their efforts (B.C. 162). But it was a peace which did not endure. In the following year the Syrian king once more invaded Palestine at the head of a great army, and, in spite of the strenuous opposition of Judas, laid siege to the Holy City. Famine soon reduced the garrison to the last extremities, and their fate would have been a hard one had not the disordered condition of Syria compelled the besiegers to accept honourable terms. Whilst the siege was in progress news came to the Syrian camp that Philip had put himself at the head of a large army, with the intention of enforcing his claims to the regency. No time was to be lost, and the king, acting on the advice of Lysias, accorded the Jews religious liberty. Jerusalem capitulated; and the same order of things was established as had existed previous to the insurrection.

Soon after these events Antiochus V. was dethroned and executed by his relative, Demetrius I. In Judea the new monarch allowed the people to retain the religious liberties granted them by his predecessor, and had he exercised more judgment in the selection of a High Priest, it would have been impossible for Judas to renew the struggle against Syria with any prospect of success. The Assidans or Pious Ones, who afterwards developed into the party known as the Pharisees, and who, while their religion was at stake, were devoted followers of Judas, were satisfied with the attainment of religious freedom. But Judas and his friends, who formed the party which afterwards became the Sadducees, considered the sacrifices that the people had already made created a new situation, and were unwilling to relax their efforts till the country was completely independent. The Assidaeans, consisting of the scribes and the bulk of the population, accepted Alcimus, the High Priest whom Demetrius had appointed, and were disposed for peace. But the senseless barbarities of Alcimus threw the Assidaeans once more into the arms of the war party, and the struggle began afresh. The High Priest was obliged to flee from Jerusalem; Demetrius sent an army to reinstate him, but Judas defeated the Syrian forces, and the Jews enjoyed a short period of repose.

Nevertheless, Judas was well aware that Demetrius would not patiently endure the discomfiture of his generals, and that in a prolonged conflict the small community of Jews would eventually be overcome. He accordingly considered it expedient to seek assistance from the Romans; and two Jewish delegates, Eupolemos and Jason, were sent to Italy to form an alliance with Rome. The Senate, which never neglected an opportunity of crippling the Syrian monarchy, accorded a favourable reception to the Jewish envoys, and acknowledged the independence of their country. It was clearly in the interests of Rome that an independent nation should separate the Syrian and Egyptian monarchies, and form a barrier to any union of their forces hostile to the Republic. While these negotiations were taking place the Syrian army again invaded Palestine. Judas went forth to meet them, and, after a desperate conflict, was defeated and slain (B.C. 161). The death of their leader shattered the party of freedom, and the Romans, probably because they saw no distinct centre of authority left standing in the country, ignored the treaty they had just made with the Jewish envoys, and left Judaea to its fate.

It was not by direct intervention that the Romans helped the Jews forward on the path of independence; it was by the disintegrating action of Roman policy on the kingdom of Syria. The Jewish leaders did not fail to take advantage of the opportunities which were thus afforded them. About nine years after the death of Judas Maccabaeus, the Romans started a new pretender to the Syrian crown in the person of Alexander Balas, a young man of unknown origin (B.C. 152). Supported by the allies of Rome, Balm was able to take the field against Demetrius, who became alarmed at the threatening aspect of affairs. Jonathan, a brother of Judas, was then at the head of the Jewish patriots (B.C. 161-142), and Demetrius attempted by concessions to win him over to his side. When the pretender Balas heard of this, he immediately outbade Demetrius, and offered Jonathan the High Priesthood as the price of his support. Jonathan sold himself to the highest bidder, and, notwithstanding further profuse promises from Demetrius, the Jewish leader remained true to his allegiance.

The war between the two rivals did not last long; Demetrius was overthrown and slain (B.C. 151), and at the marriage of the new king, Jonathan was appointed civil and military governor of Judaea. Whilst these changes were taking place in Syria, the Romans had completed the ruin of Carthage, and reduced Greece and Macedonia to the position of provinces. Jonathan who was a sagacious statesman, and had secured more for his people by diplomacy than the sword, no doubt understood the meaning of such events and dispatched an embassy to Rome. While his agents were negotiating an alliance with the Senate, Jonathan was basely murdered by a fresh Syrian pretender, and Simon his elder brother became head of the community.

Under the wise guidance of Simon (B.C. 142-135) the Jews attained a high degree of happiness and prosperity. From being a religious community, they had once more become a nation, and as a reward for Simon's services, the people at a solemn assembly proclaimed him and his descendants High Priests and Ethnarchs till a faithful prophet should arise. Simon assisted Demetrius II., king of Syria, in resisting the pretender Trypho, who had murdered his brother Jonathan; and Demetrius, in return for this aid, renounced all claim to tribute, and acknowledged the political autonomy of Judaea. Simon, however, had little faith in the promises and concessions of Syrian monarchs, and, like his two predecessors, trusted for security to an alliance with Rome. Numenius was charged with the conduct of the negotiations, and his labours were so successful, that the Romans issued a decree to all the peoples of the East, announcing that they had entered into a league of friendship with the Jews. It is not likely that this resolution of the Senate came into the hands of Demetrius, for at this period he was taken prisoner by the Parthians, who were steadily pressing westwards, and absorbing the Syrian possessions beyond the Euphrates.

Demetrius was succeeded by his brother Antiochus VII. (B.C. 141-131), a man of character and ability, who finally disposed of the pretender Trypho, and quickly made himself undisputed master of Syria. Antiochus was the last Syrian king who displayed capacity on the throne, and during his reign the Maccabaean princes had to submit to a curtailment of their authority. As long as Antiochus was engaged in fighting Trypho, he maintained a very friendly attitude towards Simon, but when this pretender was disposed of, the king altered his demeanour and demanded possession of the citadel of Jerusalem, the coast towns of Joppa and Gazara, together with the arrears of tribute which he had formerly consented to remit. Simon offered to pay a hundred talents as tribute for Joppa and Gazara, but Antiochus was not satisfied with this proposal, and sent an army into Palestine to enforce his claims in full. Simon was too old to take the field in person, but the Syrian forces were defeated by his two sons John and Judas who commanded the Jews. Simon did not long survive this victory; he was basely assassinated by Ptolemaeus, one of his sons-in-law, who was plotting to obtain the chief power (B.C. 135).

Simon's son, John Hyrcanus (B.C. 135-105), now became head of the state. He soon disposed of Ptolemaeus and his pretensions, but Antiochus was a far more formidable difficulty; he had no thought of abandoning his claims on the Jews because one of his commanders had been defeated in attempting to enforce them. Conducting a second campaign into Judaea in person, Antiochus compelled the Jews to seek shelter within the walls of Jerusalem, which he besieged. After a time hunger forced the brave defenders to sue for terms. As a result of the negotiations, the Jews had to surrender their arms, to give hostages, and five hundred talents in money, in order to be spared the presence of a Syrian garrison at Jerusalem. They had also to pay an annual tribute for Joppa and Gazara, and for some other places under Jewish rule, which were reckoned by Antiochus as a part of Syria (B.C. 134).

Hyrcanus, however, was determined at the first opportunity to set aside the arrangements which necessity had forced upon the Jews. With this object he sent three ambassadors to Rome, after the death of Antiochus (B.C. 129), to renew the treaty of friendship which had existed between the Romans and his predecessors, and to complain of the Syrians for depriving him of places, which the Senate had formerly acknowledged as Jewish territory. In accordance with the settled principles of Roman policy in the East, the Jewish mission was received in a very friendly manner, their grievances were attentively heard, and a decree was issued, ordering the Syrians to relinquish their claims to tribute, and declaring void whatever Antiochus had done in Judaea in opposition to previous declarations of the Senate. Whether the Syrians obeyed or disregarded the injunctions of the Senate is not known. In any case, the Jews had not long to wait for the restoration of what they had lost. The prolonged disorders which followed the death of Antiochus, enabled John Hyrcanus not only to resume his old position, but also to add Idumaea and Samaria to his dominions.

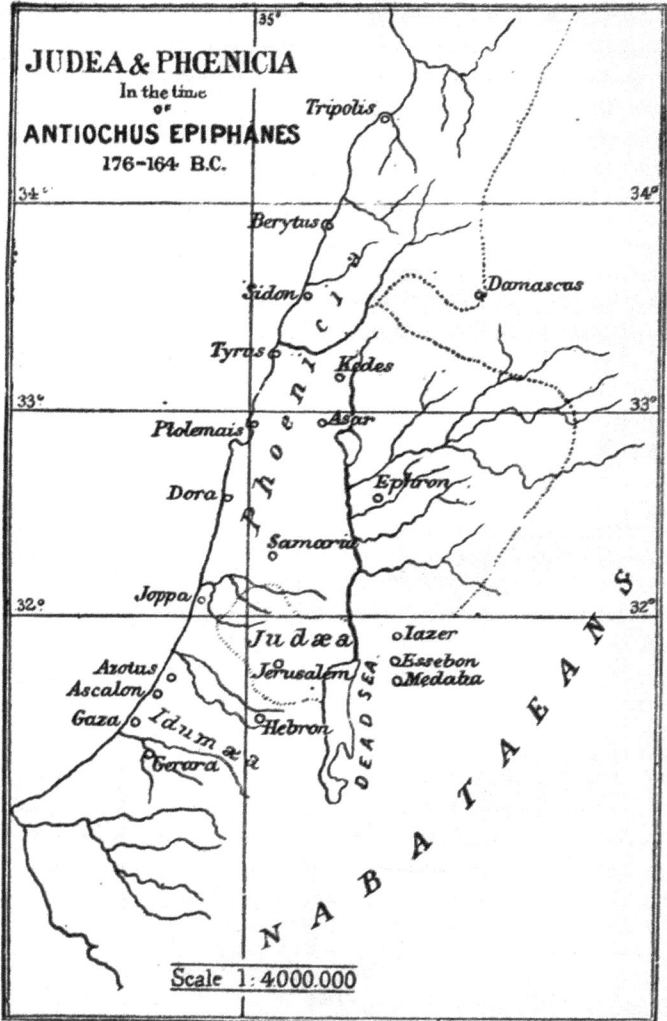

After the subjugation of these two provinces, John endeavoured to settle some parts of Samaria with Idumaean colonists. But the Samaritans resisted this line of action, and sought assistance from Antiochus Cyzikenus (B.C.

113), who was then king of what still remained of Syria. Antiochus responded to the call of the Samaritans, and, invading Judaea, captured some towns along the coast, of which Joppa was one. These coast towns had been specially recognized by the Romans as parts of Jewish territory, and John sent ambassadors to the Senate to complain of Antiochus. The Senators accordingly issued a fresh decree, ordering the Syrian garrisons to retire, and likewise forbidding Antiochus to molest the allies of Rome. But the progress of events showed that it was no longer necessary for the Jews to lean on Roman support in their contest with the decaying Syrian power. The forces of Antiochus were incapable of holding the field against the Jewish prince, and had to withdraw from Palestine.

The latter part of the reign of John Hyrcanus brings us to a period when the Jews had no longer anything to fear from the hostility of Syria. At the close of a fifty years' conflict, the Jews from being little more than a purely religious community had again become a nation, and were in possession of the ancient boundaries of the promised land. Under Hyrcanus they attained as high a pitch of prosperity, as in the famous days of David and Solomon. This success was due partly to their own heroism, and partly to a fortunate conjunction of circumstances. Nothing could exceed the bravery of the little community in asserting its claims, first to religious and then to political liberty. But the admirable qualities displayed in the Maccabaean revolt, would have been wasted in the end if the Syrian monarchy had not been in a state of embarrassment and decay. At the time the Jews began to show symptoms of revolt, and during the whole course of the struggle, the Syrians were weakened from within by dynastic troubles, and from without by the pressure of the Parthians on the east, and the Romans on the west. The resources of Syria must have been sorely exhausted by the interminable civil wars which the different pretenders to the throne waged against each other. But in spite of these internal troubles, Syria would have ultimately proved too strong for the Jews if her power had not been undermined by Roman diplomacy, and her territory constantly diminished by Parthian invasion.

At the time the Jews were fighting for their independence, the Parthians were making themselves masters of the Syrian provinces beyond the Euphrates, and the Romans were not only extorting a heavy tribute from the Syrian kings, but also compelling them to keep such a small army, that the monarchy was reduced to a condition approaching military impotence. It is doubtful if the various alliances of the Jews with Rome did much to help them forward on the path of independence. Some of these supposed alliances rest upon very slender historical foundations, and none of them, as far as can be seen, were of a very practical character. Roman professions of friendship were never backed up by Roman arms; the Senate willingly made use of the Jews to effect the destruction of Syria, but it did not desire to involve itself in adventures which would have necessitated additional conquests in the East. This is very probably the reason why Roman interference on behalf of the Jews was merely diplomatic and never military.

In the next chapter we shall see the Romans, in consequence of an alteration of the balance of power in the Republic, abandon the old policy of abstaining from military intervention in Eastern affairs. We shall at the same time find the Jews displaying an utter lack of capacity to form themselves into a homogeneous nationality; we shall also see the two parties within the young state—the Pharisees and Sadducees—producing such a condition of disorder as to lead to Roman interference, and the downfall of Jewish independence.

The Roman Conquest - B.C. 63-41

In the preceding chapter, we have witnessed the rise of the Jewish nation from a state of vassalage to a position in which it had no longer anything to fear from the hostility of Syria, and we now enter upon a new era in the history of the relations between the Romans and this remarkable people. Whilst the Jews were fighting the battle of liberty on the hillsides of their native land, the internal structure of the old Roman Commonwealth was falling into decay, and the power of the Senate or aristocracy was being supplanted by the authority of military chiefs, whose predominance resulted in the establishment of the Empire. The policy adopted by these military leaders may be described in contradistinction to the policy of the Senate as imperial rather than national; it led them in the direction of bringing fresh territories under the domination of Rome. In process of time such a policy would undoubtedly have brought the Romans into conflict with the Jews for possession of supremacy in Palestine; but the advent of this inevitable struggle was hastened by the deplorable intestine strife which broke out in the reign of John Hyrcanus between the Pharisees and the Sadducees. In the succeeding reigns this strife went on increasing in bitterness, till the Romans stepped in between the rival factions and put an end to their fratricidal war.

In the early days of the war with Syria, it was seen that a party existed among the Jews which manifested no strong desire for complete independence, but was disposed to be quite contented with the old foreign domination, after religious liberty had been fought for and obtained. But this party does not appear to have exercised a preponderating influence on the vast body of the people till the contest with the Syrians was practically over and the nation had time to direct its attention to internal affairs. From the days of Judas Maccabaeus, till the closing years of John Hyrcanus's life the party of national independence, headed by the Hasmonaeans, held the first place in the councils of the nation, and in the affections of the people. Its adherents had become the military leaders, the diplomatists, the civil administrators; in short, the ruling aristocracy of the country. By the exigencies of their position, the members of this party were brought into close contact with the civilization of Greece, which at this epoch surrounded Palestine on all sides. As diplomatists they had to be familiar with the Greek language; as generals who commanded mercenaries, they had to accommodate themselves to Gentile customs; as governors of districts containing a mixed population, they had to deal with practical affairs from a wider than a Jewish point of view. While remaining conscientiously true to the principles of the Law they did not consider it inconsistent with these principles to gratify a taste for the refinements and luxuries of Hellenic life, and their mental horizon became enlarged under the liberalizing influence of Hellenic culture. In addition to this, the Sadducees, for this is the party which we are now describing, having built up the independence of the country by a policy of prudence and diplomacy, endeavoured to uphold its interests and security by the same means, and had no hesitation in forming alliances with foreign nations for the attainment of these ends.

The Sadducees, it will be perceived, were essentially a political party, permeated, but still not dominated, by Hellenic ideas—a party of which the highest aim was to further the greatness and glory of the State it had done so much to found.

On the other hand, the central and absorbing thought of the Assidaeans, who had fought side by side with the Sadducees in the early days of the insurrection, was not the State, but Religion; and it was the same thought which burned within the heart and mind of the Pharisees, who were almost the same party appearing under another name. This, party, which was composed of the scribes and their disciples, abhorred Hellenism as subversive of the Law, and regarded the growing material greatness of the State with suspicion, fearing lest the teachings of the Synagogue should be lost amid the din and stir of political and military life. During the reign of John Hyrcanus Pharisaism succeeded in becoming a force within the nation, and towards the close of his life it began to assume an aggressive form, directing its hostility against the prince himself, who, although nominally a Pharisee, was in reality the living embodiment of Sadducaism.

The opposition of the Pharisees to Hyrcanus proceeded from causes which would among any people but the Jews have led him to be regarded with gratitude and affection. His keen desire to further the interests and dignity of his native land, his labours for the welfare and prosperity of the population, his willingness to introduce arts and sciences which had reached a higher development elsewhere than they had at home; all these things because they were not immediately concerned with the Law and the Traditions, were looked upon with disfavour by the Pharisees. It is also probable that they manifested a similar hostility to the action of Hyrcanus in forming alliances with a heathen power like Rome. These men saw in him too much of the statesman and too little of the High Priest. His secular functions appeared to cast his sacred ones too completely into the background; he had far more the aspect of a civil than of an ecclesiastical dignitary; hence the Pharisees considered that the vital interests of Judaism were suffering in his hands. It was for the God of Israel and His Law, and not for the national existence or grandeur that the

Pharisees conceived a High Priest should principally strive; but as there did not appear to be the least likelihood of Hyrcanus coming round to that opinion, the malcontents determined upon demanding the separation of the spiritual from the temporal power. It was alleged by the Pharisees that the Hasmonaean princes had no legitimate right to the High Priesthood, and, according to tradition, Eleazar, one of their number, had the boldness to tell Hyrcanus to abdicate the pontificate and to content himself with the civil government of the people. The contention of the Pharisees that the religious headship of the community did not belong to the Hasmonaeans was historically correct, but the lineal heirs to this high dignity had probably become extinct. In any case it would have been impossible for Hyrcanus to relinquish an office which in the eyes of the people invested him with a sacred character, and was one of the main sources of his authority. To a man of his experience it was manifest that he had to deal with a disaffected element in the community, and accordingly the Pharisees were expelled from the positions of influence in the kingdom.

Moulding of the So-Called Tombs of the Judges, Jerusalem.

Henceforth the Sadducees became identified even more closely than before with the cause and fortunes of the Hasmonaeans, whilst the Pharisees fell back exclusively on the people for sympathy and support. Pleading that they were contending for the faith and traditions of their fathers against a ruling house, which was supported by a party notoriously inclined to foreign customs, the Pharisees had no difficulty in arousing feelings of hostility among a fanatical population against the Hasmonaeans, and thus preparing the way for civil wars.

It is possible that Hyrcanus intended that after his death his successors should make a concession to the Pharisees, for he separated the civil from the ecclesiastical authority, leaving the kingdom to his widow and the High Priesthood to his son Judas Aristobulus.

But this arrangement did not satisfy Aristobulus (B.C. 105–4); he accordingly deposed his mother, and was the first of his house to assume the title of king. This title he used only in the non-Jewish part of his dominions, but it showed his preference for Greek customs, and was sufficient to stamp him as a partisan of the Sadducees. His partiality for Hellenism was so pronounced that he became known by the name Philhellene; yet, after conquering the Ituraeans, he retained enough of Judaism to compel his new subjects to be circumcised—a measure which in the eyes of the Pharisees may have atoned for much which they detested in his life. His, reign of one year was too brief to permit of the development of grave discontent on the part of his opponents; it was reserved for his successor to face the full force of their hostility.

Alexander Jannaeus (B.C. 104–78) became head of the nation after his brother's death, but he possessed very little of the political ability so conspicuously displayed by his predecessors; he was simply a brutal and dissipated soldier constantly involved in war. During his reign the Pharisees became the undoubted leaders of popular opinion. But Alexander paid no heed to this circumstance, and on one occasion while performing the duties of High Priest at the Feast of Tabernacles, he treated an observance enjoined on the High Priest by the Pharisees with deliberate contempt. Matters of religious ritual have always exercised a strange power over the emotions of men, and when the assembled worshippers in the Temple perceived Alexander pouring the libation on the ground, in accordance with the Sadducaean custom, instead of on the altar, their indignation knew no bounds. They immediately raised a shout that he was unworthy of his high dignity, and at the same time began to pelt him with the citrons which they held in their hands. So great was the tumult that the king would probably have been murdered by the enraged populace had not the Greek soldiers in his service come to the rescue and quelled the disturbance. As many as six thousand men fell before the precincts of the Temple were cleared. After this bloody work the Pharisees became the irreconcilable enemies of Alexander, and waited impatiently for the opportunity of heading a rebellion against him.

They had not to wait long. About a year afterwards the king lost his army in a campaign against the Nabataeans and had to return to Jerusalem, a fugitive (B.C. 94). The Pharisees immediately incited their adherents to revolt, and for six years a bloody war desolated the wretched country. After fifty thousand men had perished without leading to any decisive result, Alexander desired to come to terms with his adversaries. Nothing, however, would satisfy them but his death, and to compass this end they sought the assistance of their old enemies the Syrians. Demetrius III. invaded Palestine at the head of a powerful force and defeated Alexander who fled for refuge to the mountains of Ephraim. In this miserable plight he excited the compassion of a large body of the people who had thus far been fighting on behalf of the Pharisees. These men, whose patriotic feelings were stronger than their religious convictions, went over to the king's side when they saw the Syrians threatening to become once more dominant in Palestine. Their action immediately changed the whole aspect of the situation; Demetrius had to withdraw his forces, and Alexander again obtained the upper hand. The Pharisees, abandoned by a portion of their adherents had to flee into exile, and those who did not succeed in making their escape were crucified in a most barbarous manner by the victorious prince. He was not molested by the Pharisees during the remainder of his reign. When Tigranes, king of Armenia, overthrew the Syrian monarchy (B.C. 83), Alexander, who appears to have enjoyed the goodwill of the conqueror, was enabled, towards the close of a long career, to enlarge the boundaries of his kingdom, which, however, never comprised the whole of Palestine. Alexander had two sons, John Hyrcanus and Aristobulus, but his widow, Salome Alexandra (B.C. 78-69), succeeded him on the throne, and his elder son Hyrcanus was contented with the High Priesthood. Alexandra, a woman of prudence and resolution, reversed the policy of her husband; the Pharisees who had the ear of the masses were recalled from exile, and entrusted with a preponderating voice in the conduct of internal affairs. Under their influence, several religious customs and observances were modified to suit the ideas of the party; the marriage laws were revised, alterations were made in the law of evidence, and greater attention was paid to the education of the young. Had the Pharisees confined their activity within the sphere of legislation, it is possible that the hatred engendered during the preceding reign might have died away, but, unhappily for the peace of the nation, the Pharisees abused their power for the purpose of pursuing a policy of revenge. Their opponents were one after another condemned and put to death. The Sadducees took alarm at the fate of their companions, and placed themselves under the protection of Aristobulus, the queen's second son, who was ardently attached to their cause. Conducted by this prince into the presence of Alexandra, they implored her to put an end to the persecutions of the dominant party; at the same time reminding her of their past services to the State, and expressing their willingness to accept command of the fortresses if their presence was not desired in Jerusalem. The queen, probably grown weary of the yoke of the Pharisees, acceded to the request of her petitioners; the military strength of the kingdom was delivered over to the Sadducees, who had now simply to bide their time in order to regain their lost authority. Aristobulus, a man of enterprise and ambition, was their leader; his brother, the weak and passive Hyrcanus, was a tool in the hands of the Pharisees, and when Salome was seized with a mortal illness Aristobulus, aided by the military chiefs, overthrew his brother and became king (B.C. 69).

Under the sovereignty of Aristobulus (B.C. 69-63), the strife of parties brought the era of Jewish independence to a close, and made the Romans masters of the Holy Land. It is very probable that the bitter feud between the Pharisees and the Sadducees would have resulted much sooner in the establishment of foreign supremacy, if a strong Power had then existed in Western Asia, or if the Roman Commonwealth had not been in a state of permanent revolution, which compelled her ambitious spirits to fix their eyes upon affairs at home. From the commencement of the reign of John Hyrcanus (B.C. 135) till the revolt of the Asiatic provinces (B.C. 88), under the leadership of Mithridates, king of Pontus, the Romans had almost entirely neglected Oriental politics. But the loss of their possessions in the East aroused the patriotism of the hostile factions at the capital, and a Roman army, led by the genius of Sulla, proceeded to the scene of the revolt. Sulla quelled the insurrection, and Mithridates had to beg humbly for peace. But the restless ambition of Mithridates, as well as the Roman method of not only conquering but utterly annihilating a formidable enemy, led to a renewal of the war, which was waged with varying fortune on both sides till Pompey, a former lieutenant of Sulla's, after being invested with unlimited powers, arrived on the scene of conflict with a large army (B.C. 66). Having disposed of his adversary, Pompey boldly decided on extending the Roman frontier to the banks of the Euphrates. This decision involved the subjugation of Palestine, but its absorption into the vast empire would have taken a different, and perhaps a less bloody form, if, amid their party animosities, a common basis of patriotism had existed among the Jews.

Ruins of the Tower of Jerusalem, Formerly Palace of the Macabees, Finished by Herod

Whilst Pompey was engaged in putting a termination to the resistance of Mithridates, civil war broke out afresh in Palestine (B.C. 66). Antipater, an Idumaean of political ability, and father of Herod the Great, had obtained supreme influence over the feeble-minded Hyrcanus, whom he induced to offer concessions of territory to Aretas, king of the Nabataeans, in return for a promise of assistance to dethrone his brother Aristobulus. Aretas entered into the compact, and Hyrcanus fled with Antipater to the court of his ally at Petra. A Nabataean army invaded Palestine; the Pharisees, regardless of national independence, assisted the invaders, and Aristobulus, unable to keep the field, was besieged in Jerusalem. Whilst the Jews were destroying one another around the walls of the Holy City, Pompey's lieutenants were making themselves masters of Syria, and one of them, Marcus Scaurus, entered Juda a for the double purpose of enriching himself and effecting the pacification of the country. Both the contending princes laid their claims before the Roman general, who, from reasons of policy as well as motives of self-interest, decided in favour of Aristobulus. So great was the awe inspired by the Roman name that a word from Scaurus compelled the Pharisees and Nabataeans to raise the siege, and for two years longer Aristobulus was permitted to reign in peace (B.C. 65-63).

The arrangements made by Scaurus in Palestine were only provisional. When Pompey arrived at Damascus (B.C. 64), he took into his own hands the re-organization of the immense territories lying between the Mediterranean and the Euphrates, which were now at the disposal of Rome. As long as the supreme direction of affairs was controlled by the Senate, the object of Roman policy was not to gain possession of the East, but to break up its political unity. A different attitude was adopted with regard to foreign affairs, when the leaders of the democracy became the real heads of the Republic (B.C. 70). Unlike the oligarchy of the Senate, the chiefs of the democratic party did not consider external possessions as a necessary evil, only to be endured as helping to fill the coffers of the State; nor were they afraid of the effects upon the Roman character of a closer contact with the Hellenic communities of the East. When, therefore, Pompey began the task of restoring order and authority among the chaotic elements with which he had to deal, he discarded the old policy of the Senate, and reverted as far as possible to the organization which existed in Syria in the best epoch of the Seleucidae. The power formerly exercised by these monarchs he determined to put into the strong hands of a Roman proconsul. This decision necessitated the downfall of Jewish liberty; for Judaea in the eyes of the Romans was nothing more than a province of Syria which had been temporarily successful in asserting its independence.

Meanwhile deputations reached Pompey from the Jewish princes and people, and finally Hyrcanus and Aristobulus arrived at Damascus to urge the merits of their respective claims. But the mighty Roman did not choose to disclose his plans until he had chastised the Nabataeans. Aristobulus, putting a sinister interpretation upon his delay, showed signs of hostility, whereupon Pompey was offended, and forthwith made his legions ready for the invasion of Palestine. As the Roman troops were advancing, the unfortunate Aristobulus, trembling between hope and fear, alternately negotiated, hesitated, or made preparations for defence, till the Romans came within sight of Jerusalem. He then gave himself up, and promised to place the Holy City in their hands. But the brave and patriotic Sadducees who composed the garrison refused to admit the Roman officers; they destroyed the bridge which united Mount Zion with Mount Moriah, and, withdrawing within the fortifications of the Temple Mount, resolved to fight to the last for the liberties of their native land. The Pharisees surrendered the city itself, but for three months the soldiers of Aristobulus defied the utmost efforts of the Roman general, who would have been compelled to prolong the siege for an indefinite period, if the defenders had not put such a rigorous interpretation upon the law forbidding work on the Sabbath day. The Romans soon learned to take advantage of this extravagant literalism. On a Sabbath in the month of June, B.C. 63, a breach was effected in the walls, the Temple hill was carried after fearful slaughter by assault, and the Jewish people lay at the mercy of the conqueror. Pompey and his officers had the curiosity to enter the Holy of Holies, which had never before been seen by Western eyes. From motives of policy he immediately restored the Temple ceremonial, and for a similar reason abstained from plundering the sacred treasury.

In the so-called Psalms of Solomon we possess a poetic account of the impression produced on a large section of the people by these terrible events. "A powerful smiter," says the Psalmist, "has God brought from the ends of the earth. He decreed war upon Jerusalem and upon the land. The princes of the land went out with joy to meet him, and said to him, Blessed be thy way, draw near, and enter in peace...He entered the house of his children in peace like a father, standing in all safety. He took possession of the strong places in the land, and of the walls of Jerusalem, and while they went astray, God led him in security. He destroyed the chief men and all who were wise in council. He spilt the blood of the inhabitants of Jerusalem like unclean water. He led away their sons and daughters because they were begotten in iniquity. They did according to the iniquity of their fathers; they defiled Jerusalem and the things dedicated to the name of God."

From these and similar expressions of the Psalmist, we can gather that the bloody chastisement which the Jews had at this period to endure was regarded by the spiritual guides of the people as proceeding from the hand of God, the Romans being considered as the instruments for carrying His vengeance into effect. In the eyes of the writer, the Hasmonaeans are punished for assuming the royal dignity when it had not been promised them, and the people are also punished for condoning the transgressions of their princes, and falling with them into sin. Pompey's labours were lightened by the existence of these sentiments among a large body of the population, and more especially when he began to take into consideration the reestablishment of some settled form of government, which would satisfy the Jews, and at the same time prove amenable to the will of Rome.

When at Damascus, Pompey had received a deputation from Judaea, which made representations to him to the effect that the Hasmonaean princes had changed the form of government under which their ancestors had lived, and desiring him to restore the order of things that had formerly existed in the land. These suggestions fell in with Pompey's projected arrangements, and he proceeded to act upon them after resistance before Jerusalem was at an end. Aristobulus was deposed, and taken with his children to Rome to adorn the triumph of the conqueror (B.C. 61); the kingship, after an existence of little more than forty years, was abolished, and the Jews were stripped of all the territories (with the exception of Idumaea) which they had acquired by conquest in the era of their independence. In this way Samaria, the commercial cities along the Mediterranean coast, the Decapolis in the northeast of Palestine, and many Hellenic communities on the eastern banks of the Jordan, were liberated from a yoke which they detested, and which at times forced Judaism upon them at the point of the sword. By the inhabitants of these places Pompey was looked upon in the light of a deliverer. The self-government which they had formerly enjoyed he, according to Roman custom, restored to them; and the rule of the Roman pro-consul was mild and beneficent when contrasted with the despotism of the Jewish kings. Judaea itself was placed under the authority of the Roman governor of Syria, who, with two legions at his command, was responsible for the peace and order of the newly-acquired territories. The Jews had now to pay tribute to Rome in the same way as they had previously done to Syria; but they were freely permitted to manage their own internal affairs, and to live in accordance with their own laws. As a reward for his fidelity to Roman interests, Hyrcanus was reinstated as High Priest, receiving at the same time the civic title of Ethnarch, a name by which his predecessors had been known before they assumed the prouder dignity of king.

In estimating Pompey's conduct it must be borne in mind that, if his arrangements pressed severely on Jewish pride, they were on the whole a blessing to the peoples of the East, who were rescued from chaos and instability, and enabled, after years of anarchy, to enjoy the fruits of peace. High above the petty princes with which Syria was filled there now stood the Roman governor to keep them all in awe; complete liberty within their own dominions was freely accorded them, but they were now effectually restrained from preying on their weaker neighbours. These princes became in reality Roman procurators, responsible to the proconsul for the just exercise of their powers. With the advent of peace, ruined cities were restored and repopulated; communities which had groaned under the yoke of petty despots were allowed to manage their own affairs; commerce could now take a wider sweep; the facilities for human intercourse were vastly enlarged; and civilization in those regions was enabled to extend its influence and blossom forth in higher forms. Even in the case of the Jews, if Pompey destroyed the ideal boundaries of the Holy Land, this was done simply because a Gentile element predominated outside the borders of Judaea; in fact he was only restoring to the population of these districts, the liberty of which they had lately been deprived. Nevertheless he permitted the Jews to retain complete possession of their own territory, that is to say, the territory which they inhabited after the return from Babylon, a period which must be considered as a fresh starting-point in their national career. It is true he made the Ethnarch Hyrcanus a tributary prince, a proceeding which deprived the people of their liberty. Still it was plainly impossible for Pompey to allow an aggressive power, as the Jews had shown themselves to be, to exist with independence in the very heart of acquisitions which he had just placed under the protection of Rome.

It was not however to be expected that the Jewish patriots would look at the situation from this point of view, and accordingly we find Alexander, a son of the dethroned Aristobulus, a few years after Pompey's departure, rallying his dejected countrymen, and taking the field against the Romans at the head of more than ten thousand men. At this period Gabinius (B.C. 57–55) was at the head of affairs in Syria, and as Hyrcanus was unable to put down the insurrection, the proconsul entered Judaea and utterly defeated Alexander, who afterwards fell into his hands. At the close of the revolt, Gabinius made some alterations in the government of the country. Hyrcanus was deprived of temporal power and confined to his spiritual functions. The country was also divided into five districts, each district being ruled by a separate council, composed of the leading citizens, who were responsible to the proconsul. Many towns which the Jews had destroyed were rebuilt and repopulated, among them being Samaria and Scythopolis, the latter of which afterwards became the most important place in Galilee. By filling the country with a non-Jewish population, and by creating local centres of administration entirely independent of one another, Gabinius hoped to produce provincial rivalries, and to destroy the desire for political unity and independence.

Before the arrangements of Gabinius had time to produce any practical results, Aristobulus escaped from Rome, and headed a fresh revolt (B.C. 56). But his raw levies were unable to withstand the disciplined bravery of the legions, and in spite of heroic efforts on his part the insurrection was crushed, and he had once more to go back into captivity. Nothing daunted by his father's ill-success, Alexander his son, resolved a second time to try the arbitrament of war (B.C. 55). Gabinius was engaged in an expedition against Egypt, Syria was in consequence depleted of troops, and the Jewish army was assisting the Romans as auxiliaries. Alexander conceived that a favourable moment had arrived to strike another blow for freedom, but his hopes were quickly shattered, for Antipater succeeded in persuading many adherents of the prince to desert him, and Gabinius on his arrival in Palestine defeated and dispersed the rest. In the Egyptian campaign Antipater had been of the utmost service to the Romans. By him the expedition was provisioned and fitted out; through his instrumentality, the roads were left open, so that the invaders had no hostile manifestations to encounter on the march. It was in all probability as a reward for these signal services, that Gabinius, after the restoration of peace, arranged the affairs of Palestine in accordance with the views of Antipater, who had now become the virtual ruler of the land. These arrangements restored Hyrcanus, or rather his wily minister Antipater, to the most important position in Southern Syria.

View of Bethlehem

Whilst these events were transpiring in Palestine, three of the most powerful Roman citizens, Caesar, Pompey, and Crassus, renewed an agreement known as the Triumvirate (B.C. 56), the effects of which were shortly afterwards felt throughout the whole of Western Asia. No power was left standing capable of resisting the united action of these three men, who accordingly assumed supreme control of the Republic, and selected the most distinguished positions for themselves and their adherents. Each of them inwardly cherished the vast ambition of becoming one day undisputed master of the State. Crassus, who far outstripped his colleagues in riches, wished also to rival them in military achievements, and be the first to grasp the dignity they all were plotting to obtain. Caesar was already occupied in subduing the West, and in that region there were no more laurels to be won, but mighty kingdoms in the East were still unconquered; and the recent outbreak of the Parthian war offered Crassus an opportunity, admirably suited to his present purposes and ulterior designs. In his eagerness to reach the scene of action, Crassus proceeded to the East before the expiration of his consulate, and taking over the government of Syria B.C. 55—53) from Gabinius, entered with a light heart on an expedition against the Parthians, which proved fatal to his reputation and his life. Before crossing the Euphrates the proconsul took no pains to leave a contented people behind him on whose goodwill the Romans could rely. What Pompey had possessed the wisdom to spare, his avarice was unable to resist. The Temple of Jerusalem was plundered in violation of his oath, producing bitter feelings of resentment against the Romans, who soon afterwards experienced the evil effects of Crassus' greed. In the arid wastes of Mesopotamia he was defeated and slain. His brave lieutenant Cassius led back the remnants of the shattered legions to Syria.

The Jews smarting under a sense of injustice rose once more to revolt, and endeavoured to co-operate with the victorious Parthians who were bent on driving the Romans out of Asia. Never did the Jews obtain a more favourable moment for asserting their right to independence, for the Roman forces in Syria under the command of Cassius (B.C. 52—5 I) did not now exceed ten thousand men, and the impending hostilities between Caesar and Pompey prevented him from being reinforced with troops from Italy. But even in these circumstances the fortune of war declared itself against them; and Cassius after suppressing the insurrection sold thirty thousand Jewish warriors in the slave market, and at the suggestion of Antipater executed the leader of the rebels (B.C. 52).

Whilst the Jews were vainly attempting to determine the form of rule in Palestine, a vaster question involving not only the political future of this principality, but of the whole civilized world as well was rapidly approaching a solution at Rome. The death of Crassus put an end to the triumvirate; the ties of family the only ones which bound together the dissimilar characters of Caesar and Pompey were broken by the death of Pompey's wife, Caesar's daughter Julia, and Pompey was now anxious to settle their conflicting claims to the empire by an appeal to the sword. Caesar did not fear this ultimate appeal, still he did not desire it. Pompey and the aristocrats, however, left him no choice. By the violence of their measures they forced on a rupture and the great civil war began. It is said that Caesar before crossing the boundaries of his province hesitated when he reflected on the miseries the war would cause, and the judgment posterity would pass upon his act. At last hesitation gave way before resolve, and turning to his friends he is reported to have said, "Let us go whither we are called by the presages of the gods and the iniquity of our enemies. The die is cast."

At the head of only five thousand men and three hundred horse he marched with startling rapidity upon the capital. Pompey and the aristocratic party fled from Rome in consternation, and crossed the Adriatic into Macedonia. In sixty days Caesar without shedding a drop of blood was master of the whole of Italy. Immediately afterwards he set out for Spain, the centre of Pompey's strength. "I go," he said, describing his tactics, "against an army without a general; afterwards I shall proceed against a general without an army." Spain, after a brilliant campaign, was subdued in forty days. Caesar then transported his legions into Greece, and after many vicissitudes completely overthrew his rival in the plains of Pharsalia (B.C. 48). Pompey fled from the field of battle and sailed for Egypt, but, on landing he was basely assassinated by order of the Egyptian king. Caesar, at the head of a small force, arrived in Alexandria, in pursuit of his vanquished foe; but on his arrival he learned that Pompey the Great was dead.

Whilst Caesar was at Alexandria, the Jews, under Antipater, were able to perform a signal service for him at one of the most critical moments of his military career. When the ministers of the Egyptian king saw that he was in command of a little more than three thousand troops, they attacked him with a large army, aided by the mob of Alexandria. Caesar was compelled to burn his ships, and was ultimately blockaded in one quarter of the city both by land and sea. His position was fast becoming desperate, when a miscellaneous army from the principalities of Syria succeeded in forcing its way to his assistance. By far the most important personage in this army was Antipater, whose contingent of three thousand men gave stability to the whole. He also procured help from the Arab tribes along the line of march, and it was by his efforts that the large Jewish colony at Alexandria was induced to come to Caesar's aid. But Antipater was more than a clever diplomatist; in this campaign he displayed conspicuous gallantry in the field. He was the first to storm the walls of Pelusium, and it was he who, turning the tide of battle outside Alexandria, enabled Caesar to effect a junction with the relieving force, a movement which resulted in the utter discomfiture of the Egyptians' (B.C. 47).

Caesar at the commencement of the war against Pompey released Aristobulus, who was a prisoner at Rome, and appointed him to the command of two legions, with instructions to proceed to Syria, and create a diversion in favour of his patron. But the unfortunate prince was poisoned by Pompey's party, and his son Alexander beheaded about the same time. Antigonus, his younger son, after victory had declared itself for Caesar, laid the claims of his house before the conqueror; but the recent services of Hyrcanus and Antipater outweighed the pleas of Antigonus, who had to retire into obscurity and wait for better times. Caesar, when settling the affairs of the East, willingly overlooked the circumstance that the Jews had in the first instance sided with his opponent. He placed them in the most favoured position which any community subject to Rome could hold. The land was freed from the tribute imposed upon it by Pompey; the Roman garrisons were withdrawn, and the population exempted from military service in the legions. Religious liberty was assured to the Jews both in Palestine and throughout the East. At home they were permitted to live in accordance with their own laws, and could only be judged by their own tribunals. The power of self-government was granted them, which made them masters of their internal affairs. The walls of Jerusalem, which Pompey had destroyed, they were allowed to rebuild; the important seaport of Joppa was restored to them, as well as all the places along the coast which had not been acquired by conquest. Hyrcanus was elevated to senatorial rank, and the ethnarchy made hereditary in his family. Antipater received his share of honour by being made a Roman citizen, and granted immunity from taxation. Caesar did not make him a Roman official, as some have supposed, but he confirmed the astute Idumaean in the position of Prime Minister to Hyrcanus. Owing to the weakness of his master's character, this position invested him with supreme power in the State, Hyrcanus being little more than a tool in his hands (B.C. 47).

During the remainder of his life Antipater adopted the only policy possible to a protected State—a policy which consisted in attempting to make the Jews contented with their position as an autonomous people within the vast empire of which Caesar had become the chief. In the political condition of the world at that period, not to speak of the irreconcilable divisions among the Jews themselves, the independence of Judaea was utterly impracticable, and it would have spared the unfortunate population much bloodshed and misery if the Jewish aristocracy had quietly accepted the altered order of things. But these men, jealous of Antipater's influence and power, did their utmost to hamper him in his efforts to pacify the country. In order to cripple the father they assailed his son Herod, a young man of twenty-five, who had just earned the gratitude of the peaceable inhabitants of Northern Palestine, and the goodwill of the Syrian proconsul by dispersing the robber bands of Galilee and executing their chiefs. As this latter measure was taken without authority from Jerusalem, he was summoned before the aristocrats of the Sanhedrin, who possessed sufficient influence to secure his banishment. But Herod was not a man to be easily crushed. He withdrew to Damascus, entered the Roman army, and was appointed by Sextus Caesar. (B.C. 47–46) military governor of Coelo-Syria. In this new and important office he was able to overawe the opponents of his family, and to strengthen his father's hands in Jerusalem.

Roman politics were now as important to the Jewish people as the course of events within their own borders, and the vicissitudes of parties at the imperial capital were distinctly felt in the remotest provinces of the East. Caesar was not satisfied with exercising the authority of a king, he had the weakness to desire the name as well. It was a weakness which sealed his fate. The old Republic was no doubt dead, but republican forms were still deeply rooted in the heart of the aristocracy. A plot was laid against his life by a band of senators, and on the Ides of March (B.C. 44) the Dictator was assassinated. Once more the Roman world, which had begun to taste the sweets of peace, was thrown into disorder and convulsed with civil war. Among the people the desire for the old constitution was extinct, and Caesar's murderers had to flee from Rome. One of the principal conspirators, Cassius, retired to Syria, the pro-consulate of which he had received from Caesar. Syria was then in a very unsettled state; a partisan of Pompey's, Q. Caecilius Bassus, had raised an insurrection (B.C. 46); Sextus Caesar, the proconsul, was assassinated by his own troops, who went over to Bassus, and war was going on between Herod and Bassus when Cassius arrived (B.C. 44) and reconciled their conflicting interests. Cassius soon showed himself a hard master. On Palestine alone he levied a contribution of seven hundred talents, and as Antipater was unable to pay the whole sum within the allotted time, the inhabitants of several Jewish towns were ruthlessly seized and sold as slaves. Herod, on the other hand, won the proconsul's good will by the alacrity with which he paid the one hundred talents that fell upon him. He was rewarded with the procuratorship of Coelo-Syria, and a promise of the Jewish crown if fortune favoured Cassius in his impending conflict with the Caesarians.

The death of Caesar did not destroy Caesarism, which sprang up with the decay of the spirit of liberty, and Octavian, a nephew and heir of the mighty

Dictator, aspired to play the part which was left vacant by the murder of his illustrious relative. In conjunction with Mark Antony, one of Caesar's lieutenants, he resolved to effect the overthrow of Cassius, and the rest of the conspirators. The armies of the contending factions met in the plains of Philippi; Cassius was defeated and committed suicide, and the Roman world lay at the disposal of Antony and Octavian. The victors divided the spoils between them; the West was allotted to Octavian, then a young man of twenty-one, and Antony became sovereign lord of all the Roman conquests in the East. When the tidings of Cassius' defeat reached Palestine, the Jewish aristocracy believed the moment had at last arrived which would rid them of the Herodian family. Antipater they had already

The Tower of Hippicus, a Fortification of Jerusalem

succeeded in poisoning, but his two sons, Herod and Phasael, in spite of insurrections' and discontent, continued to hold high positions, and Herod, through his betrothal to Mariamne, the beautiful granddaughter of Hyrcanus, became a member of the royal house. Deputations from Judaea reached the headquarters of the Roman general to complain of the Idumaean brothers for usurping the power which belonged to the ethnarch. But Hyrcanus raised his voice in defence of the accused, and Antony thereupon elevated the sons of his old friend Antipater to the rank of Tetrarchs (B.C. 41).

In looking back upon the period which had elapsed since the Jewish people fell under the domination of Rome, it will be seen that they must necessarily be involved in the confusion and unsettlement inseparable from the downfall of old Roman institutions, and the uprising of an imperial system on their ruins. The Romans themselves suffered terribly in life and fortune from the revolution then in progress in their midst, and Judaea did not escape the turmoil arising out of a change in the centre of authority from the ancient oligarchy to the new monarchy. But Rome on the whole exercised greater severity towards her own citizens than towards her dependents in the provinces. Judaea, during this troubled time, had to suffer much, but it was due to the wisdom of Antipater that she did not suffer more. To his honour it must be said that he made the utmost of the difficult and perilous circumstances in which the Jews were then placed, and by abandoning a hopeless struggle with Rome obtained the most favourable conditions possible for the people whose interests he had in charge. Personal ambition, no doubt, entered into his calculations it is an element in the character of almost everyone who aspires to rule but the important fact remains that he possessed a clearer view of the times in which he lived, and utilized his knowledge in the performance of far greater services to the Jewish nation than the Jewish aristocracy who reviled and opposed him. By futile insurrections and by fostering discontent the aristocracy added vastly to the miseries of the population. By their opposition to the Romans, they were in reality throwing themselves across the path of the Divine purpose which was working itself out in history by binding the Mediterranean peoples under one form of civil rule, as a preliminary to the advent and propagation of the Christian faith. The Pharisees, whether consciously or not, displayed a wiser appreciation of the tendency of events by withdrawing altogether from public life. When Rome became supreme, political affairs ceased for a time to have any interest for them, and rabbinical tradition passes over in silence the entire political history of this period. Their attitude was summed up in the maxim of the famous rabbi Schemaiah, "Love work, eschew domination, and hold aloof from the civil power."

The Roman Vassal King - B.C. 41-4

Before the battle of Philippi, the agents of Cassius had entered into negotiations with the Parthians, for the purpose of securing their co-operation against the partisans of Caesar. The loss of this action was a fatal blow to the republican cause. Still its adherents at the Parthian Court succeeded in inducing King Orodes to undertake, in the following year (B.C. 41), the invasion of Syria, which contained many Roman garrisons hostile to Antony. A powerful army under the command of Quintus Labienus, a Roman noble, and Pacorus, the king's son, crossed the Euphrates, won over most of the Roman troops in Syria, and quickly overran the whole province. The two generals shortly afterwards (B.C. 40) divided their forces; Labienus pushing westwards into Asia Minor, and Pacorus turning his hordes of horsemen against Palestine. Whilst these unexpected events were shaking the foundation of Antony's power, the new ruler of the East was in the first transports of his notorious amour with Cleopatra, queen of Egypt, then in the very flower and full perfection of her charms. When tidings reached him that the Parthians were carrying all before them Antony was living under the enchantments of the queen at Alexandria in a giddy whirl of license and prodigality, but he was unable to tear himself from the fatal woman who henceforth became the evil genius of his life.

Left without counsel or assistance from their protector at a time when they were in grievous need of both, it now went hard with the new tetrarchs who had to confront a hostile population as well as the horsemen, of Pacorus. The struggle was too unequal to be of long duration. Herod, after desperate fighting, succeeded in making his escape from Jerusalem with his household, to a place of safety the fortress of Masada on the south-western shores of the Dead Sea. His brother Phasael dashed his brains out in a Parthian prison; Hyrcanus was captured and sent into exile beyond the Euphrates. Antigonus, the son of Aristobulus, who had formerly urged his claims upon Caesar, received the Jewish crown by making most shameful promises to Pacorus, and the whole structure of government raised by the Romans in Palestine was shattered at a blow (B.C. 40).

At last, however, the infatuated Antony was roused to action, and, leaving Alexandria, he proceeded to Tyre, the only city in Syria which still held out against the Parthians. There he learned that his position in Italy was imperiled by the headstrong conduct of Fulvia his wife. This violent and imperious woman had quarreled with Octavian, and in the disturbances which ensued Antony's friends were driven from Italy, and his colleague obtained a preeminence which was regarded by Antony as full of danger to himself. He accordingly set sail for Italy (B.C. 40) to demand explanations from Octavian, and a fresh civil war seemed imminent, when the legions, who were now weary of decimating one another, compelled the two generals to arrange a peaceful settlement of their differences. Whilst the triumvirs were engaged in re-dividing the Roman world, Herod arrived as a fugitive in the capital. After providing for the safety of his family, he had wandered through Idumaea to Alexandria, and, on finding Antony had gone, immediately made haste to Rome. From the triumvirs, who knew the value of his services, Herod met with a cordial welcome, and it was decided to elevate him to the royal dignity. In the Senate, orators of distinction spoke in his behalf, and Antony himself urged upon the assembly that, in view of the approaching Parthian war, Herod should be proclaimed a king. This proposal was unanimously approved of by the senators, and Herod, who was sitting in their midst, was then escorted by the triumvirs and the consuls to the temple of Jupiter on the Capitol, where he offered sacrifice in accordance with a custom of the Roman magistrates on their entrance upon office. This imposing ceremony must have been a proud moment in the life of the new king, who did not dream of attaining such high honours when he arrived in Rome. But the kingdom was his own as yet only in name; he now hastened from the capital to make it his own in reality (B.C. 40).

Antony, after his reconciliation with Octavian, was able to give his attention once more to Eastern affairs. Publius Ventidius Bassus, one of his best lieutenants, was placed in command of a fresh army destined to operate against the Parthians. Fulvia being dead, Antony, to seal the peace, had just married Octavian's sister, a woman of pure and lofty character, and was staying with her at Athens watching the development of events both in the East and West. The Parthians were not really formidable when away from their wide-extending plains, and Ventidius,

Roman Soldiers in Action

sweeping them like dust before him, soon regained possession of the invaded provinces (B.C. 39). When Herod was ready to commence operations in Palestine, the land was cleared of the Parthian horsemen, and the adherents of Antigonus were the only opponents the new king had to meet. Collecting troops with money kindly lent to him by a rich Jew of Antioch, and entering Galilee, he took the offensive with success. Ventidius sent him a detachment of Romans to assist in completing the conquest of the country. From them, however, he derived little real assistance. Silo, the commander, was bribed by Antigonus to remain inactive, and it was a relief to Herod when this force was recalled. Afterwards Ventidius dispatched two legions to his aid in command of another officer, but this man proved more corrupt than Silo. Herod had, in consequence, to contend with disheartening circumstances till he received help from Antony who was now in Asia Minor, and had taken into his own hands the supreme command of military affairs 1 (B.C. 38). Caius Sosius succeeded Ventidius as, Legate of Syria, and Antony entrusted him with the task of placing Herod on the Jewish throne. Sosius, with a large army, marched through Phoenicia upon Jerusalem, which, after a most heroic defence, was at last carried by assault. Antigonus became a prisoner, but at the urgent entreaties of his rival he was soon afterwards put to death (B.C. 37).

Whilst Herod was engaged in the formidable operation of suppressing discontent and re-organizing his kingdom, Antony fell once more under the spells of Cleopatra (B.C. 36)—an event of evil omen for the Jewish king, as well as for his Roman master. Antony's ambition now took the form of attempting to found a vast Oriental Empire after the manner of Alexander the Great satraps and vassal princes were to act as governors, and his children by Cleopatra as kings. The fair Egyptian now assumed the lofty title Queen of Kings, and in order to maintain her state required an extension of territory and an increase of her revenues. As Judaea had formerly been in possession of her family, and as it lay close to her own dominions, she set her heart upon obtaining it. With this fixed purpose she laboured strenuously to damage Herod in the estimation of Antony, and plotted with the king's relations in the expectation of accomplishing his downfall. Considering the influence which she possessed over her lover, it is remarkable that she did not speedily attain her end. Her failure can only be accounted for on the ground of Antony's unshakeable esteem for the monarch of his own creation. Once, however, her efforts to compass Herod's destruction were almost crowned with success, and the king looked upon himself as a lost man. In obedience to her importunities, Antony, while making preparations for his expedition against the Parthians which ended so disastrously, summoned the Jewish king to Laodicaea to answer a charge of having caused the death of his youthful brother-in-law Aristobulus. On Herod's arrival Cleopatra employed all her arts to secure his condemnation; but her sagacious victim succeeded in mollifying the displeasure of the Roman, who said a ruler must not be constantly interfered with in the exercise of his authority. Contrary to all expectation he returned to Jerusalem, still enjoying the favour of Antony; but he had to go on patiently enduring the machinations of Cleopatra and her intrigues with his nearest relatives as long as Antony continued at the head of affairs in the East. Eventually the queen obtained one of the fairest portions of Herod's kingdom, the famous palm groves and balsam gardens around Jericho which he had afterwards to lease from her. He had also to become surety for the tribute arising from her recent acquisitions in Syria; and his position was growing more and more precarious, when hostilities, which had been long foreseen, at length broke out between the two masters of the Roman world (B.C. 31).

Since the renewal of his relations with Cleopatra, Antony's proceedings in the East had begun to produce a deep feeling of irritation and resentment at Rome. Quitting the toga of his people for a purple robe, Antony assumed the manner of life of an Oriental despot, and appeared to have forgotten that he was a Roman. He celebrated his triumph over an Asiatic prince in Alexandria an act which deeply wounded Roman pride and frequently made his appearance in the city, which was now the rival of Rome, in the costume of the god Osiris, or arrayed in royal garments with a diadem on his head. The prudent and calculating Octavian was in the meantime engaged in restoring tranquility to the West, and consolidating the basis of his power. By the mild and temperate character of his policy, all classes were conciliated; and he waited patiently till the effects of Antony's extravagant folly rendered him intolerable to the Roman people. When the time for decisive measures at last arrived, Octavian openly denounced his colleague in the Senate (B.C. 32); and in the following year Cleopatra was declared a public enemy. In the war which ensued it was the foolish behaviour of this fatal woman that precipitated Antony's ruin. She retarded his preparations for the great contest, and at Actium (B.C. 31) prevailed on him to fight on sea where he was weak. While the battle was at its height she fled from the scene of action with sixty ships and made for Alexandria, thus converting a doubtful contest into a crowning victory. Worst of all, she had so demoralized the warlike spirit of Antony that when he saw her vessel take to flight he forgot his duties as a brave man and a general, and joined her. Octavian was now at the summit of his power, and the destruction of his rival was only a matter of time.

Fortunately for his future career, Herod was not allowed to participate actively in the hostilities which culminated so disgracefully at Actium. That the forces of the Jewish prince were then engaged in operations against the Nabataean Arabs was the work of Cleopatra. Conscious of Herod's military capacity, she was determined to prevent him from establishing additional claims upon the gratitude of the man who had at last become her husband; it was her intention to claim Judaea as her portion of the spoil at the conclusion of the war, which she expected would terminate in favour of Antony. Events, however, did not adapt themselves to the avaricious anticipations of the queen. After the disaster at Actium, the respective positions of herself and Herod became suddenly inverted, and her husband's last hope now hung on the fidelity of the very man whom she had doomed to destruction. Herod, for his part, on hearing of Antony's discomfiture, seized the first opportunity of freeing himself for the future from the menaces of Cleopatra by abandoning a lost cause. When Antony was informed that the Jewish king, in whom he placed implicit confidence, had deserted him, he relinquished all thoughts of continued resistance. Feeling that his end was near, he tried the consolations of philosophy; soon finding them ineffective, he drowned despair in dissipation, and as he had in past days lived with Cleopatra "the Inimitable Life," he now formed with her at Alexandria a society called "the Inseparables in Death." In this mood he waited the approach of his successful rival.

Octavian was apprised of Herod's defection, and of the valuable assistance he had rendered the Syrian proconsul by compelling a band of gladiators faithful to Antony to lay down their arms. Consequently when the Jewish king appeared at Rhodes in the following year (B.C. 30) to make his submission to the victor, who was then completing preparations for an advance on Alexandria, he found the politic Octavian favourably disposed towards him. Octavian appreciated the excellent services which the Idumaean family had formerly rendered to Caesar in the Alexandrian war; and being about to engage in a similar enterprise himself, he gladly welcomed such an important ally as Herod, who was accordingly confirmed in his authority. After this successful interview, Herod hastened homewards and made magnificent preparations for the advance of the legions through his territories upon Egypt. It is very probable that this duty, as it was a preliminary to the final overthrow of Cleopatra, possessed a certain attraction for the king, who had already advised Antony to put her to death, as being the cause of his misfortunes. Meanwhile Cleopatra was conducting secret negotiations with Octavian in the hope of being permitted to retain the crown. By her orders, Pelusium, the key of Egypt, opened its gates to the conqueror; and in the hour of battle her soldiers proved faithless to Antony, who, surrounded on all sides by treachery and defection, and having nothing to expect from the clemency of his opponent, returned to Alexandria and put a termination to his existence. Cleopatra now hoped to purchase the grace of Octavian with the dead body of her husband, but being secretly informed that the victor intended taking her to Rome to adorn his triumph, she followed Antony's example, and was found dead at his tomb. With the conclusion of the Egyptian war the troubled and bloody period of transition from republican to monarchial institutions came to an end. Octavian was now undisputed master of the whole empire. His victory over Antony was hailed with acclamation as the beginning of a new and brighter era for distressed humanity; of war and convulsion the world was weary, and the great poets of this period give noble utterance to the universal aspiration for repose and peace (B.C. 30).

For the next forty years Octavian or to use the name of honour conferred upon him by the Senate—Augustus remained at the head of affairs, and utilized his unique position in founding and developing the institutions of the new empire. While professing the utmost reverence for ancient constitutional forms, he assumed under old names a monopoly of supreme power, and in the guise of restoring liberty to the oppressed republic, in reality transformed it into an Oriental despotism. His long reign is replete with interest both to students of literature and of political institutions; but, above all, it will continue to be memorable, in the history of mankind, as the era in which the Founder of Christianity was born.

It was under the political system created by Augustus that the Christian religion found scope to spread itself throughout the Western world. His character and aims in consequence acquire a significance which does not attach to any of the previous Roman rulers of Palestine. With all his admirable qualities of mind and temper, Augustus cannot be called a genius; and though his wonderful faculty for utilizing men and circumstances compels respect, yet he remains one of those cold and calculating natures it is impossible to love. With him every action was the result of premeditation; nothing was spontaneous; he even wrote down what he intended saying to his wife, and his ideal of life appeared to be to avoid committing a mistake. Antony accused him of being deficient in courage: this, however, cannot be asserted with justice; it undoubtedly required courage of a very high order for a youth of nineteen to come forward as heir of the murdered Caesar a step which threw him into the very heart of the Titanic strife let loose by the Dictator's death. It was not, however, in keeping with his principles, using his own expression, "to hazard much for the sake of little." The quick flash of impulse he regarded with a certain dread, and his boldest enterprises were always the outcome of cool and patient calculation. In dealing with men politically, this habit of mind was of the highest value to Augustus, but it utterly failed him in the loftier domain of religion, and the reforms which he inaugurated in this sphere produced no lasting fruit, because the reformer was simply actuated by motives of state, and not by the sacred flame of love for what is good. His private life belied the stringent laws enacted against the immoralities of the time: and if the simplicity of his table and home was a bright example in a luxurious age, he was in other respects soiled and tainted with the odious vices of his contemporaries. His pretended zeal for moral purity gives a painful air of hypocrisy to his character, of which he appears to have been conscious when he asked the friends admitted to his deathbed if he had not played his part well in the pantomime of life.

In his public capacity Augustus had an admirable opportunity after Antony's death of constituting the empire which had become a necessity—upon a broad and enduring basis; and although this was apparently his intention, events proved that he did not possess the statesmanship or self-renunciation requisite for such a task. In the old Roman institutions, for which he professed so profound a reverence, were to be found nearly all the materials for the erection of a sound constitutional fabric, free alike from the excessive decentralization that had ruined Greece and the despotic autocracy inseparable from Oriental forms of civilization. Out of the materials which lay at hand, and of which he must have been cognizant, Augustus might have created a stable government, directed by competent public servants, assisted and controlled in their administration by the intelligent co-operation not only of the inhabitants of Rome or Italy, but of every freeman within the dominions of the empire. On this path, which would probably have saved Europe ten centuries of darkness and barbarism, Augustus did not choose to proceed; and the only institution which he founded on the ruins of the Republic was the absolute will of the emperor too frail a bulwark to prevent the rapid dissolution of ancient society. Tacitus gives a lucid and concise account of the method adopted by the emperor for concentrating all authority in his own person, and of the willingness of all classes to accept the yoke.

"The defeat of Brutus and Cassius," says the historian, "destroyed the republicans; Sextus Pompey had succumbed in Sicily; the fall of Lepidus and the death of Antony left Augustus as sole chief of Caesar's party. Renouncing the title of Triumvir for that of Consul, Augustus, for the purpose of protecting the people, was at first contented with the tribunitian power. Soon afterwards, having gained the soldiers by his largesses, the people by distributions of food, and all orders of the State by the sweets of peace, he grew bolder by degrees, and drew to himself without opposition the whole power of the Senate, the magistrates, and the laws. The bravest of the nobility had perished in battle or by proscription; the rest won over to servitude by riches and honours, preferred the present with its safety to the past with its dangers. These changes did not displease the provinces; they dreaded the rule of the Senate and people, on account of the rival ambitions and cupidity of the magistrates, who were feebly checked by laws which were powerless against violence, corruption, and wealth."

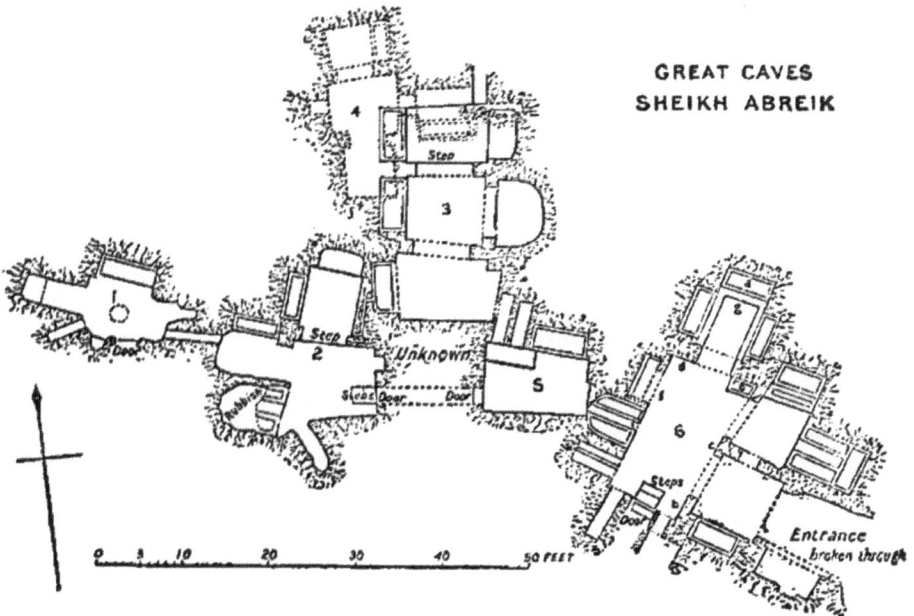

GREAT CAVES
SHEIKH ABREIK

Such, then, was the character of the ruler with whom Herod had for the future to deal; and such the nature of the empire into which Palestine became incorporated for several centuries to come. At the close of the Alexandrian expedition Augustus had to arrive at a determination respecting the government of his new acquisitions in the East. He renounced the designs of Caesar and Antony for carrying Roman arms beyond the Euphrates. The countries immediately contiguous to the Mediterranean formed a natural boundary for an industrial and commercial empire such as Augustus had conceived; his eastern policy therefore resolved itself into the question of establishing a stable authority on the Egyptian and Syrian line of coast. Of Herod's competence to assist him in this task the emperor was well aware. The Jewish king, it is true, in the struggle between contending factions, had frequently changed sides, but he had always remained faithful to Rome; although he espoused Antony's cause, he did not oppose Augustus in the field, and his hatred of Cleopatra went far to atone for his familiar relations with her lover. In addition, the excellent arrangements Herod had made for the comfort of the troops in the recent campaign were fresh in the emperor's memory, and policy as well as gratitude pointed to the Jewish prince as the fittest man for guarding Roman interests in Western Syria. At all events, such was the opinion of Augustus, who possessed a rare aptitude for the selection of able subordinates. Herod, accordingly, was not only confirmed in his kingdom, but it was also enlarged by the addition of Samaria, the Jewish possessions of Cleopatra, portions of territory east of Jordan, and the whole coastline from Gaza to the future city of Caesarea. A few years afterwards, when Augustus was further convinced of the wisdom of his choice, Herod received fresh accessions of territory. His power then extended eastward to Damascus and northward to the sources of the Jordan, the whole kingdom forming a vaster dominion than had at any previous time been ruled from Jerusalem, even in her palmiest days.

In the internal administration of his extensive possessions, Herod became a zealous imitator of his imperial master, and Palestine, as well as Italy, could boast its Augustan age of order, civilization, and peace. In the turbulent regions of the northeast, the king successfully accomplished the difficult task of pacification, utterly dispersing the hordes of robbers who had made this district their refuge and home. He amply satisfied the primary test applied by Augustus to all his subordinates namely, their fitness for maintaining order and tranquility. It was no easy matter to achieve this end among the disaffected and fanatical population over which he ruled; but Herod was a man of infinite resource, who thoroughly understood the temper of his subjects, and knew what precautions would prove effective in the contingency of revolt. The defenses of the capital were strengthened to overawe the inhabitants, a military colony was planted in Samaria for the same purpose, and a strategical system of fortifications established throughout the rest of the country, His Roman masters had long since taught him how to dispose of opponents; and during the reign of Antony he freely decimated them by proscriptions, which served the twofold purpose of supplying the triumvir with gold, and of striking terror among the disaffected. Under Augustus, who had grown weary of blood, the king pursued, except with his own family, a different method, which con listed in covering the land with a network of spies. It is said that he sometimes played the spy himself, mixing among the people in disguise at night, the better to ascertain their true feelings towards the government. Despotism, by stifling the free and open expression of opinion, is invariably driven to these dark courses, and Augustus is reported to have adopted even more shameful means than Herod to feel the real pulse of public sentiment. As a safeguard against sedition and discontent, Herod had great faith in keeping the people occupied; large assemblages were forbidden, as tending to conspiracy and disorder; the use of torture was not infrequent; punishments were as a rule severe; and, especially in Judaea, terror and force were the ultimate and only foundations of authority.

It would, however, be taking an imperfect view of the king's administration to look only at the equivocal methods adopted by him for upholding order and curbing disaffection. It is certain that he was also animated by a sincere desire to promote the welfare and prosperity of his subjects, and that, under his rule, Palestine, like other portions of the empire, entered upon an era of unwonted affluence. Measures were put in operation to augment the productiveness of the country. Trade was encouraged, new commercial centres were established, cities restored and founded, and, to facilitate communication between Syria and Egypt, a magnificent harbour was constructed at Caesarea. The building operations at Caesarea were on an immense scale; and the choice of site reflects high honour on the king's foresight, for the place rapidly grew into an important city, and eventually displaced Jerusalem as the capital of the country. His influence with the Roman administrators was also exerted in behalf of the Jews (the Diaspora) who had settled in different parts of the empire, and through him valuable privileges and immunities were secured for them. At home the king lightened taxation when he believed it was becoming burdensome, and during a famine which committed terrible ravages in the land, he displayed admirable qualities both of head and heart. By him vast supplies of food were obtained from Egypt for the starving population; the tender, the aged, the infirm were the objects of his assiduous care; and as the treasury was empty, he sold the whole of his costly plate and furniture stripping the royal palace of its grandeur in order to supply the people with the necessaries of life.

Herod's success in maintaining order and promoting prosperity among his subjects induced Augustus to lay upon him the much more delicate and difficult duty of attempting to Hellenize them as well. The external unity of the empire had been achieved, but it as yet possessed no internal cohesion, and the only thing which prevented the huge structure from falling to pieces was the invincible constraint of Roman arms. Augustus wished to create an internal bond of union among the heterogeneous populations under his sway, and to attain this end adopted the project of permeating the unhellenized portions of the East with the tastes, habits, and customs of Greece and Rome. Herod, as far as his dominions were concerned, became a willing instrument of his imperial master, and made vigorous efforts to impart a Roman character to the land. In the Gentile portion of his government he erected splendid heathen temples, and dedicated them to Caesar. Roman spectacles were introduced, Roman theatres and amphitheatres constructed for the amusement of the populace; the military roads were studded with Roman monuments; cities, towns, palaces, and public edifices received Roman names, and especially the names of the imperial family Samaria became Sebaste, Straton's Tower became Caesarea, and the entire country presented the appearance of being thoroughly Romanized. In Judaea the king, who knew the temper of the inhabitants, went to work more warily, but even in this province he ventured to build a huge amphitheatre not far from the Holy City, and here the games instituted by Augustus in honour of his victory at Actium were celebrated in a magnificent manner. Contests with gladiators, chariot races, wild-beast fights could now be witnessed in the very heart of Judaism on a scale and with a splendour which compelled the admiration of the Gentiles themselves.

People from all parts of the empire were invited to these novel spectacles. Jerusalem ceased to be a city given up to priests, rabbis, and doctors of the law; it was unwillingly opened out to the more diversified life of the West. Foreign mercenaries from Galatia, Germany, and Thrace were now to be seen in its streets; foreign envoys and retainers were always frequenting the royal palace, and Western habits of life became more and more

Portion of the Wall That Surrounded the Temple

common and prominent in the capital; Greek orators, sophists, and historians gave an air of intellectual distinction to Herod's court; and two brothers, both able men, Nicolaus and Ptolemaeus, of Damascus, held high positions in the administration. Ptolemaeus did not possess the brilliant gifts of his brother, but he was of the utmost service to the king in the practical conduct of affairs, and exercised a wholesome influence on his passionate and suspicious nature. Nicolaus was Herod's confidential agent in his dealings with Augustus and the Roman officials He was a man of exceptional acquirements, at once a diplomatist, courtier, poet, and philosopher; he had also published well-known works on geography and history, and was a naturalist of repute besides. Other Greeks of lesser note also found their way into Herod's favour, some for good and others for evil, but all of them contributed towards Hellenizing the capital and giving a Western tone to the conduct of affairs.

44

While pursuing this line of policy Herod felt that he was inflicting deep wounds on Jewish religious susceptibility, and in order to allay public discontent pretended to be acting in obedience to commands from Rome. To a certain extent this excuse may be correct, for during the supremacy of Antony, he displayed little liking for works of art or Western modes of life, and his newborn zeal under Augustus probably proceeded from motives of statecraft and a desire to please his imperial master. Still, it is also worthy of being remembered that Herod was only half a Jew. By education he was a Greek. During his reign he surrounded himself with Greeks, and openly preferred them to his Jewish subjects. He delighted in their applause, loved to adorn their cities, restore their temples, subsidize their games, and, although his mind was never deeply penetrated by Hellenic culture, he had been taught to regard it as the highest and best. But with all his Gentile leanings, Herod was too much of a statesman to carry Hellenism beyond the point which his Jewish subjects could endure, and carefully avoided repeating the blunders of Antiochus Epiphanes. On the contrary, he tried to make political capital out of Jewish beliefs, especially those connected with the Temple and the Messianic hopes.

At this period it was a prevalent idea among the Jews that the Messiah when He appeared would erect a far more splendid temple than the one at present in existence; and the Book of Enoch, then very popular, sustained this belief by prophesying that the Messianic age would be inaugurated by the building of a house to the praise of a great king for ever and ever. Herod took hold of these expectations and set himself to utilize them for dynastic purposes. In the fifteenth year of his reign (B.C. 20) he summoned a great assembly of the people, and after delivering an oration to them on the blessings which had accompanied his rule, announced his intention of rebuilding the Temple and superseding the old structure of Zerubbabel by a far more glorious edifice. His proposition was received with mingled feelings of apprehension and dismay, but Herod succeeded in dissipating the fears of the people. Thousands of priests and workmen were engaged, the materials for the new edifice were collected before the old Temple was demolished, and for eight years the great work of re-construction was proceeded with. Huge blocks of marble, which afterwards aroused the wonder of Christ's disciples, were transported from a great distance to the Temple Mount; the priests were taught masonry, so that no unclean hands should touch the inner courts, and the king himself was forbidden to approach the most sacred portions of the new edifice. At last the great undertaking was completed. Its consecration was celebrated with unequalled pomp and magnificence, and national pride was gratified by the spectacle of its extraordinary beauty. When the morning sun burst upon the white marble of the Temple, Mount Moriah glittered like a hill of snow; and when its rays struck the golden roof of the sacred edifice, the whole mount gleamed and sparkled as if it were in flames. Whoever has not seen the Temple of Herod, said the rabbis, has seen nothing beautiful; pious legend went further, and declared that it was built amid manifestations of Divine approval.

Notwithstanding the momentary satisfaction produced among the people of Judaea by the re-erection of the Temple, Herod never really enjoyed more than a temporary popularity in this, the most rigid and fanatical part of the kingdom. It was not so much his despotism which made the dwellers in and around Jerusalem his irreconcilable enemies. The despotism of several of the Maccabean princes had been far more brutal; it was not the king's Hellenism, for the Maccabees had been as ardent Hellenists as he; it was not even his usurpation taken by itself, but the fact of his being an Idumaean, a stranger in the gates of Israel.

Among no people of antiquity did race antipathy exercise so potent an influence as among the Jews of Judaea. Among them national exclusiveness had become one of the most vital elements of religion, and their racial kinship with the Edomites added bitterness to this exclusive spirit, instead of tending to break it down. It was sufficient that Herod was one of the hated children of Edom to ensure his being detested by the Jews; no services of his could possibly wipe out this stain. It would have proved fatal to the popularity of any prince however excellent, and the Jewish deputy who accused the king before Augustus was expressing the heartfelt convictions of his countrymen, when he said that the generation which lived under Herod endured more tribulation than all their forefathers together since the return from Babylon.

Unquestionably Herod put down religious outbreaks with a strong hand, and drowned every uprising of fanaticism in blood; his measures were sometimes terribly severe, but they were essential to the one supreme demand of Augustus—the maintenance of peace. Herod's rule shows many a dark blot on its pages, but it was the only rule then possible except the direct sovereignty of Rome; and if his administration is compared with the condition of things which immediately preceded it, or even with the latter period of independence, it will come forth from the ordeal with additional lustre. It has to be conceded that his government was not based on the people's will, but it has likewise to be remembered that to Jews had proved in the most glaring manner their total incapacity to govern themselves, and their choice actually lay not between, despotism and self-government, but between despotism and anarchy.

Herod evidently knew the reason why he was so bitterly hated by his Jewish subjects, for he burned the archives of Jerusalem where the genealogies were preserved, and pretended to be a descendant of a distinguished family of Babylonian Jews. Nicolaus of Damascus even drew up a Jewish pedigree for the king, but the device was too transparent to deceive any one, and he was known to the last in popular language as the Hasmonaean slave. But, after all, Judaea was only a small portion of his dominions, and the hostility which he experienced there is in marked contrast with the goodwill accorded him in Samaria and Galilee, and the gratitude of the Jews abroad. The Samaritans were warmly attached to him, and Samaria was his favourite residence;

46

the absence of fortifications in Galilee is a proof that he had nothing to fear from the high-spirited and warlike inhabitants of the north, and he was recognized by the Jews of the Dispersion as their friend and protector. In face of these circumstances it is hardly possible to avoid the conclusion that sentimental antipathies, joined to an innate spirit of turbulence, distorted the popular judgment in Judaea, and led the inhabitants to see Herod in a perverted light.

It is remarkable that public virtues are sometimes found in conjunction with a disreputable private character, and this was to a certain extent the case with Herod. In many respects his long reign was a distinct blessing to the Jews, and if his family life with its dreadful tale of murder and woe had remained unchronicled, history might have accorded him a place among the select band of sovereigns who have deserved well of their country. Something in the human conscience rebels against the dictum that a ruler's private life is a matter of indifference so long as it does not injuriously affect his public action, but this appears to have been the light in which Herod was regarded by Augustus and his minister Agrippa. With only one short interval he enjoyed the confidence of the emperor to the last, and on more than one occasion he gave substantial proof that this confidence was deserved. It was through Herod's timely assistance that a disastrous expedition sent by Augustus to the Red Sea did not terminate more disastrously, and on the only occasion in which the king was visited with the imperial disfavour, Augustus discovered afterwards that the error lay with himself. So striking was his faith in Herod's judgment in Eastern affairs that the proconsuls of Syria, men of the highest eminence in the empire, were enjoined to undertake nothing of importance within the province without first consulting the Jewish king, and Josephus relates that Augustus esteemed Herod next to his son-in-law Agrippa, and that Agrippa who had visited the king's dominions and seen his great undertakings valued him next to the emperor.

It is in Herod's family life that the darkest elements of his character are most distinctly seen. His great palace at Jerusalem presented the outward appearance of a Grecian edifice, but within it was an oriental harem full of the plots and jealousies of women, eunuchs, and slaves. When the king entered this polluted atmosphere his usual sagacity utterly failed him, and he frequently acted like a man bereft of reason. His palace was little better than a pandemonium; a women's war was continually going on among the different members of his family; the air was full of rumours, whisperings, and secret intrigues, all of which were poured into Herod's ears in exaggerated forms, till he imagined himself surrounded by an invisible network of conspiracy. His jealous and suspicious nature was worked upon by skilled intriguers who knew the weak spots in his character, and roused him into transports of fury and revenge. It was at such times that he gave orders for those terrible executions of his own kindred, which remain without a parallel in history. In these fits of rage he spared neither age nor sex, and neither affection nor the sacred ties of fatherhood and wedlock were allowed to stay the hand of the executioner. Wives, brothers, children, were all hurried to an untimely doom when once his suspicions were successfully aroused. By Herod's command his beautiful wife Marianne perished in the flower of life; his children Alexander and Aristobulus met with a like fate as they were entering upon manhood, and their great-grandfather Hyrcanus while he was tottering to the grave. Besides these victims, Marianne's mother, his brother-in-law Costobar, his uncle Joseph, and his eldest son Antipater were all executed. Some of them—as, for instance, his mother-in-law Alexandra and his diabolical son Antipater probably deserved their fate; but the others were sacrificed to the jealousy and suspicion of the king. Remorse generally followed these executions, and the miserable man was to be seen wandering about heartbroken and inconsolable, calling aloud to his victims as if they were still alive. Augustus sometimes tried to compose Herod's family disputes, but with little permanent success, and at last he came to the conclusion that it was better to be one of Herod's swine than his son.

In Herod's old age the arbitrary and bloodthirsty side of his character obscured those more estimable qualities which have obtained for him the name of Great, and when he died at Jericho (B.C. 4) about the age of seventy, after a reign of thirty-four years, the earlier and more brilliant period of his life was forgotten; and he lived in the popular imagination simply as the instigator of atrocity and woe. By the gospel writers who place the birth of Christ in the concluding years of his long reign, he is represented as a jealous and suspicious tyrant, and a similar account of him is preserved in an old fragment of Jewish literature written probably a short time after the king's death. In prophetic tones a writer under the pseudonym of Moses, after pronouncing sentence of condemnation on the Maccabees for their impiety which brought about the usurpation of Herod, proceeds thus to describe the king, and his tyrannous deeds: An insolent king shall succeed them who is not of the race of the priests—a daring and godless man. And he will judge them as they deserve. He will extirpate their eminent men with the sword, and will bury their bodies in unknown places, so that no man shall know where their bodies are. He will kill the aged and the young and not spare. Then shall a great fear of him be among them in their land, and he shall execute judgment among them as the Egyptians did among them, and shall chastise them for thirty or forty years. And he will beget sons who as his successors shall rule a shorter time."

Of these sons and their relations with the Romans we shall in the following chapter proceed to speak.

The Roman Tetrarchs - B.C. 4 to A.D. 37

Immediately after Herod's death Augustus sent Sabinus, a Roman official, to superintend the administration till he came to a decision respecting the future government of the country. Before the arrival of this functionary a dangerous tumult had already taken place in Jerusalem, in which three thousand citizens lost their lives; and, to complicate the situation, the authority of Sabinus, which was apparently ill-defined, was ignored by Herod's old officers. This step was taken in accordance with instructions from Archelaus, the king's son, who was then on his way to Rome to obtain the assent of Augustus to his father's will. After the arrival of Sabinus in the capital, the disorders throughout the country became so alarming, that Quintilius Varus, the Syrian proconsul, had to overawe the disaffected with his legions,

Masada from the Northwest

and before his departure he left a strong garrison in Jerusalem to uphold the authority of Rome. But the spirit of revolt was abroad; the turbulent had no longer the fear of the old king before their eyes. Sabinus was arbitrary, and the wild forces of fanaticism which were gathered together at the Feast of Pentecost (B.C. 4) shut up the Roman garrison in one of the fortifications of the Holy City. Sabinus, seeing the critical nature of his position, dispatched pressing messages to Varus to come to his relief; meantime the revolt assumed larger proportions, and, with the exception of Samaria, the whole of Palestine was in open rebellion. Bands of robbers and marauders, headed by pretenders and slaves, sprang up in different parts of the country. Herod's palace at Jericho was looted, the armoury at Sepphoris, in Galilee, fell into the hands of the insurgents, and the whole of Palestine was plunged into anarchy when Varus began his march to rescue the garrison of Jerusalem. As in former revolts, the desperate bravery of the insurgents was of no avail against the disciplined valour of the West. Varus inflicted severe chastisement upon the rebellious districts; several towns were burnt, many Jews were sold as slaves, and, as a terrible warning to the disaffected, two thousand rebels were taken and crucified.

It appears that Sabinus had for some reason incurred the displeasure of the proconsul, for when he approached the Holy City at the head of his troops, Sabinus did not dare to meet him, but retired to the sea coast, and Varus, with the assistance of one of Herod's old generals, succeeded in restoring a temporary tranquility to the unhappy land.

While these events were transpiring in Judaea, most of the members of Herod's family had arrived in Rome, and were intriguing against one another for possession of the old king's inheritance. Herod had made a will shortly before his death disposing of his property and dominions, but his arrangements possessed no validity till they received the sanction of the emperor. Augustus placed himself in the position of a suzerain towards the princes, who were allowed to remain in authority in different parts of the empire, according them a wide discretion in internal affairs, but reserving certain questions for settlement by himself alone. Among these were the questions of peace and war and of succession to the throne. In the case of Herod's family it was difficult for the emperor to arrive at a decision, owing to the discord prevailing amongst them and their accusations against one another. Whilst he was considering the best methods for disposing of the old king's dominions, the situation was complicated by the appearance in Rome of a Jewish deputation, composed of citizens who were hostile to a continuance of Herodian rule, and whose aim it was to induce Augustus to place the country under the immediate control of a Roman governor. In order to obtain more light on the affairs of Palestine, Augustus summoned the sons of Herod and the deputies from Judaea to meet him in conference on an appointed day in the Temple of Apollo. Here, surrounded by the imperial officials, he heard the complaints of the Jewish delegates, as well as their proposals with respect to the future government of Palestine. The defence of the Herodians was undertaken by Nicolaus of Damascus, who not only rebutted the charges of the delegation, but also accused the Jews of taking pleasure in disorder and sedition, and of being unwilling to submit like peaceful citizens to the lawfully constituted authorities. A few days after the termination of these proceedings Augustus publicly announced his intention of adhering to the main provisions of Herod's will. Archelaus was accordingly made ruler of Judaea, Idumaea, and Samaria, with an annual income of one hundred and twenty thousand pounds, but without the title of king; his brother Antipas obtained the provinces of Galilee and Peraea, with power to raise a revenue of forty thousand pounds annually; while his half-brother Philip became ruler of the wild districts of Batanaea, Auranitis, and Trachonitis, in the northeast of Palestine, and had an annual revenue of twenty thousand pounds. Other members of the family were also suitably provided for by the emperor, and the whole of Herod's dominions, with the exception of the coast towns of Gaza, Gadara, and Hippos, remained in the hands of his relatives and children.

Of Philip's long reign (B.C. 4 to A.D. 34) there is little left on record. His mother was Cleopatra of Jerusalem, whom Herod received into his harem more on account of her beauty than her birth. Philip was educated at Rome along with his half-brothers Archelaus and Antipas, and from what is recorded of his character, he seems to have been the best disposed and most estimable of the Herodian family. While Archelaus was in Italy with the object of gaining the assent of Augustus to his father's will, the government of Palestine was left in Philip's hands, and during the interregnum he struggled manfully with the disturbances which arose. During this troubled period the high qualities of the young prince won for him the esteem of Varus, the proconsul, who recommended him to the favourable consideration of the emperor, and at the same time advised him to go and look after his interests at Rome. Philip accepted this counsel. The portion of the late king's possessions which Augustus allotted to him was in extent the largest, but in other respects the poorest, the most unsettled, and the most difficult to govern. It contained a mixed population of Arabs and Syrians, interspersed with Jewish and Idumaean colonists, who had settled in these regions in the preceding reign for the purpose of holding the predatory instincts of the wild inhabitants in check. Philip, like a wise ruler, made the most of the position in which he stood, and of the indifferent material with which he had to deal. Avoiding all schemes of territorial aggrandizement, the young tetrarch concentrated his attention on affairs at home, and acquired the reputation of a sober-minded and discreet ruler, who watched like a father over the welfare of his people. It was a custom of this excellent prince, accompanied by his trusted advisers, to make occasional visits to the different parts of his dominions. At such times he readily attended to the complaints of his subjects, and administered justice to them at a moment's notice. He apparently possessed the secret of ruling the intractable population of his tetrarchy, for during a reign of many years (B.C. 4 to A. D. 34) an era of peace and tranquility prevailed among a people whom the Syrian proconsuls had in vain attempted to reduce to order.

Philip's capital, Caesarea Philippi, originally bore the name of

View of Nazareth

Paneas, and was situated in a beautiful and picturesque district among the mountains of Lebanon, near the sources of the Jordan, where Herod the Great had built a temple in honour of Augustus. Philip, who was under the necessity of choosing a chief town for the centre of his government, selected this place, and in order to increase the population, declared it an asylum where all could flee to and find security. At a critical period in His public ministry, Jesus had occasion to retire from Galilee to this neighbourhood, and it was here that He asked His disciples the momentous question, Whom do men say that I am? The village of Bethsaida, on the northeastern shores of the sea of Galilee, was also enlarged by the tetrarch, who changed its name to Julias, in honour of the notorious daughter of the emperor. He considered himself as a Gentile ruler, his coins being stamped with the head of Caesar and an impression of the heathen temple of Paneas. Of his marriage with Salome, a daughter of Herodias, there was no issue, and when he died in the reign of Tiberius (A.D. 33-4), at the age of fifty-five, his territories were incorporated with the pro-consulate of Syria.

Herod Antipas (B.C. 4 to A.D. 39), Tetrarch of Galilee and Peraea, was also a man of a peace-loving disposition, and would in all probability have died in the position to which Augustus appointed him if he had regulated his private life with the same prudence as he conducted public affairs. He was a son of Herod the Great by Malthace, a Samaritan woman, and a full brother of Archelaus, who was a little his senior in age. Like most of Herod's children he received a Roman education, and at one time it was the old king's intention to appoint him sole heir of his possessions. It is probable that his father discerned signs of ability in the young prince, or perhaps he had the good fortune not to incur the morbid suspicions of the aged king. He was better liked in Herod's family than Archelaus, and his relatives made every effort to induce Augustus to carry out the king's earlier intentions with regard to the succession.= But these efforts utterly failed, probably because Augustus no longer felt the necessity of preserving a large kingdom on the eastern frontiers of the empire, but more likely because he did not wish to interfere with the final arrangements of the deceased king. Accordingly Antipas, in spite of powerful voices being raised in his behalf, had to rest content with the provinces which his father finally assigned to him.

Antipas was only seventeen years of age when he began to reign (B.C. 4). His territories did not lie compactly together like the dominions of Archelaus, but they were not so difficult to govern, although the Galileans were a warlike and high-spirited people. In many respects Galilee was highly favoured by nature, and enjoyed a certain amount of commercial prosperity, but shortly before passing into the hands of its young ruler it had suffered severely, in consequence of the unsettlement of the whole country after Herod's death. Ruined towns and villages bore witness to the heavy chastisement inflicted on the people by the legions of Varus, and the fact that Antipas was sent to govern them by the same power which had so lately perpetrated these barbarities was not calculated to ensure him a warm welcome from his new subjects. He did not, however, meet with active opposition, and perhaps the people, after their recent experiences of war and disorder, were glad of any change which promised a restoration of the tranquility they had for so many years enjoyed. In the late troubles the important town of Sepphoris had been reduced to ruins, and its inhabitants sold as slaves; Antipas showed the people his desire to do the utmost for the welfare of the land, by rebuilding it and making it the seat of government. In the province of Peraea, which was exposed to the incursions of the wild sons of the desert, the tetrarch erected the fortress of Julias, on the eastern banks of the Jordan, opposite Jericho; and to still further ensure the safety of his possessions in this region, he allied himself by marriage with a daughter of Aretas, the Nabataean king, whose dominions here bordered on his own.

During the lifetime of Augustus (B.C. 4 to-A.D. 14) Antipas, who knew that his princely position depended solely on his ability to preserve peace and contentment among the population, acted with prudence and caution, and no complaint was made against him to the emperor. Still he never succeeded in securing the confidence of Augustus to the same extent as his father; and when his brother Archelaus was deposed, Judaea and Samaria were not placed under his control, as he probably had anticipated, but were incorporated with the province of Syria. The sacred ties of blood had very little influence with the children of Herod, and one of the worst characteristics of Antipas was his utter want of fraternal feeling. When his brother Archelaus was accused of tyranny by his subjects, Antipas, instead of attempting to shield him, in all probability did his best to procure his banishment (A.D. 6).

The accession of Tiberius to the imperial throne (A.D. 14 to A.D. 37) was an event of much importance to the tetrarch, for it changed the coldness of his previous relations with the imperial court, and ultimately exalted him into the position of a confidential agent of the new Caesar. Tiberius was a man of a soured and suspicious temperament, who never thoroughly trusted his officials, and Antipas served the emperor's purpose as a kind of spy on the Roman authorities charged with the administration of affairs in the East. It is probably on this account that he was hated by Pontius Pilate, who was Procurator of Judaea during the latter part of the reign of Antipas; for Pilate, who understood the character of Tiberius, would be well aware of the general nature of the correspondence which passed between the gloomy man on the Tiber and his vassal in Palestine. Vitellius, the Proconsul of Syria, also knew that Antipas was in the habit of sending secret communications to the emperor, and disliked him quite as much as Pilate. On one occasion he was deeply incensed at the underhand conduct of the Jewish prince. The proconsul had been requested by Tiberius to endeavour to conclude a treaty with the Persian king, Artabanus, and after he had carried the emperor's wishes to a successful issue he was mortified to find that Antipas, who accompanied him to the Euphrates to meet the Persian king, had dispatched an account of the whole proceedings to Rome which anticipated his own. On the death of Tiberius, the proconsul made Antipas feel that he had not forgotten his resentment.

Notwithstanding the hostility of the Roman officials Antipas retained the goodwill of the emperor to the last. As a token of gratitude to his patron he built a new capital on the western shores of the Sea of Galilee, and called it Tiberias. While the building operations were in progress, it was unfortunately discovered that an old graveyard occupied a portion of the site, a circumstance which caused the rabbis to declare the place unclean; and it was some time before the Jews in any numbers could be induced to settle in the new capital. Although situated in one of the most beautiful districts of Galilee, it had the reputation of being unhealthy; still, in spite of this serious disadvantage, the new city grew in a short time to be one of the most important places in Palestine. It was constructed in the Greco-Roman style of the period; its inhabitants were mainly Gentiles, and besides the royal palace the public buildings consisted of an amphitheatre, an arsenal, and latterly a synagogue.

While Antipas was at the summit of his prosperity he set out on a journey to Rome which proved to be the beginning of all his future misfortunes. During his stay in the imperial city, he lived at the house of his half-brother Herod (Boethus) whose wife Herodias was a granddaughter of Marianne, whom Herod the Great had executed in a fit of jealousy. Herodias was an ambitious woman, and disliked the private station to which her husband had been consigned by his father's will. Antipas, although no longer young, was unable to resist her charms, and it was secretly arranged between them that Herodias should desert her husband and become the tetrarch's wife. One of the stipulations in this guilty arrangement was that Antipas should divorce the daughter of the Nabataean king, to whom he had been married for a great number of years. By some means or other knowledge of this immoral compact reached the ears of the unfortunate princess, who was to be its principal victim, and she anticipated the action of her faithless husband by at once fleeing from his dominions to the court of her father at Petra. Aretas, who had not been on harmonious terms with Antipas for some time, on account of a territorial dispute, now decisively broke with him, and made preparations for war. Antipas, on his side, was not idle, but when the two armies came to blows, the forces of the tetrarch were thoroughly defeated, and he had to fall back for protection on the friendship of Tiberius.

It is very probable that Antipas had obtained the emperor's sanction to his new matrimonial arrangements, for he at once espoused the cause of his servile vassal, and gave orders to Vitellius to declare war against Aretas, and execute him or send him to Rome in bonds. To all appearance fortune was once more smiling upon the schemes of Antipas: Vitellius had completed the necessary preparations for the campaign; the Roman legions were on the march; the fate of Aretas was trembling in the balance, when all of a sudden the situation was completely changed by the unexpected news that Tiberius, the tetrarch's protector, was dead. It was now that Vitellius found the long-sought-for opportunity of requiting Antipas for disclosing the contents of the Parthian treaty. He knew that the operations in which the army was engaged were intended to avenge the Jewish prince; accordingly the proconsul, on the pretext that he was without orders from the new emperor, immediately declared the campaign at an end, and withdrew to Antioch. To be baffled in this manner when the victim was almost in his grasp must have been a bitter disappointment to Antipas, if it did not also fill him with a presentiment that his own downfall was nigh at hand.

The war with Aretas was not the only difficulty in which Antipas became involved through his marriage with Herodias; this unfortunate alliance also led him to deliver over John the Baptist to imprisonment and death. It was within the tetrarch's dominions, in the province of Peraea that the preacher in the wilderness exercised his public ministry, and in the course of his admonitions he felt it a duty to rebuke the moral delinquency of a ruler whose relations with Herodias were equally opposed to the Law of Moses and the conscience of mankind. Notwithstanding the solemn condemnation of his unlawful union, Antipas continued to respect the Baptist. It was only when he began to dread the political consequences of John's missionary activity, that he listened to the advice of Herodias and cast the fiery preacher into prison. The place of confinement selected for the illustrious captive was the fortress of Machaerus on the Arabian frontier, chosen probably because it was far away from the religious excitement which was at that moment so profoundly agitating Jewish life. Here John was permitted a certain amount of freedom; his disciples were allowed to visit him, and through them he was enabled to communicate with the outside world. Antipas was not a man of a cruel or bloodthirsty disposition, and it is not probable that he ever intended to put the Baptist to death his imprisonment of John being rather a measure of precaution than an act of punishment but it was not easy for him to defeat the settled purpose of a woman like Herodias. Her heart was set upon accomplishing the destruction of the man who had dared to lift up an accusing voice against the propriety of her actions. John had been a few months in confinement when the opportunity for satisfying her revenge unexpectedly arrived. It was on the occasion of Antipas' birthday. To celebrate this event the prince entertained the chief dignitaries of his dominions at a feast in the course of which the graceful dancing of Salome, Herodias' daughter, so pleased the excited reveler that, in Oriental fashion, he promised the charming dancer anything she chose to ask, even to the half of his possessions. At the instigation of her mother the princess, to the tetrarch's great astonishment and consternation, asked to be presented with the head of John the Baptist, and Antipas was weak enough to satisfy this atrocious request. The executioner soon did his work, and Herodias could at last exult in the fact that the burning words of the preacher in the wilderness would trouble her uneasy heart no more.

John's execution occurred before the defeat of the tetrarch's army by the Nabataeans, and this defeat was attributed by his subjects to the foul manner in which he had taken the life of a man whom they all looked upon as fulfilling the sacred mission of a prophet. It is very likely that Antipas himself shared the feelings of his subjects with respect to this bloody decd. It is certain that the Baptist's death weighed heavily upon his mind, for when the fame of Jesus soon afterwards began to reach his ears, he seemed stricken with remorse, and said, "It is John the Baptist; he is risen from the dead." Within the tetrarch's dominions the greater part of Jesus' public ministry took place. Here the first Christian community was formed, consisting almost exclusively of the subjects of Antipas; and such was the commotion created among the people by the teachings of its Founder that the alarmed prince is said to have meditated making Jesus share the fate of John. This report, however, was very probably circulated by the enemies of Jesus, and had little or no foundation in fact. Antipas was not the kind of man to repeat an experiment which had already gravely endangered his popularity, and might easily have led to the downfall of his throne.

Still, we can gather from the expression which Jesus uses concerning Antipas, that he had no faith in the fox-like character of the man. He avoided the capital of this prince, and although Antipas had a great desire to see Him, that desire was not gratified till he beheld Jesus as a prisoner at Jerusalem in the closing hours of His earthly life. Antipas was in the Holy City when Jesus was arrested and brought before the Roman procurator, and Pilate imagined it would be an easy way of escaping the responsibility of condemning One whom he believed to be innocent by sending Him for judgment to the ruler under whose jurisdiction He had passed the greater portion of His public life. But Antipas, although he availed himself of the opportunity of gratifying a long-standing curiosity, and permitted Jesus to be brought before him, took care at the same time to express no definite judgment upon the case, and left Pilate to bear the odium of pronouncing a condemnation in which he disbelieved.

The death of Tiberius (AD. 37) was a severe blow to the fortunes of the Jewish prince, and soon after the accession of

Fascimile of Portion of Codex Alexandrinus

Caligula to the empire the foolish ambition of Herodias brought about the tetrarch's deposition and banishment. The same feeling which prompted this restless woman to desert her former husband now urged her on to torment Antipas into seeking the royal dignity from the new emperor. Caligula before ascending the throne was a bosom friend of Agrippa, a brother of Herodias, and when he became emperor, Agrippa (A.D. 37) was made ruler of the territories formerly in possession of Philip, being likewise elevated to the position of a king. Her brother's sudden rise of fortune aroused the jealousy of Herodias, and although Antipas had no desire for additional honours, she

56

persuaded him against his own inclinations to go with her to Rome, and sue the new emperor for the name of king. Agrippa, on hearing of the departure of his relatives for the imperial city, determined, if possible, to defeat the object of their journey and foil his sister's cherished wish. In former days when Agrippa's future was overcast, and his position one of poverty and embarrassment, Antipas, although for a time befriending him, at last subjected the unfortunate prince to gross indignities which he would not readily forget. Agrippa's time had now come; while Herodias and her husband were on the way to Rome, he dispatched a messenger to his patron, the emperor, with the information that Antipas was a disloyal vassal, and had at that moment in his arsenals a stock of arms sufficient to equip seventy thousand men. In his interview with Antipas the emperor asked him if these allegations were true. As the tetrarch was obliged to admit that he had a large quantity of war material in his fortresses, Caligula concluded that Agrippa's accusations were well founded, and that Antipas was making preparations to throw off the imperial yoke. It is extremely improbable that the tetrarch had any ideas of the kind; still he had committed the fatal mistake of arousing suspicion; his doom was sealed. Caligula forthwith deposed him, confiscated his private property, which, along with his dominions, he bestowed upon Agrippa, and banished the hapless prince to Gaul for the remainder of his life (A.D. 39). When this crowning calamity fell upon her husband, Herodias rose superior to her antecedents, and acted with the greatest magnanimity. She had been the immediate cause of his misfortunes, and she was willing to be the sharer of his fate. When Caligula told her that she should be allowed to retain her estates and live where she pleased, she answered him in these noble words, "The love which I have for my husband prevents me, O Caesar, from accepting of thy favour; and since I have been his partner in prosperity it is not right for me to abandon him in misfortune."

It has already been narrated that Augustus, after Herod the Great's death, appointed Archelaus with the title of Ethnarch (B.C. 4 to A.D. 6) to the most important division of his father's kingdom the provinces of Judaea and Samaria. This prince's reign was brief and inglorious. He was the elder son of Malthace, the mother of the tetrarch Antipas, and was born, as far as can be ascertained, about the year 21 B.C. It is evident that Herod at one time did not intend him to occupy the high position which afterwards fell to his lot, for when he was sent to Rome with his brothers Philip and Antipas to receive a Western education, his father put him under the care of a Roman unconnected with public affairs. Herod's elder children while in Rome had lived with Asinius Pollio, a man of consular dignity. They had also the option of making Caesar's palace their home, but the king, having in view the humbler future of his younger children, deemed it sufficient to place them in less illustrious hands. When Archelaus returned to Palestine towards the close of his father's life (B.C. 5), the evil genius of the Herodian family, his elder brother Antipater, made insidious accusations against him to the aged king. Even after Herod had discovered the lying villainy of Antipater, so suspicious was

57

his nature, that he could not shake off the feeling that Antipater's calumnies had some foundation, and in his last will but one he excluded both Philip and Archelaus from all share in the inheritance, appointing as his successor their younger brother Antipas. But in the closing days of his life the bewildered king, feeling probably that he had committed an injustice again altered his mind, and Augustus confirmed the unhappy old man's final arrangements with respect to Archelaus, only withholding from him the title of king till he showed signs of deserving that distinction.

At the time of Herod's death Archelaus was only eighteen years of age, and troubles began to thicken on his path at the very outset of his public career. The people felt that the heavy hand of his father was removed, and discontent began to show itself before Augustus had confirmed the young prince in his new position. Archelaus attempted to satisfy the malcontents by assuring them that their grievances would be taken into consideration after his return from Rome. But the people were impatient for an immediate settlement of their wrongs, and at last their attitude became so menacing, that Archelaus found it necessary to disperse them by force (B.C. 4). The execution of this measure was accompanied with such terrible severity, that the prince immediately alienated not only his future subjects, but the members of his own family as well. His aunt Salome had been making efforts to win over the people after Herod's death by a policy of mercy; but all these attempts at conciliation were forever frustrated by the ill-considered barbarity of Archelaus. Salome now became his pronounced opponent, and on his arrival at Rome he had many hostile influences standing between him and the favour of the emperor. His claims to the inheritance were resisted by almost all his relatives, as well as by Sabinus, the imperial procurator, and a body of representatives from Judaea whom Varus had allowed to go to Rome for that purpose. Augustus hesitated in the face of so strong an opposition; but, finally deciding to abide by the main provisions of Herod's will, he exhorted Archelaus to make a mild use of his authority.

It is possible that the emperor's counsels produced a certain impression on the newly-appointed ethnarch, for we do not find him violating Jewish religious feeling to the same extent as his father. In his reign no offensive heathen edifices were constructed, and if heathen amusements were still permitted, they did not exist on a scale calculated to outrage national ideas. The coinage of the period is perfectly free from the heathen symbols which Philip did not fear to use in the north of Palestine. He followed his father's footsteps by frequently effecting changes in the high-priesthood. But his action in this respect may have proceeded as much from prudence as from choice, although the growth of the synagogue was no doubt imperceptibly undermining the political importance of the high priest. A hereditary love of magnificence induced the ethnarch to rebuild the palace at Jericho, which had been destroyed in the late civil convulsions; and from a desire to hand down his name to posterity he founded the town of Archelais, a little to the north of the newly-restored palace. Archelaus' deference to the Law did not prevent

58

him from setting its ordinances aside when they stood in the way of his passions. It is expressly laid down in the Mosaic legislation, that a man shall not marry his brother's widow if her marriage has been blessed with children. But Archelaus treated this injunction as if it did not exist, and putting away his own wife, he allied himself with his brother's widow, Glaphyra, who was already the mother of two children. At Rome such a proceeding would have been perfectly legitimate, and was not an uncommon occurrence. But a prudent prince would have avoided Roman precedent, and followed the sentiments of his own subjects, even if he had ceased to share them. In other respects this marriage was imprudent. Glaphyra, during her previous residence in Jerusalem as the wife of Herod's son Alexander, had been a fruitful source of irritation in the

Samaritan Inscription Found at Amoas (Translation: "Blessed Be His Name Forever.").

Herodian family, and the folly of her behaviour was one of the causes which aroused Herod's suspicion, and led him to take the terrible step of putting his son to death. Time, however, appears to have worked a change for the better in the character of this princess, for on her return to Jerusalem, the city where she had spent the first days of married life, her mind began to brood on the wrongs she had done her murdered husband. In her dreams she saw him once again; she heard his reproaching voice; a sickness fell upon her and she died.

The wise admonitions of Augustus did not have a permanent effect on the conduct of his vassal in Judaea. Despotism and barbarity were essential elements in his character which could not be effectively restrained. His rule at last became so intolerable that the Jews and Samaritans for a time abandoned the spirit of antipathy which had separated them for centuries, and united together for the purpose of securing the deposition of Archelaus and freedom from his odious tyranny. In this enterprise they were assisted by the relatives of Archelaus, and a deputation from Palestine represented to Augustus that the ethnarch had disregarded the imperial commands, and was a tyrant among his subjects. These reports incensed the emperor, and Archelaus's agent in Rome was sent to Palestine with orders to bring his master back to Italy to answer the charges preferred against him. Archelaus had a presentiment that his downfall was near at hand, and appears to have been brooding over it when the summons calling upon him to proceed to Rome arrived. His guilt was established to Caesar's satisfaction; he was banished to Vienne in Gaul, the ethnarchy was abolished, and Judaea became a Roman province (A.D. 6). The despotic character of Archelaus is alluded to in the Gospel narrative, where it is mentioned that the holy family on their return from Egypt avoided his dominions and settled in Galilee, under the milder rule of his brother Antipas.

The Roman Procurators - A.D. 6-37

The deposition and banishment of Archelaus deprived Judaea of the external appearance of an independent state, and the humblest peasant in the country could now clearly realize that the land which had been promised to his fathers, and for which the Maccabees had so heroically shed their blood, was once more in possession of the Gentiles. For about one hundred and fifty years Judaea had possessed the outward semblance of an independent existence. Although the nation was for a portion of that time in a position of vassalage to the great empire of the West, that position was but slightly felt by the vast body of the people, and was to some extent obliterated by the outward brilliancy and enterprise which illustrated the long reign of Herod the Great. As long as the Herodian family reigned in Jerusalem it was possible for the population of Judaea to cherish the illusion that they were a free people; but with the disappearance of the ethnarch and the advent of a Roman governor, the eyes of all were opened to the fact that the era of liberty had come to an end. Still, the change was of their own creation; the new order of things was not forced upon them from without. For many years it had been the ardent wish of the popular leaders to get rid of the Idumaean dynasty, and they must have known that when this desire was gratified the pressure of Roman rule would be felt in every corner of the land. The deputation which asked Augustus to depose Archelaus was anxious to be placed under the immediate jurisdiction of Rome; and it is possible that Augustus would have satisfied Jewish feeling at an earlier date if he had not been bound by a pledge to Herod to the effect that he would carry out the provisions of the king's will with respect to the succession. The tyrannical conduct of Archelaus absolved him from further obligations to the dead king, and he now possessed a free hand in dealing with Jewish affairs. Strangely enough the wishes of the Jewish delegates coincided with the drift of imperial policy. Augustus was discovering the inconveniences connected with the existence of vassal states within the empire, and their extinction was only a matter of time.

In all probability the men who had succeeded in obtaining the deposition of Archelaus anticipated that Judaea would be incorporated with the neighbouring province of Syria, and that the Jews, except in the matter of taxation, would practically possess the management of their own affairs. Augustus, however, quickly dissipated all such expectations. The territories of Judaea were too extensive to be left without strict imperial supervision; the population was too turbulent; the strategic importance of the country as a highway between Syria and Egypt was too great. Besides, the pro-consulate of Syria was already the most important in the whole empire, and it was against the principles of the administration to put additional power in the hands of the great military governors, as they might be tempted to use it for the purpose of opposing Caesar himself. Augustus accordingly decided to form the territories of Archelaus into an independent province of the second rank, and to place an imperial procurator at the head of civil and military affairs (A D. 6). Publius Sulpicius Quirinius, Governor of Syria, was charged by Augustus with the task of constituting Judaea into an imperial province, and of re-organizing the administration upon Roman principles. Quirinius did not belong to an ancient family; but the tendency of the empire was to abolish all privileges of birth, and to throw open the highest offices to every citizen. Quirinius, by the exercise of soldierly talents, and by his zeal in the service of the state attracted the attention of the emperor, who raised him to the rank of senator and consul, and finally promoted him to the governorship of Syria. Before his nomination to this important position he had repeatedly served in the East, and possessed a large and varied experience in the conduct of affairs in this part of the Roman dominions.

The first business of Quirinius on his arrival in Jerusalem was to make preparations for taking a census of the population, with a view to ascertain the wealth of the province and the extent of its capacity for taxation. The Roman method of arriving at this result consisted in dividing the country into a certain number of districts;

Head in White Marble, From Sheikh Abreik

each district had to furnish a return of the population and property contained within its limits, and to submit it to the governor. On the basis of this return taxation was afterwards levied. The principles upon which taxation was imposed were founded on the nature of the relations which the Romans considered to exist between themselves and the provincials. According to Roman ideas, when a people had been overthrown and made incapable of further resistance to Roman arms, both the people and their possessions became the absolute property of Rome. But it was found impracticable to carry out this theory after the conquerors had become masters of large portions of the globe.

Accordingly the conquered nations were allowed to retain their liberty subject to the payment of a capitation or poll tax *(tributum capitis)*, and also their property subject to the payment of a tax on the produce of the soil *(tributum soli)*. Other taxes, chiefly for local purposes, such as the mainte-

61

nance of roads and bridges, were also levied, but the largest part of the revenue was derived from the land and the poll tax. The poll tax was regarded as a most degrading form of impost, and was considered to emphasize the fact that the people who paid it were no longer in possession of liberty. The poll tax was not, however, so burdensome as the land tax, which ranged in amount from a tenth to a fourth of the whole harvest, if it was not, as frequently happened, commuted to a fixed sum, which the provincials agreed to pay to the imperial treasury.

In the days of Herod and Archelaus the Roman system of taxation was not in operation in Judaea, and it is very unlikely that the Jews had any payments or returns to make to the imperial treasury as long as these princes conducted their affairs. The leaders of the disaffected who waited upon Augustus were undoubtedly aware that one of the first consequences of incorporation would be an alteration of the existing fiscal system, and its assimilation with the fiscal arrangements which were in force in other parts of the empire. But this important fact was unknown to the bulk of the population, and when the news spread throughout the province that every Jewish householder would have to render a complete account of his property to Gentile officials, the greatest consternation immediately ensued. It was certainly not the intention of Augustus to act harshly towards a people that had just been imploring him to take them under his immediate protection and control, but the administration of the new province had to be carried on; for this purpose taxation had to be imposed, and in order to make it equitable it was indispensable to have a census of the population and an accurate return of their property. In carrying out the instructions of the emperor, Quirinius, with his experience of the East and its peculiarities, would no doubt take Jewish susceptibilities into consideration as far as this was practicable, but he appears to have overlooked, or been unaware of, the fact that a census taken after the Roman manner involved a violation of the Mosaic Law. It was from this point of view that it was regarded by the masses, and the punishment which Jehovah inflicted on David for numbering the people would not be forgotten. Besides, if it was absolutely necessary to obtain a census of the population, why should it be taken in conformity with heathen custom? why were the regulations which the Law laid down to be discarded, and the people exposed to the chastisement of God for their neglect? These were questions which must have deeply agitated multitudes in Judaea, when the time came for filling up the required returns, and it needed all the authority of the High Priest Joazar to induce them to comply with the demands of the Roman governor.

Although the census was in the last resort submitted to as inevitable, the enforcement of it created a widespread spirit of discontent, and led to the formation of an intransigent party, whose one rallying cry was irreconcilable hatred of Rome. This new party was mainly recruited from the ranks of the Pharisees, and the program of its leaders consisted in a determination to carry out in the political domain the Pharisaic principle, that the payment of taxes to the foreigner was an act of dishonour to the God of Israel. The

Scribes shrank back from the practical application of their doctrines, and contented themselves with holding up the collectors of taxes (the publicans of the New Testament) to the moral reprobation of their co-religionists; but the Zealots, the name adopted by the new party, were not satisfied with these paltry and ineffective methods; they were resolved to resist Roman domination by force of arms. According to the teaching of the Zealots, Jehovah was the only and supreme ruler of Israel, His elect people; to Him alone was tribute due, and in order to maintain this doctrine they were prepared to stake their lives and shed their blood. Both the Zealot and the scribe believed that the dominion of the Gentiles over God's chosen people was a transitory disaster which must come to an end. But while the scribe resigned himself to heathen supremacy in the full conviction that God would speedily deliver Israel, and lift His people into an exalted position among the nations, the Zealot became impatient of this passive attitude, and proclaimed the principle that God would deliver them when He saw them making exertions to deliver themselves. Many diverse elements entered into the composition of the party of the Zealots. Its higher forces consisted of patriots, enthusiasts, and exalted visionaries; but by its proclamation of war to the knife against Rome and every friend of Rome, Zealotism also enrolled under its standard a class of men who, in the guise of religion and patriotism, were playing the vulgar part of robbers and assassins. It was a party which grew in popularity as the inexorable character of Roman rule became better understood, and it is a remarkable circumstance that Simon, a disciple of Jesus, was at one time a Zealot.

The man who stood at the head of this new movement, and to some extent originated it, was a certain Judas, called the "Galilean," a native of Gamala, in Gaulonitis. He was a passionate enthusiast, whose sole idea was to propagate the great cause he had in hand. The fiery intensity of his convictions exercised a marvelous fascination over the masses, and numbers of young men placed themselves under his leadership. It is probable that Judas was in Jerusalem when Quirinius arrived and proclaimed his intention of instituting a census, and that this announcement kindled his slumbering patriotism into flame. At all events he forthwith set himself in opposition to the new government, and inflamed the passions of the ignorant and fanatical population by declaring to them that the proposed census was nothing but the first step towards slavery. In exalted tones he adjured them to uphold their liberties, and repudiating the passive doctrines of the Pharisees, he declared that none but cowards would pay tribute to Rome. The passionate exhortations of the Galilean met with a warm response; an insurrection broke out, Judas perished, and his followers were dispersed. But the Zealots did, not die, as Gamaliel imagined, with the fall of their first leader; the flame of his teaching still burned in the hearts of the people, and when at last the terrible war broke out which terminated in the destruction of Jerusalem, the Zealots became the soul of the resistance, and Rome had no rest till they were utterly exterminated.

When the revolt of Judas was quelled, and Quirinius had completed the arrangements connected with the formation of Judaea into an imperial province, the duty of carrying on the government fell into the hands of Coponius (A.D. 6-9), a Roman knight who was appointed by Augustus administrator of the country. As Judaea was constituted into a province of the second rank, the head of the administration was not chosen from the same class, and did not hold such a distinguished position as the senatorial proconsuls and the imperial legates. In order to mark the difference between him and these high officials, he was known by the title of Procurator, but he performed substantially the same functions as the imperial legates. Like them he was entrusted with full military and judicial powers. The troops at the disposal of the procurator of Judaea never amounted to more than three thousand men; the main body was stationed at Caesarea, which now became the capital; the rest, consisting of a small detachment, formed the garrisons of Jerusalem and Samaria. On the recurrence of the great Jewish festivals, and especially at the feast of the Passover, the garrison of Jerusalem was strengthened in order to overawe the tumultuous multitudes that then crowded into the Holy City from all parts of the empire.

On these occasions the procurator generally went up to Jerusalem at the head of the reinforcements, and resided in one of the Herodian palaces, where he administered justice and transacted affairs. The procurator also visited every part of the province at least once a year, and in the principal towns heard the complaints of the provincials and redressed their grievances. For these services the procurator received an annual salary from the imperial treasury, and was forbidden to accept bribes or presents from the people over whom he ruled. He had to superintend the collection of the taxes, but he had no power of increasing them. These measures were adopted by the emperors for the protection of the provincials from the terrible extortion to which they were frequently subjected in the days of the Republic; and if a governor went beyond the limits of his authority it was in the power of the people whom he had oppressed to call him to account for his misdeeds at Rome. But the habit of extortion had taken deep root among the official classes, and in spite of all the regulations of the Caesars some of the Judaean procurators committed gross acts of tyranny and corruption, and had no small share in fostering the disaffection which led to the downfall and destruction of the Jewish state.

It is difficult to say with certainty whether the procurators of Judaea were in a position of subordination to the governor of Syria, or whether they were entirely independent of him. It seems more probable that they occupied a position of official independence, and were responsible for the administration of affairs within the province to the emperor alone. In certain cases the legate of Syria did undoubtedly interfere in Judaea, but these interferences only took place when he was invested by the emperor with extraordinary powers. As a rule the functions of the two officials appear to have been quite separate and distinct, and the fact that the governor of Syria required to be armed with special authority from Rome before he could take legal action in Judaea, goes far to show that the heads of the two provinces, although different in rank, were completely independent of one another in ordinary circumstances. The procurator was, like the Syrian legate, appointed directly by the emperor, and acted as his immediate representative in accordance with strictly defined instructions. He had to keep his imperial master regularly informed of everything of importance that occurred within his jurisdiction, and was not allowed to act on his own initiative in matters of serious moment till he had received instructions from Rome. These arrangements produced a most salutary effect upon the government of the provinces, and went a great way towards holding in check the hereditary instincts of rapacity which characterized Roman officials.

ROMAN
AND
MEDIÆVAL RUINS
KAISÀRIEH

During the ascendency of the Romans Judaea was divided for administrative purposes into ten or eleven districts or toparchies. Local councils consisting according to the extent of the locality, of from seven to twenty-three members, were in existence throughout the province, and these councils enjoyed considerable authority both in criminal and administrative affairs. Over these local bodies stood the Senate or Sanhedrin of Jerusalem as a kind of superior council for the whole province. This council, besides exercising a spiritual authority which was co-extensive with Judaism, was also empowered to give legal decisions and to frame administrative regulations within Judaea in all matters which lay beyond the competence of the smaller provincial councils. All criminal offences committed by Jews were within the jurisdiction of the Sanhedrin, but when the punishment decreed against an offender involved his execution, this extreme sentence required to be confirmed by the procurator before it could legally take effect. Charges of blasphemy and of transgressing the Law were heard by this tribunal, and even Roman citizens accused of profaning the Temple had to appear before it.

The Sanhedrin also maintained a police force; and in all matters of faith, custom, and law, where Roman interests were not at stake, this council, as well as the inferior provincial councils, possessed a wide-extending and effective power. The procurator, however, was not in any way bound by the decisions of the local bodies, and he could nullify their action, when such a course seemed to him expedient. As the representative of Caesar, he had power to nominate or dismiss the high priest, a power which was frequently exercised. He alone possessed full jurisdiction over Roman citizens, and a sentence of death had no legal force till it was confirmed by him. But notwithstanding these restrictions, the Jewish authorities enjoyed more local liberty under Roman rule than they had done under their own princes, for it was a fixed principle with the imperial government to leave the enforcement of local laws and the management of national institutions as much as possible in the hands of the subject races.

For some length of time the Roman system of administration appears to have worked with comparative smoothness. The deep-seated opposition to Gentile rule was so promptly checked by the defeat of Judas the Galilaean that it did not dare to manifest itself in open acts of hostility. Under Coponius the old feud between the Samaritans and the Jews acquired fresh life. Certain Samaritans, wishing to be avenged on the Jews for the calamities which they had inflicted on Samaria, came to the Temple at dead of night and scattered dead men's bones in the sacred edifice. It is not said that the desecrators were brought to justice, but Coponius, Lasing that a repetition of such acts might bring popular passion to a dangerous height, took care to have the Temple more closely guarded for the future. Shortly after this disagreeable incident a new procurator was appointed Marcus Ambivius (A.D. 9-12),but his administration proved uneventful; and, whilst his successor, Annius Rufus (A.D. 12-15), an equally unimportant personage, was at the head of affairs in Judaea, the long reign of Augustus came to an end.

In the course of his reign Augustus had steadily displayed a friendly interest in the Jews, and although he had no love for Judaism, or indeed for any foreign religion, he adopted a conciliatory attitude towards every form of faith, and allowed perfect liberty of worship to the Jewish communities which existed among the heathen populations of the empire. In Judaea itself he exhibited the same consideration for the religious ideas and customs of the inhabitants the imperial family sent presents of sacred vessels for the use of the Temple, and a burnt sacrifice of a bullock and two rams was daily offered up at the emperor's expense in honour of the God of Israel. On the other hand, the Jews, after the incorporation of the province, had to offer sacrifices for Caesar and the Roman people, and, as far as the Law permitted, to invoke the Divine blessing upon them in the services of the synagogue. These obligations were no doubt irksome to many of the rabbis, but the performing of them was lightened by the consciousness that the emperor was a generous benefactor and protector of the Jewish race.

Augustus was succeeded in the cares of the empire by Tiberius (A.D. 14-37), the eldest son of his wife Livia by a former marriage with the Senator Tiberius Claudius Nero. The new emperor was a man of great experience both in civil and military affairs, and had reached the mature age of fifty-six when he began to reign. In the course of his previous career Tiberius had filled with success the most important offices of state. He was equally fortunate as a general and an administrator, and although Augustus disliked his sombre and intractable temper, he cast aside personal feeling, and in the interest of the commonwealth adopted Tiberius as his successor. For the first ten or twelve years of his reign Tiberius conducted the affairs of the empire with much mildness and moderation, but after the death of his son Drusus (A.D. 23) the plots and intrigues of an ambitious aristocracy aroused his fears, and the fierce, implacable elements of his nature spent themselves in mercilessly decimating his political adversaries. If we look only at the summary and terrible manner in which Tiberius got rid of his opponents, it must be admitted that he played the part of an atrocious tyrant; it has, however, to be remembered that he was surrounded by a network of conspiracies and had no alternative but to kill or submit to be killed.

These bloody proceedings of Tiberius, although they rightly shock the conscience of mankind, only affected the higher personages in Roman society and did not touch the great mass of the people, for the emperor was in other respects an excellent ruler and made the public welfare the supreme object of his solicitude. He continued the humane policy of Augustus with regard to the provinces, and watched over their interests with assiduous care. Capable governors were appointed to rule the provincials; and after giving proof of their fitness for the task Tiberius allowed them to remain for a long period in the exercise of their functions; the incapable and extortionate, on the other hand, were immediately dismissed and punished. He also prevented the provinces from being weighed down with new burdens, and took care that the old ones were collected by the officials without avarice or cruelty.= All his laws, except the statutes against treason, were framed simply with a view to promote the public good. He made it one of his most important duties to attend to the complaints of the provincials, and they appreciated his efforts in their behalf.

The Jews had at first no reason to be dissatisfied with the new occupant of the imperial throne. Tiberius continued, with respect to them, the mild and conciliatory policy of his predecessor Augustus. Shortly after his accession, the procurator, Annius Rufus, was replaced by Valerius Gratus (A.D. 15), who remained for eleven years at the head of affairs in Palestine. Gratus was no doubt an experienced and trustworthy official, for Tiberius was very careful to select competent men as his subordinates; and the fact that Gratus retained his position so long proves that he discharged the duties it involved to the satisfaction of his imperial master, and in accordance with the humane principles which Tiberius endeavoured to infuse into the administration of the provinces.

The new procurator experienced considerable difficulty in finding a high priest with whom he could co-operate harmoniously, and in the space of four years he had four times to change the religious head of the community. But these frequent changes were of secondary importance to the masses, and in no way disturbed the tranquility of the land. Public attention was at this moment (A.D. 17) concentrated upon material interests; the burden of taxation was becoming irksome, and in concert with the Syrians, the Jews of Palestine begged the emperor to diminish the tribute. In response to this appeal and in order generally to place Eastern affairs upon a more satisfactory footing, Tiberius entrusted his nephew, Germanicus, with extraordinary powers, and sent him to Syria to inquire into the grievances of the provincials. Whether Germanicus considered it necessary to lessen the amount paid by the Jews to the imperial treasury or not is unknown. He died amid suspicious circumstances before his mission was completed (A.D. 19).

About this period Tiberius banished the Jewish colony from Rome (A.D. 19), because four of their number, under the guise of religion, had succeeded in defrauding a Roman matron, named Fulvia, a woman of high position who had embraced the Jewish faith. In accordance with a decree of the Senate, four thousand Roman Jews fit to bear arms, were drafted into the legions and sent to repress brigandage in the inhospitable island of Sardinia; the rest of the community were allowed a certain time to quit Italy, or abjure their faith. These harsh proceedings did not materially affect the policy of the emperor towards the population of Palestine, but they show that he had no predilection for the Jewish race, and was not sorry to find some plausible pretext for driving Jewish settlers from the capital. In fact, it was not the intention of the Caesars to allow the Jews to establish themselves in the Latin-speaking portion of the empire, where their race peculiarities would inevitably stir up the same antipathies as existed in the Greek cities of the East. Accordingly they lost many of their privileges when they migrated westwards, and the immunities which they were permitted to retain, such as permission to plead before their own tribunals and exemption from military service, were granted them as matters of favour and not of right.

Seven years after the expulsion of the Jews from Italy, Pontius Pilate (A.D. 26–35)—a name inseparably associated with the most momentous events in Christian history was appointed to succeed Valerius Gratus as procurator of Judaea. No authentic information exists respecting the previous career of this official, and he probably owed his appointment to his success as a soldier and administrator in other parts of the empire. In Judaea his procuratorship was a failure from the commencement; the cause of his insuccess consisting for the most part in a profound disdain for the people over whom he ruled. He apparently made no effort to understand the new world of ideas into which he was placed, or if he did apprehend the import of Jewish feeling and conviction, he acted on the principle that they were to be as far as possible frustrated or ignored. He conducted the government of the province simply with a view to secure the approbation of Tiberius, and as the drift of imperial policy, when Pilate was made procurator, seemed to be adverse to Judaism, one of his first official acts consisted in an attempt to get the people of Jerusalem to tolerate the presence of heathen symbols in the Holy City.

It had been the custom of former procurators to respect the susceptibilities of the population in the matter of graven images, and the imperial standards were divested of all such ornaments when Roman troops had occasion to enter Jerusalem, in order to take up their quarters in the citadel. Pilate believed the time had now come for setting this custom aside, and probably considered that it would advance his interests with the emperor if he succeeded in his design. Accordingly, when a change took place in the Jerusalem garrison, Pilate commanded the fresh troops to enter the Holy City by night and to retain the silver busts of the emperor on the ensigns. On the following morning the people were horrified to find that the Holy City was being profaned, and that heathen rites were being celebrated in sight of the Temple.

The whole population was struck with consternation and dismay, and a feeling of intense indignation flew through the city and communicated itself to the fanatical peasantry of the province. At any moment the excitement might have ended in an outbreak of rebellion, for the party of Judas the Galilean had many devoted adherents who would have gloried in resorting to extremities at once. Fortunately, the counsels of extreme men were not adopted, and it was decided to send an imposing deputation to the new capital, Caesarea, to implore the governor to respect their ancient laws and remove the ensigns. On their arrival, the supplicants discovered that they had to encounter a man who was totally out of sympathy with the Jewish race, and was determined before yielding to put the strength of their convictions to the test. Pilate spoke of their request as an indignity to Caesar, and refused to listen to it. The petitioners, on the other hand, were resolute; they would not accept the procurator's answer, and for five days and nights hung around his footsteps reiterating their request in attitudes of abject humility. Pilate, wearied with their persistent entreaties, adopted fresh measures and tried to stop their clamour with intimidation. He invited the complainants to meet him in the circus, and when they came forward to renew their petition, his soldiers, who lay in concealment, surrounded them at a given signal and threatened the hapless Jews with instant death if they still persisted in their demands. But death had lost its terrors for this pertinacious band; instead of dispersing, as the procurator had hoped, they bared their necks to the Roman weapons and professed their willingness to perish rather than outlive the profanation of their laws. Pilate, who did not anticipate such a display of resolution, at once gave way, and the standards were ordered back to Caesarea.

AQUEDUCTS
near Jericho.

Although the procurator was baffled for the moment by the determined attitude of the Jews, he did not abandon his purpose of forcing the people of Jerusalem to admit heathen symbols into their midst. His next attempt in this direction was of a milder character, and took the form of introducing into the old palace of Herod on Mount Zion the governor's residence during his stay in Jerusalem votive tablets dedicated to the emperor. These tablets only con-

70

tained the names of the emperor and the person who had dedicated them, but the rabbis saw in them a dark design on Pilate's part to familiarize the people with Caesar worship, which had become general in other parts of the empire. It is not at all unlikely that this was the procurator's real intent. The empire was a vast agglomeration of different nationalities possessing no common bond of union, and the aim of Roman statesmen was to create such a bond by lifting the emperor out of the ordinary rank of mortals, and making him a common object of adoration for all his subjects to whatever race they might belong. In the other provinces of the Roman world this policy had met with a gratifying measure of success; in Judaea alone it had not even been tried, and Pilate, who had probably just left some region where the cultus of the Caesars had grown into an established institution, was evidently animated with the desire of placing it ultimately on a similar footing in Palestine.

It is hardly to be supposed that the procurator, in the prosecution of his religious policy, was merely gratifying a feeling of personal animosity at the cost of adding immensely to his difficulties as a ruler. Such is not the course which a man of Pilate's experience was likely to adopt. It seems more reasonable to believe that he was acting in the character of a Roman official anxious above all things to augment the strength of the empire by promoting its internal unification. Among polytheistic populations, where the dividing line between gods and men was but indistinctly traced, the apotheosis of the emperor had no religious or intellectual difficulties standing in the way of its acceptance; to the Jews, on the other hand, it was a blow aimed at the fundamental principle of their faith the unity and majesty of Jehovah. The commotion which Pilate's action immediately created among all classes plainly shows that the affair of the votive tablets was regarded in this light by the entire Jewish community. Even the sons of Herod, princes whose devotion to Rome was above suspicion, joined in the outcry, and implored the procurator to retrace his steps. It was impressed upon him that he was driving the people into rebellion. He was asked to show the imperial edict which empowered him to act as he was doing. He was threatened with the exposure of all the misdeeds he had committed since he became governor, but neither threats nor entreaties nor expostulations produced the slightest effect on Pilate's determination, and Tiberius was finally appealed to. Although the emperor was probably not displeased as the Jews imagined at the experiment made by his subordinate, he perceived that in the present temper of the people it was destined to fail, and Pilate accordingly received orders to remove the obnoxious symbols from Jerusalem to Caesarea.

Twice had Pilate been defeated in his attempts to override the religious feelings of the Jews, but he was evidently a man possessed of great tenacity of purpose, for his previous failures, instead of being a source of discouragement, had the opposite effect of stimulating him to fresh efforts. In order to maintain the worship at the Temple in all its dignity and splendour, large offerings of money were sent to the Temple treasury from every Jewish community throughout the world. Pilate believed that a portion of this money might be usefully expended in providing the Holy City with a pure and abundant supply of water, which would also be of much service to the Temple itself, where the refuse arising from the sacrifices must necessarily have been great. It does not appear that he consulted the Sanhedrin or the priests as to the expediency of this great undertaking, but whether he obtained the acquiescence of these important bodies or not, his scheme met with a determined resistance from the population. The fanatical masses were roused to a high pitch of fury by the thought that money dedicated to sacred uses should be expended at the will of a heathen on objects of a secular character.

Pilate, when he made his appearance in Jerusalem, was assailed by the abuse and clamour of a multitude numbering many thousands, who were bent on repeating the pertinacious tactics which had succeeded so well at Caesarea. Pilate, perceiving this, skillfully distributed a number of troops disguised in Jewish garments among the crowd, and, as soon as the clamour was renewed, the soldiers began

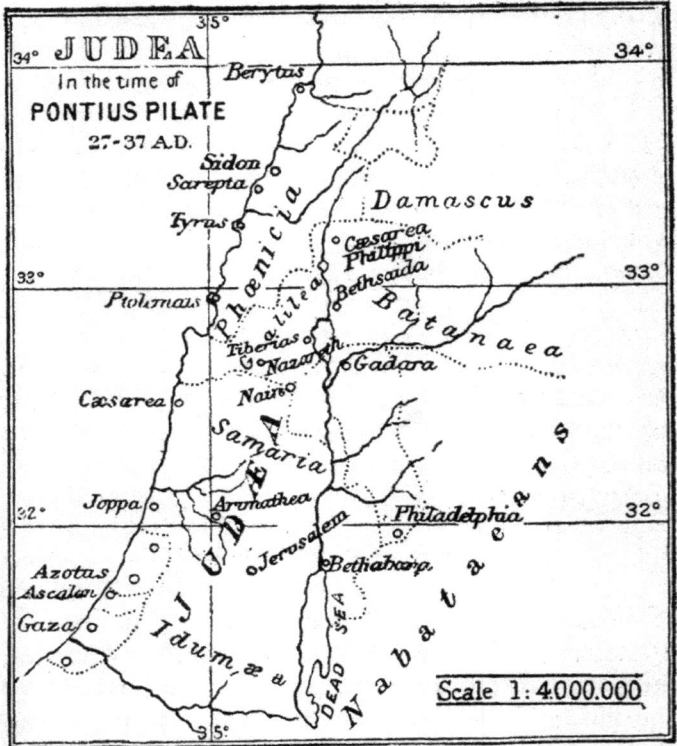

to beat the agitators with their clubs, and so disconcerted them that they lost heart and fled. He was afterwards able to go on unhindered with the work which, when completed, formed a magnificent aqueduct several miles in extent. Nevertheless, if the Tower of Siloam, which fell and killed eighteen people, formed a part of Pilate's undertaking, it is certain that the rabbis looked upon the whole structure as lying under the curse of God.

But all these proceedings sink into insignificance in comparison with the part played by the procurator at the trial of Jesus. The influence of Jesus at this period was fast becoming a power among the masses, and both the rabbis and the priestly aristocracy, whose system He was menacing, were anxious on religious grounds to see Him put to death. But they knew it was futile to charge Him with blasphemy before a Roman judge, who would certainly have told them, like Gallio, that he would be no judge of such matters.

Still, these men believed it necessary at all hazards to compass their ends; the real charge against Jesus was left in the background, an accusation of a political character was substituted for it, and at the Feast of the Passover—a time when the procurator always made his appearance in Jerusalem for the purpose of maintaining order Jesus was arraigned before him as a seditious demagogue who was plotting against the authority of Rome. Pilate, however, was well aware from his previous experience of Jesus' accusers, that they would regard any movement hostile to Rome as a virtue and not as a crime, and he no doubt listened to their evidence with the utmost skepticism. In fact, all the proceedings of that fatal day conclusively show that Pilate was convinced of Jesus' innocence. Why the procurator did not immediately release Him is incomprehensible: His conduct in pronouncing a sentence of condemnation against One whom he knew to be guiltless cannot be accounted for on the ground of Pilate's deference to Jewish feeling, for the whole period of his procuratorship clearly shows that he paid no regard to it whatever. It is not, therefore, likely that he would do so in this instance alone. Neither can it easily be explained on the principle that he feared the representations the Jews would make against him to Tiberius. He was not the man to quail before such threats. In short, his condemnation of Jesus appears to have been pronounced in a moment of inconceivable weakness, when the ordinary motives which influence and control human judgment were in abeyance. This, however, does not lessen his responsibility for the crime in reality a judicial murder the guilt of which will forever rest on Pilate's head.

The procuratorship of Pilate was brought to a termination in consequence of certain repressive measures which he deemed it necessary to adopt in Samaria. The Samaritans were thrown into a state of intense excitement by the appearance of a religious impostor in their midst, who said that he would show them the vessels of the Tabernacle which, according to a Samaritan tradition, had been buried by Moses on Mount Gerizim. As the finding of these sacred vessels was regarded as a prelude to the advent of the Messianic kingdom, and as Messianic hopes were at this moment running high in Palestine, great multitudes of Samaritans made their way to Gerizim, the holy mountain of their people, in the full conviction that a mighty transformation of the world was at hand. But the movement was not merely religious, it evidently possessed a marked political character as well, for the people assembled in arms, and a widespread discontent existed against the Roman government. Pilate, whose eye was fixed on the doings of the Samaritans, was afraid lest their excitement should culminate in a revolt. Troops, probably drawn from the garrison of Samaria, were dispatched to Mount Gerizim to overawe and disperse the excited crowds. A conflict took place between the Roman soldiers and the people. Many of the Samaritans were killed, and several of the ringleaders who were taken prisoners were afterwards executed by order of the governor.

These events took place while Vitellius was pro-consul of Syria (A.D. 35-39), and as he had been entrusted by Tiberius with extraordinary powers in the East, Pilate lost the independent position usually held by the procurators of Judaea, and became a subordinate of the Syrian governor. The members of the Samaritan provincial council were aware of the change that had taken place in the procurator's status, and being much incensed at the manner in which he had dealt with their countrymen, they sent a deputation to Vitellius, and accused Pilate of murdering loyal and peaceable subjects of the empire. As the Samaritans had always enjoyed the reputation of being faithful vassals of Rome, Vitellius considered that their charges against the procurator were worthy of serious examination. He was suspended and sent to Rome to justify his conduct; but before his arrival in the imperial city Tiberius had died, and Pilate at the same time disappears from the pages of authentic history (A.D. 37).

Destruction of the Jewish State - A.D. 37-73

A feeling of relief and satisfaction ran through the whole empire when it became known that the gloomy Tiberius was dead. His successor Caligula, then in the twenty-sixth year of his age, assumed the responsibilities of power amid the acclamations of the Jewish provincials as well as the citizens of Rome (37-41). The new emperor began his career as a ruler under the happiest auspices. The senate, the people, the provinces, hailed the young monarch's advent to supreme authority with delight; his first public utterances produced an excellent impression, and for a short time it was believed that a new and brighter era had begun. These illusions were of brief duration; the true character of Caligula revealed itself as soon as he was securely seated on the throne, and he proved as his discerning predecessor had prophesied both a curse to himself and to the community. It may be said with a near approach to certainty that Caligula soon after he became emperor was mad; the unspeakable vices to which he was addicted are hardly compatible with sanity, and the abominable cruelties and caprices of his reign are clearly the aberrations of a disordered mind.

Unfortunately for the Jews, Caligula among his other peculiarities seriously imagined that he was a god. At Rome he sat among the statues of the divinities for the purpose of receiving public adoration. At Alexandria, where there was a large and important Jewish colony, he compelled the rabbis to admit his statue into their synagogues, and practically changed them in spite of all remonstrances into temples for the worship of himself. Orders were also sent to Petronius (A.D. 39), who had succeeded Vitellius as governor of Syria to place the imperial statue in the Temple of Jerusalem, and to crush out by force of arms any resistance which the Jews might offer to such a step. The cordial relations Vitellius had established by his conciliatory measures after the fall of Pilate were once more snapped asunder, and the Jewish people suddenly found themselves confronted by the same dangers as had menaced their ancestors when Antiochus Epiphanes polluted the sanctuary with the image of Olympian Zeus. But in the two centuries that had elapsed since this act of desecration a decided change had taken place in the feelings of the Temple aristocracy. They had now become as ardent upholders of Judaism as the Pharisees and the common people; and even the family of Herod joined with the rest of the nation in resisting the insane folly of Caligula.

In face of the tremendous and menacing opposition which immediately manifested itself in Judaea, Petronius, the governor, hesitated to carry out the imperial commands. He foresaw from the desperate temper of the people that it would be impossible to place Caligula's statue in the Temple without inflicting terrible misery on the unhappy country, and involving it in all the horrors of a religious war. In these circumstances this humane officer, well knowing the extreme peril in which he was placing himself, resolved to ask Caligula to rescind the obnoxious decree. While Petronius's letter was on its way to the emperor, King Agrippa, at a feast which he gave at Rome in honour of Caligula, adroitly interceded for his co-religionists; and orders were sent to the Syrian governor to proceed no farther with the project for erecting the emperor's statue in the Temple. When, however, the tyrant discovered that Petronius was also acting in behalf of the Jews, and that he had shrunk from executing the imperial will, a message was sent to him in which he was commanded to put himself to death. Fortunately for Petronius, Caligula was assassinated before the fatal message reached its destination; it came into his hands soon after the welcome announcement that the hateful monster was no more (A.D. 41).

Although all immediate danger was now at an end, the persecutions of Caligula produced a profound feeling of disquietude among the Jews. It was perceived on all sides that their religious liberty rested upon a frail foundation, and might at any moment be overthrown by the caprice or vanity of a heathen emperor. These apprehensions were fruitful ground for the operations of the Zealots, who had since the death of Judas the Galilean been actively and successfully propagating the doctrine of armed resistance to the Roman oppressor. The warlike teaching of these enthusiasts was rapidly superseding the passive doctrines of the Pharisees, and the latter were in consequence beginning to lose their accustomed hold upon the confidence of the masses. The people were becoming impatient of the fine distinctions drawn by the Pharisees on the subject of Roman domination. Why should they continue to wait any longer for the advent of the Messiah in order to be forever rid of the accursed heathen and all their works? Would it not be better, as the Zealots said, to follow the example of Mattathias, the noble father of the Maccabees, and once again win freedom at the point of the sword. It was not perceived by the fanatical masses that the historical conditions were entirely different, and that the mighty empire of the West, with its splendid military resources, was not for a moment to be compared with an effete Eastern monarchy in the last stages of decay. It was enough for the ignorant population that Caligula had been playing the same part as Antiochus Epiphanes; the hateful Roman with his heathen images was another type of Antichrist, and his dominion over God's elect people must no longer be endured. Such were the convictions which were fast ripening in the popular mind when Caligula was succeeded by his uncle Claudius (A.D. 41-54), then fifty years of age.

Byzantine Capital

The personal character of the new Caesar made him in many respects as unfitted as his predecessor for the immense task of governing so vast an empire. For fifty years he had lived in comparative obscurity, and when the praetorians carried him into their camp and proclaimed him emperor, he was destitute of any real practical experience of public affairs. On account of bodily and mental infirmities, which had afflicted him from childhood, he had always been looked upon by his imperial relatives with feelings of pity or contempt; and when he became master of the Roman world, so weak, timid, and irresolute was his character, that he soon fell under the domination of women and slaves. Very little was to be expected from a ruler so unhappily constituted, and yet the policy which Claudius at first adopted in Judaea was singularly wise and opportune. Instead of sending a procurator, who with the best intentions would probably have added to the existing state of exasperation, Claudius fell back upon the methods of Augustus, and decided to manage Jewish affairs by means of a prince who understood the peculiarities of the people.

In King Agrippa who already ruled the two tetrarchies in the north of Palestine, formerly held by his uncles Philip and Antipas, Claudius found a man admirably suited to his purpose. Agrippa was a loyal friend of the imperial family; he had been of signal service to Claudius when he was proclaimed emperor, and gratitude as well as policy induced the new Caesar to extend the dominions of Agrippa, who was accordingly made ruler (A.D. 41) over all those territories which had formerly been administered by his grandfather, Herod the Great. As a precautionary measure Roman troops continued to garrison Caesarea and Samaria. The appointment of Agrippa had a mollifying effect upon the population, and his sagacious conduct of the government dissipated all fears of a revolt. At Jerusalem where he took up his residence, he lived in accordance with the strict principles of the Pharisees, and exercised his authority with mildness and moderation. The powers of the Sanhedrin were extended, the doctors became guests at the royal table, the populace was treated with affable generosity, and national sentiment gratified to a degree which brought the king into collision with Rome. Excepting the Christians whom he persecuted and put to death, all classes of the community were devoted to Agrippa, and when he died after a brief reign of little more than three years there was grief and lamentation throughout the land (A.D. 44).

The affairs of Palestine had been so successfully conducted by the deceased king, that Claudius decided to send Agrippa's son, then a youth of seventeen to occupy the vacant throne. Had the emperor possessed sufficient strength of mind to carry out this wise intention, and had he also withdrawn the Roman garrison which was mostly composed of Syrians, the elements of friction between Rome and Judaea would have been to a great extent removed. It is even possible that such a policy would have so far satisfied Jewish national aspirations as to avert the terrible insurrection which was already looming in the distance. Agrippa with Maccabaean blood in his veins had rehabilitated the Herodian family in the eyes of the populace; all but a few extreme fanatics would have joyfully submitted to the authority of his son.

Unhappily for the peace of Palestine, Claudius allowed himself to be overruled by his advisers; the youth of Agrippa's son, who was then being educated in Rome, was alleged as a reason for not transferring him to so responsible a position. The old method of governing the country by procurators was again resorted to. The Zealots were not slow to take advantage of the error which had been committed by the counselors of Caesar. Agrippa's reign though brief had indirectly furthered their cause by imparting a fresh impulse to patriotic feeling, and when the new procurator, Cuspius Fadus, (A.D. 44—46) entered upon his duties, he immediately found himself confronted with disaffection and disturbances.

In spite, however, of the outbreak of insurrectionary movements among that portion of the population over which the Zealots had gained so great an ascendency, the emperor and his procurators still went on with the work of conciliation. The vestments of the high priest, which except for a brief interval after Pilate's deposition had always been in charge of the garrison in the tower of Antonia, were handed over to the Temple aristocracy. The power of nominating the high priest was taken away from the procurator, and in order that there might be no conflict between the civil and ecclesiastical authorities, Claudius appointed Herod, prince of Chalcis, a brother of the late king, to supreme control over all religious affairs. After the departure of Fadus, who had succeeded in restoring order, and in repressing a movement of a Messianic character, Claudius rightly discerning that Jewish discontent was at bottom of a religious nature, nominated Tiberius Alexander (A.D. 47), a nephew of Philo the philosopher, to the office of procurator. The emperor may have hoped that this officer, understanding the idiosyncrasies of his countrymen, would be competent to keep them within the bounds of order and law. But his mission proved a failure; a serious revolt of the Zealots took place; James and Simon, two sons of Judas the Galilean, were captured and crucified, and when Alexander was succeeded by Cumanus (A.D. 48-52), the situation in Judaea had become more menacing than ever. In fact, the procuratorship of Cumanus is little else than a painful record of robberies, murders, race hatreds, and insurrection. At last matters became so serious that the legate of Syria, Ummidius Quadratus felt himself compelled to interfere. This official had been entrusted with extraordinary powers in the East, and after investigating into the conduct of Cumanus, with respect to a bloody feud which had broken out between the Jews and Samaritans, he suspended the procurator, and sent him to Rome to justify his proceedings before the emperor. Once again Claudius gave evidence of his anxiety to conciliate the Jews. The Samaritans were condemned, Cumanus was banished, and a tribune named Celer, who had made himself offensive to the Jews, was sent back to Jerusalem to be executed.

It was no doubt believed in imperial circles that the people of Judaea would be appeased by the unwonted spectacle of a Roman officer perishing in obloquy at the scene of his misdeeds. The spirit of revolt, however, was not to be so easily allayed; every day it was gaining a firmer hold upon the popular mind, and the enemies of Rome had now become too numerous and implacable to be satisfied with anything short of national independence. The Temple aristocracy, it is true, still held aloof from the ideas of the Zealots, but it had become a rotten and effete caste, ever ready to plunder the poor and helpless, and as the trial of St. Paul before Ananias shows, very brutal in the exercise of its powers. Such men were regarded by the people as oppressors, and were utterly without influence. The Pharisees retained the respect of the masses, but they too were unable to stem the tide of popular feeling. It had become impossible to get the people to wait any longer for the advent of the Messianic king, and although they still believed that he would come to their deliverance they were determined in the meantime to begin the task themselves. The Zealots, in fact, were now triumphant, and the Zealots had opened their ranks to all who would swear eternal hatred against Rome. Robbers, brigands, assassins, the malefactor who murdered for hire as well as the honest patriot burning to be free, were all equally welcomed by the Zealots...It was not so much the hardness of Roman rule as the fact that they were being ruled by aliens which was driving the Jews into rebellion. The time for concessions was at an end, and the only course now open to the emperor was to garrison the disaffected province with an overwhelming force, and to place a resolute procurator at the head of it. This stern line of policy Claudius did not deem it necessary to adopt, and under Felix, who succeeded Cumanus, the bonds of social order were dissolved.

The choice of Felix (52—60) at such a critical period was most unfortunate. It was said even by the Romans that he exercised his powers in the spirit of a slave; St. Paul was one of the many victims of his avarice; and his remedies for the disorders of Palestine only aggravated the disease. Under his procuratorship the Zealots and their allies, the Sicarii, or assassins became bolder and more defiant, and measures of severity produced no permanent result. Even in Jerusalem itself the procurator was incapable of holding the forces of anarchy in check. The functions of government were at times in abeyance; riot and bloodshed defiled the streets; assassinations took place with impunity within the Temple courts, and the worshipper at the feasts was in constant dread of having a dagger plunged into his heart by some mysterious hand. In the country districts the same lamentable disorder prevailed. Villages were sacked and burned down, houses plundered, the peacefully disposed were terrorized; the friends of Rome murdered whenever an opportunity presented itself. Passionate appeals were made to the people to revolt, and acquiescence in the established order of things was regarded as a crime. A feverish exaltation existed in the popular mind; the air was filled with rumours of the supernatural, and multitudes were ready to follow any deluded visionary who undertook to verify his vocation by the performance of some miracle or the revelation of a sign from heaven. On the Mount of Olives, a Jew from Egypt was able to collect a great number of people to witness the lofty walls of Jerusalem fall down at his command.

His followers, like the adherents of another fanatic named Theudas, were dispersed or slain; but the atmosphere of miracle which then hung over Palestine was fatal to the teachings of experience, and as soon as another visionary assumed the part of his baffled predecessor he immediately found a credulous multitude eager to espouse his cause.

Two years after the appointment of Felix to the procuratorship, Claudius was poisoned at the instigation of his wife Agrippina (54); and her son Nero, in whose interest this crime was perpetrated, was presented to the soldiers and proclaimed emperor (A.D. 54-68). But the change which had taken place in the occupant of the throne produced no alteration in Roman policy with respect to Palestine. Felix remained for some time longer at the head of affairs, and was eventually replaced by Porcius Festus (A.D. 60-62). The new procurator found himself confronted with a population in a state of anarchy, and although he made strenuous efforts to restore an outward semblance of order, the Zealots still continued to gain ground, visionaries still retained their hold upon the masses, and when Festus died (62) the disorder and confusion had become more deeply seated than before? Till the arrival of a successor to Festus, Ananus the high priest assumed supreme authority, and exercised it with extreme barbarity. James the Just and many other Christians were sentenced to be stoned; even the Jews felt his conduct to be intolerable, and the people impatiently longed for the arrival of Albinus, the new procurator (62-64). Albinus achieved as little success as his predecessors, and, judging by the nature of his proceedings, it is questionable if he expected much. He allowed sedition to go on unchecked as long as he was paid by the seditious to overlook it; he willingly accepted bribes from the Zealots to release their imprisoned companions; by practicing extortion on a wide scale he no doubt increased the number of the disaffected, and he was to all appearance more anxious to enrich himself than to pacify the distracted province.

Gessius Florus (64-66), the last of the procurators, proved even a greater scourge than Albinus. Under his administration the patience of the people became exhausted, and the revolt, which terminated in the destruction of the Jewish state, began.

The smallness of the Roman garrison, as well as the mutinous temper of the masses, who had now gone over in a body to the Zealots, combined to render the revolt inevitable, but its approach was accelerated by the arbitrary conduct of the procurator. Whole districts were plundered and reduced to desolation; all guarantees for the safety of life and property had disappeared; and numbers of the peaceably disposed inhabitants, finding the condition of Judaea becoming more and more intolerable, forsook the country and sought a home elsewhere. The first outbreak took place in Caesarea. It assumed the form of a street fight between the Jews and Greeks, which the Roman commander was not able to suppress. The flame of revolt spread to Jerusalem, and became most menacing when it was known that Florus had just taken seventeen talents from the Temple treasury. Florus soon appeared upon the scene, and made this seditious movement in the Holy City a pretext for letting loose his soldiers on the inhabitants. A sad scene of pillage and murder was the result; many eminent Jews were crucified, and by pursuing a policy of exasperation, Florus hoped to incite the populace into acts of rebellion. In this design he partially succeeded; serious fighting occurred in the streets of Jerusalem, the Zealots gained possession of the Temple Mount, and the Roman garrison was confined to the fortress of Antonia. Quiet, however, was for a time restored. Florus left the city, and Cestius Gallus, the legate of Syria, who had been ap-

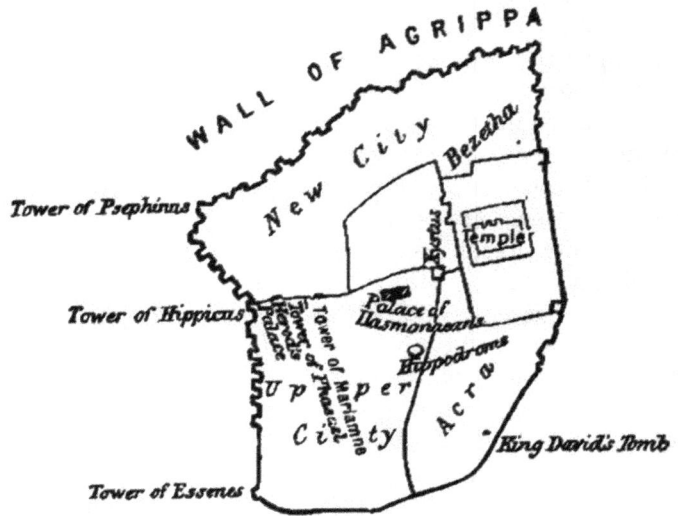

Scale 1: 25000

prised of the dangerous posture of affairs, sent one of his officers to Jerusalem to inquire into the true nature of the disturbances.

When Neapolitanus, the officer charged with this duty, arrived in the Holy City, accompanied by Agrippa II., the tumult had abated, and he w s received by the people with many outward tokens of respect. After his departure, Agrippa, conscious of the burning passions that lay beneath this momentary calm, exhorted the populace in impressive language to remain at peace with Rome. But no amount of persuasion would induce them to submit for the future to the authority of Florus. For venturing upon such a suggestion, Agrippa was stoned by the multitude, and had to flee from the city. Every day the breach between Rome and Judaea was becoming wider, and, in spite of every effort of the friends of peace, the Zealots were rapidly making any pacific solution impossible. Headed by Menahem, another son of Judas the Galilean, they captured the fortress of Masada, and Put the Roman garrison to the sword. In accordance with their principles, the daily sacrifice which had been offered for the emperor since the days of Augustus was discontinued—a step which was equivalent to a declaration of war with Rome.

Many of the priests now joined the ranks of the disaffected, and Eleazar, the son of Ananias the high priest, placed himself at the head of the war party in Jerusalem. Most of the notables in the Holy City were terrified at the prospect of a rebellion, and Agrippa sent them three thousand men to assist the Roman garrison and hold the Zealots in check. But Agrippa's soldiers were unequal to the task, and after a series of bloody conflicts in the streets, they had to lay down their arms. In the midst of the disorder the public records were destroyed. The palaces of the high priest and the Herodian family were burnt to the ground. The opponents of the Zealots had to flee into hiding-places, and Ananias the high priest was discovered and slain. It was now a capital offence for any Jew to be suspected of desiring to live at peace with Rome. Flushed with their success over the forces of Agrippa, the Zealots now directed their efforts against the Roman garrison; the Romans were so small in number and so hard pressed that they offered to surrender on condition of being permitted to withdraw from the country. These terms of capitulation were solemnly accepted by the Jewish leaders, but the Romans had no sooner laid down their arms than they were basely massacred. It was a war of extermination upon which the Zealots had entered; Palestine must, they declared, be purified from the pollutions of the heathen; frightful massacres took place in different parts of the country, and the non-Jewish population, when unable to defend itself; was mercilessly put to the sword.

When tidings of these events began to arrive at Antioch, the capital of the proconsulate of Syria, the Romans quickly realized the gravity of the situation, and Cestius Gallus immediately made preparations for suppressing the revolt. With a force of twenty thousand Roman soldiers, and at least an equal number of auxiliaries, he commenced his march upon Jerusalem. In the month of September (A.D. 66) the Roman army appeared before the walls of the Holy City. But Gallus met with such an obstinate resistance that he determined to abandon the siege. His retreat was most disastrous, and terminated in a headlong flight. In addition to losing over six thousand men and several superior officers, his war material, baggage, and military chest fell into the hands of the victors, who returned triumphantly to Jerusalem laden with the spoils of war. Fired with the success of the Zealots, all classes now espoused the cause of national independence. The aristocracy placed themselves at the head of it. The whole of Palestine was for the present free, a government was organized, and vigorous preparations were made for the approaching conflict with Rome.

The disastrous expedition of Cestius Gallus compelled the Roman government to take a serious view of the rebellion, and it was decided at the court of Nero to send an officer of the highest rank to Palestine for the purpose of suppressing it. Titus Flavius Vespasian, a general of great sagacity and experience, who had achieved distinction in Germany and Britain, was invested with the powers of an imperial legate, and appointed to command the army destined to operate against the Jews. In the spring of the year A.D. 67, Vespasian assembled his forces, numbering about fifty thousand men, at Ptolemais on the sea coast, and made preparations for the reduction of the neighbouring province of Galilee. Here Josephus the historian was in command of the Jews, but the Zealot John of Gischala was the soul of the revolt. In the first campaign Galilee was brought into subjection; Josephus fell into the hands of the Romans, and John fled with a number of his followers to Jerusalem. While the Roman army was in winter quarters (A.D. 67-8), a terrible state of anarchy prevailed in the Holy City. John of Gischala, with the assistance of wild Idumaean hordes, overthrew the aristocratic government, massacred the most distinguished inhabitants, and literally drenched the city with blood. Vespasian was pressed by his subordinates to utilize this fratricidal strife for the advantage of the Roman arms. But he preferred allowing the Jews to continue weakening their powers of resistance, and was conscious that the appearance of a hostile army before the city walls would be a signal for all factions to rally round the common cause.

When the Roman general again took, the field, he deferred marching on Jerusalem till all effective opposition had been crushed out in Peraea, Samaria, and Idumaea. In the early part of the summer these operations were successfully accomplished; the rear of the Roman army was now secure from hostile assaults, and Vespasian was making dispositions for a close investment of the Holy City, when tidings reached the camp that the emperor Nero was dead (June, 68). As Vespasian was now without orders, all active operations were suspended, and the Zealots were able for some time longer to continue the work of self-destruction. For the moment the rebellion in Judaea ceased to occupy the first place in Vespasian's thoughts; civil war had broken out respecting a successor to Nero; the legions were at variance as to the choice of a new emperor. Galba Otho and Vitellius were set up and rapidly overthrown (A.D. 68–9); and finally the legions in the East proclaimed Vespasian, and seated him securely on the throne (A.D. 69-79).

For a period of nearly two years the war in Judaea remained at a standstill. At the expiration of that time Vespasian, whose hands were now free determined to complete the task he had undertaken in the reign of Nero, and to restore imperial authority within the walls of Jerusalem. An army consisting of four legions, besides a body of Syrian auxiliaries assembled at Caesarea, and the emperor's son Titus, then about thirty years of age, was appointed to the chief command. At the head of this force Titus advanced through Samaria, and about the Feast of the Passover (A.D, 70) the Roman troops encamped before the Holy City. Jerusalem was strongly fortified; to capture it was a formidable undertaking. It was protected on all sides by a triple circle of walls; in the interior of the city there were besides the massive fortifications around the Temple three mighty towers of enormous strength. The garrison consisted of the

The Arch of Titus, Rome.

most determined and fanatical adherents of Judaism, whose desperate valour compensated to a great extent for their want of discipline. The defenders of the city were also sustained by the belief that the God of Israel would aid them in preserving His sanctuary from the pollutions of the heathen, and would intervene at the appointed moment to confound the enemies of His people. These lofty hopes, however, did not prevent the Zealots from dividing themselves into hostile and embittered factions during the long interval of respite which elapsed between the departure of Vespasian and the arrival of Titus. Instead of utilizing this period in strenuous preparations for defense, it was in great part wasted in bloody encounters between the rival parties which had sprung up within the ranks of the Zealots themselves. Ultimately the struggle for supremacy lay between John of Gischala, who held the Temple, and a certain Simon of Geraza, who held the city. Many of the followers of these two chiefs had perished in the daily conflicts which took place in the streets, and these conflicts continued till the appearance of the Roman army before Jerusalem compelled both parties to act in concert for its defense.

Titus, after an ineffectual attempt to treat with the insurgents, assailed Jerusalem from the north, and in a few weeks his soldiers obtained possession of the two outer walls and the lower portion of the city. The Romans now pushed forward upon the remaining fortifications, but failing in their efforts to storm the tower of Antonia, they surrounded the city with a wall, so as to starve the defenders into submission. As soon as this work was completed they renewed their operations against Antonia, and on the 5th of July it was carried by surprise. Fully another month elapsed before the Temple which was burnt down during the assault upon it fell into the hands of the Roman commander (August 10th). The loss of the Temple was a grievous blow to the Zealots, and entailed upon them an immense sacrifice of life. Some of them succeeded in joining their comrades in the upper city, where a terrible famine was raging, and although hope was now wellnigh extinguished, the insurgents were resolved to hold out to the very last. Three weeks after the destruction of the Temple the Romans delivered a final assault on the upper city; the Jews offered but a feeble resistance, and after an unprecedented struggle of five months' duration Jerusalem lay once more at the feet of Rome (Sept. 7, 70). Titus ordered the place to be demolished. A number of the captives, and among them John of Gischala and Simon of Gerasa, were reserved to adorn the triumph of the conqueror; the rest either perished in the Roman amphitheatres, or were transported to Egypt to labour in the mines. The capture of Masada, a Jewish fortress on the southwestern shores of the Dead Sea, put a termination to one of the fiercest struggles recorded in history (A.D. 73).

The implacable attitude of the Zealots had taught Vespasian that it was no longer possible to govern Judaea in accordance with the principles of his predecessors. The policy pursued by them of allowing the Jews to manage their internal affairs subject to the cursory supervision of a procurator was liberal in its aim, and had proved successful in other parts of the empire, but it failed in Palestine in consequence of the political aspect which religious feeling had assumed in the minds of the population.

The perfect freedom enjoyed by the doctors of the Law under a system of local autonomy enabled them to turn the synagogues into schools of sedition. An ignorant and fanatical multitude had been trained from childhood to consider that it was at variance with their religion to accept a foreign yoke. It is not therefore surprising that every true son of the Law felt a burden upon his conscience till he was in arms against the power of Rome. This dangerous condition of popular feeling remained for the most part unknown to the Romans, and if symptoms of disaffection at times became manifest, they were probably treated by the Roman officials with a lofty disdain. In their eyes it no doubt seemed impossible that a petty Oriental nationality would ever venture into open conflict with the colossal forces at the command of the

Caesars. The Romans, accustomed to regard human society from a secular point of view, had no notion of the overwhelming potency of religion in the Jewish mind, and remained unconscious of the deep and powerful passions which religious sanctions were implanting in the Jewish heart. It was not till the rebellion had been crushed that the Romans recognized the nature of the people with whom they had to deal.

A state which could produce such men as the Zealots, who were just as irreconcilable after defeat as they were before it, was seen to be a constant source of menace to the empire, and its continued existence as an organized community was clearly incompatible with imperial order, stability, and peace. If the smaller organism was not to cripple or paralyze the larger one, the only course before Vespasian was to decree the dissolution of the Jewish state. It was a harsh measure, but the necessities of imperial policy demanded it. Accordingly all the outward symbols of a separate nationality were as far as possible obliterated. Jerusalem and the Temple were purposely left in ruins. The High Priesthood and the Sanhedrin were also abolished, and no centre of authority was permitted to remain. Even the Jewish Temple, which had existed for some centuries in Egypt, was now shut up; it was determined to prevent this sanctuary from becoming a new source of disturbance and disaffection. The Temple tax, which the Jews had been in the habit of sending as a pious offering to Jerusalem, had now to be paid into the imperial treasury. The transformation of this offering into a Roman impost was probably intended to remind the Jews of their true position in the empire. In pursuance of the policy of completely severing Palestine from its past, a colony of veterans was settled near Jerusalem, the chief cities of the province were reorganized upon Western principles, and a determined effort was made to Romanize the whole land. The results of Vespasian's policy were only partially successful; a large force had to be maintained in the country, and the Jews, after all their disasters, were still the most important element in the community.

The Final Conflicts

After the destruction of Jerusalem Titus left Judaea, and one of his lieutenants was entrusted with the task of extinguishing the last embers of resistance. In the autumn the victorious Roman celebrated the birthday of his brother Domitian and of his father Vespasian in a manner which rather belies his reputation for humanity. At the festivities which took place at Caesarea and Berytus in honour of these events thousands of Jewish captives were placed in the public arena, and either perished at the gladiatorial shows or in combats with wild beasts. But at Antioch and Alexandria, both of which cities he soon afterwards visited, Titus was restored to a better frame of mind, and would not listen to the solicitations of the Gentile population when they asked him to deprive the Jews of their ancient civil privileges.

"How can this be done," he said to the people of Antioch; "their country is now destroyed, and no other place will receive them." At this time Titus was deeply enamoured with a Jewish princess of the Herodian family, Berenice, one of King Agrippa's daughters, and a woman of great personal beauty and charm. This princess succeeded in fascinating the Roman soon after his arrival in the East; she became his inseparable companion, and, although her character for virtue was at a low ebb, it was currently believed that she would one day become his wife. It is possible that Berenice may have exerted her influence in favour of the Jews outside Palestine, but, as they had remained passive during the progress of the insurrection, there was no reason why they should be punished for the sins of their co-religionists in Judaea. The love of Titus for Berenice did not unfit him, like the famous amour of Antony and Cleopatra, for the serious business of life. A rumour arose after the fall of Jerusalem that Titus was aiming at the overthrow of Vespasian, and this rumour received fresh currency when it became known that he had worn a diadem during some religious festival in Egypt. Titus, in order to dispel these unjust suspicions, hurried home to Rome, and, appearing unexpectedly before the aged emperor, exclaimed, "I am here, my father, I am here!"

Immediately after his arrival in the capital Titus and Vespasian celebrated the triumph which the Senate had decreed them for their victories in Palestine. The triumphal pageant was organized on a scale of unusual magnificence, and the Roman populace were invited to gaze on representations of the battles which had been fought as well as on the actual trophies captured in the course of the campaign. Among these trophies were the spoils of the Temple the sacred vessels, the golden candlestick, and the rolls of the Law. Seven hundred of the tallest and most handsome among the Jewish captives walked in front of Vespasian and Titus, and when the great procession reached the temple of Jupiter Capitolinus, it stood still until a tragic ceremony had been performed. It was an ancient Roman custom that the enemy's general should be put to death while the people waited at this sacred spot. On this occasion Simon Bar Giora, one of the principal leaders of the Zealots, was the hapless victim, and when the messenger arrived to announce that the Jewish captain was slain, the multitude sent up a shout of joy, and prayers and sacrifices were forthwith offered up with great solemnity in the Temple. To commemorate the overthrow of the Jews gold, silver, and bronze coins were also struck. On some of these pieces we find the image of a Jewish warrior with his hands bound; Judaea is also represented in the form of a woman sitting in desolation under the shade of a palm tree, while around is the sad inscription, "Judaea captive." The sacred ornaments of the Jewish Temple were deposited in the Roman Temple of Peace, and the Book of the Law was kept in the imperial palace. All these tokens of the humiliated people have long since passed away, but the magnificent arch which was soon afterwards erected in Rome to commemorate the exploits of Titus still bears witness in all its shattered grandeur to the downfall of the Jewish national cause.

When Titus returned from the East he was admitted by his father Vespasian to a share of the supreme power. Amid the responsibilities of empire Titus still retained his affection for Berenice; she was invited to visit him at Rome, and for some years lived in the imperial palace as if she were his wife. The amour had become so notorious that the Athenians erected a statue in her honour, bearing the inscription, "The great queen daughter of the great king, Julius Agrippa." But the people of Rome were not so complaisant as the Greek provincials; they had a peculiar hatred of Eastern women, and after a time Titus, in deference to a rising tide of popular feeling, was obliged to break off his connection with the Jewish princess. After the death of Vespasian (A.D. 79) and the accession of Titus Berenice again appeared in Rome, animated with the hope of renewing the old relations with her lover. It is possible that Titus, when they unwillingly separated, held out this prospect before her, but time and prudence had produced an alteration in his designs, or perhaps he was resolved to show the Romans that their emperor had the power of sacrificing affairs of the heart to the imperative demands of state, for it is related that Berenice exercised her blandishments upon him in vain. This princess was the last of the Herodian family who played a conspicuous part before the world, and after the death of her brother Agrippa, who held a small principality in the northeast of Palestine, the Herodians sank back into obscurity.

The reign of Titus was of short duration (A.D. 79-81), but in the brief period to which it was confined he succeeded to such an extent in gaining the affection of all classes that he was afterwards spoken of as the Delight of the human races Feeling that his end was approaching, he opened the curtains of his litter on his way to the Cutilian springs, and, looking wistfully into the heavens, pathetically exclaimed that he did not deserve to die, for, with one exception, there was none of his acts that needed to be repented of. Titus was succeeded by his brother Domitian (A.D. 81-96), a man whose character was full of contradictory elements. During the first half of his reign Domitian administered the affairs of the empire with wisdom and firmness, but in the latter part the innate ferocity of his disposition gained the mastery over him, and led him at times to perpetrate the most wanton and barbarous atrocities.

At this time many of the Jews who had sought a refuge in Rome after the destruction of their country had to live in a condition of the most abject poverty. They inhabited the lowest quarters of the city, and all their earthly possessions consisted in a basket and a bed of straw. It was only by resorting to begging at the houses of the wealthy that these wretched outcasts were able to eke out a miserable and precarious existence. In these circumstances it is not surprising that many of them, in order to evade the small tribute that Vespasian had imposed upon the race, either dissimulated their origin, or did not make the statutory public declaration of the fact. The agents of Domitian, who were embarrassed for want of money towards the close of his reign, sometimes resorted to the most stringent measures in order to collect the Jewish tax, and Suetonius, the Roman historian, says that, when he was a youth, he once saw an imperial procurator in the midst of a large crowd compel an old man of ninety to pass through the degrading ordeal of proving whether he was circumcised or not. The painful impression which this incident produced upon the historian shows that such arbitrary proceedings were not usual with the Roman administration, and it is probable that it was the isolated act of an over-zealous official, and not part of any organized system for extorting the Jewish tribute. On the other hand, however, Domitian visited the utmost penalties of the law upon certain Romans who were charged with Judaism.

According to Roman ideas to renounce one's religion was equivalent to renouncing one's country, and at a period when all religions, with the exception of Christianity the universalistic principles of which were then almost unknown were national and a part of patriotism, the Roman view of the matter was substantially correct. In accordance with a statute, probably dating from the time of Vespasian, which forbade Judaizing, Domitian caused two Roman nobles, Flavius Clemens and Acilius Glabrio, to be executed. But in instituting proceedings against these senators it is very likely that the tyrant was merely actuated by political motives, for Clemens was his relative, and Glabrio was also accused of fighting with wild beasts in the arena, an accusation quite inconsistent with the other charge of Judaism. At the time the sentences were inflicted Domitian was aware that the Romans had become weary of his hateful yoke; conspiracies and plots were thickening around him, and he no doubt hoped that a few acts of vigour would strike terror among his enemies. But in these expectations he was disappointed, and a few months after the death of Clemens, Domitian perished by assassination (A.D. 96).

The Senate selected one of its own members, Marcus Cocceius Nerva (A.D. 96-98), as Domitian's successor. The new emperor had reached the age of sixty-five when he was called to supreme power, and although he had occupied high positions in the State he was neither distinguished by great talents nor conspicuous services. It is very probable that he was chosen by the senators on account of the well-known mildness and moderation of his character. When Nerva assumed the imperial purple he did not belie his antecedents, and the humane measures which characterized his short reign of sixteen months were in signal contrast to the harshness and barbarity that disgraced the name of his predecessor. His accession was a welcome change to the Jews, and although the Jewish tribute was not remitted it was henceforth levied with so much discretion and forbearance that coins were struck to commemorate the fact. During this period the friends of Judaism could also breathe more freely, and it was no longer permitted, as in the time of Domitian, to bring accusations against them because of their beliefs. It was perhaps fortunate for Nerva that his reign was short; his excessive mildness degenerated into mere weakness and timidity, and it was said by a competent witness that the empire was falling to pieces under his rule. Nerva, however, had the wisdom to perceive that he needed the assistance of a stronger hand than his own, and accordingly adopted Trajan, the most distinguished general of his time. Three months after this event Nerva died, and Trajan was accepted as his successor by the army and the Senate (A.D. 98).

In selecting Trajan (A.D. 98-117) Nerva rendered a most important service to the Roman people. The new emperor is one of the most commanding and attractive figures in the history of ancient society, and his character is equally worthy of admiration, whether we look at him as a soldier, as a statesman, or in his private capacity as a man. Brave and intrepid in the field, just, laborious, and economical as an administrator, genial, affable, and modest as a companion, Trajan, with his fine figure and noble countenance, happily united in his own person all the highest qualities of the Roman race. To Trajan has been ascribed the lofty sentiment that it is better the guilty should escape than that the innocent should suffer, and such was the veneration in which his memory was held by later times, that it became a custom with the Senate on the accession of a new emperor to hail him with the salutation, "May you be more fortunate than Augustus and better than Trajan! " From such a prince the Jews had nothing to fear and it is likely that they participated in the general prosperity which distinguished his reign. But the destruction of the Holy City and the demolition of the Temple had awakened feelings of resentment which even an era of unwonted prosperity could not mollify or assuage, and after a truce of nearly fifty years the Jews once more resolved to measure themselves against the colossal force of Rome. It was whilst Trajan was engaged in war with the Parthians that the Jews broke out into revolt (A.D. 116), and on this occasion the insurrectionary movement was participated in by the whole Jewish population of the East. The Parthian war was not of Trajan's seeking. For forty years the Romans had acquired the right of placing a king on the throne of Armenia, but in the year 114 the Parthian monarch set aside the prince appointed by Trajan, and conferred the kingdom of Armenia on one of his own nominees. Sometime before this signal affront to Roman pride the attitude of the Parthians had frequently been one of ill-concealed hostility, and although Trajan was now about sixty years of age he determined to take the field in person to chastise the insolence of his enemy and strengthen the frontiers of the empire. In the spring of 115 the old emperor having restored discipline among the Syrian legions and reinforced them with veterans from Pannonia, began his march from Antioch to the Euphrates. After futile negotiations with the Parthians Armenia was made a Roman province, and the whole of Mesopotamia submitted without a blow. In the following year Trajan pursued his way along the banks of the Tigris: Ctesiphon, the Persian capital, fell into his hands, and his progress was only stopped by the waters of the Persian Gulf. Seeing a vessel about to sail for India, and recollecting the exploits of Alexander, he is reported to have said, "Were I yet young I would not stop till I, too, had reached the limits of the Macedonian conquest." But these aspirations, if it is true that Trajan ever cherished them, were soon dissipated by the news that the populations behind him had risen in revolt. Trajan hastily retraced his steps, and after much severe fighting in which one legion was cut to pieces, the emperor succeeded in mastering the insurgents.

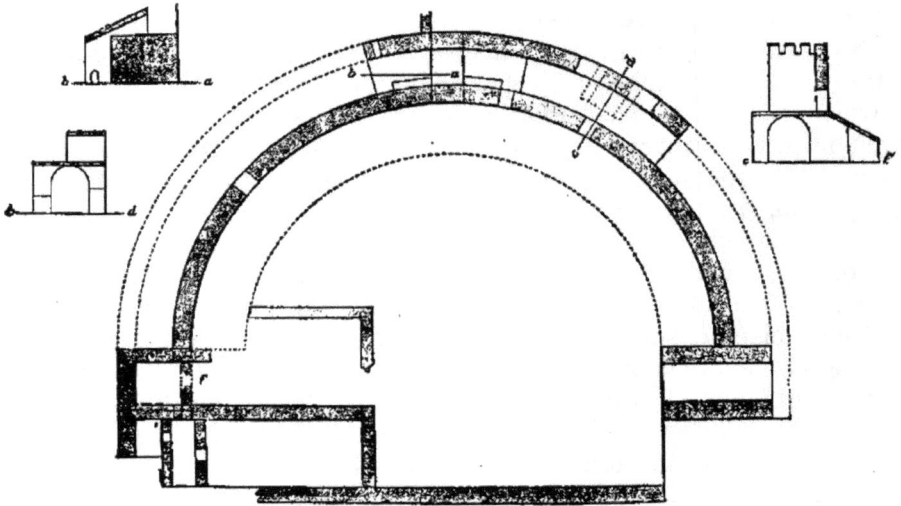

Roman Theatre Mamas

Among the most determined of Trajan's opponents in the course of this insurrection were the Jews of Mesopotamia. Lucius Quietus, one of the emperor's most trusted lieutenants, operated against them, and received orders from his chief to expel the Jewish population from the province. While Quietus was endeavouring to carry these instructions into effect news arrived at the Roman headquarters of the alarming revolt that had taken place among the Jewish colonists on the eastern shores of the Mediterranean (A.D. 116). Concerning the immediate cause of this widespread outbreak it is impossible to speak with certainty; it must have been to some extent preconcerted, otherwise it would not have sprung into existence almost simultaneously in so many districts. The revolting atrocities which characterized the conduct of the Jews tend to show that they were largely under the sway of a wild and aimless fanaticism, and if they had any settled purpose it apparently consisted in a resolve to exterminate their Gentile fellow-citizens, and to found an independent Jewish state amid the desolation they had created. In the island of Cyprus alone the Jews put two hundred and forty thousand of the native population to death, and in Cyrene on the African coast more than two hundred thousand Greeks and Romans were brutally massacred. In both of these provinces it is probable that the Jews outnumbered the rest of the inhabitants. After the revolt was quelled Cyrene had to be re-colonized. Wherever the Jews obtained the mastery they behaved like hordes of cannibals, eating the flesh of their victims and smearing themselves with their blood.

90

The moment for revolt was well chosen, and the temporary success which attended it was no doubt owing to the fact that the exigencies of the Parthian war had almost depleted the Eastern provinces of Roman troops. When the insurrection extended to Egypt the Prefect Lupus was unable to hold the field, and had to take refuge among the fortifications of Alexandria. Here he awaited the arrival of Martius Turbo, who was dispatched by Trajan with powerful reinforcements to the scene of hostilities. Turbo was an able officer, and once more taught the Jews that the frantic onset of Oriental fanaticism was unavailing against the cool bravery of the West. After a bitter and somewhat prolonged struggle the Roman commander succeeded in rescuing the oppressed populations of Egypt, Cyrene, and Cyprus; everywhere he cut down the insurgents without mercy, and at Alexandria the rebel population was almost annihilated. As a result of their atrocities, the Jews were henceforth forbidden to set foot on the island of Cyprus, and the feeling of resentment against them had reached such a pitch among the inhabitants that even shipwrecked Jews were threatened with death.

The rebellious attitude of the Jews had seriously interfered with the success of Trajan's policy in the East. From a military point of view the Euphrates was not a satisfactory frontier, and Trajan considered that the empire would enjoy greater security if its boundaries were extended to the banks of the Tigris. The line of the Tigris was much more easy to defend against incursions from the East, and it was not so much lust of conquest as the exposed position of the Romans in that quarter of the world which led the emperor to involve himself in a Parthian war. But the formidable outbreak of the Jews in Mesopotamia and on the Mediterranean contributed not a little to throw the emperor's great designs into confusion, and when he returned to Antioch (A.D. 117) with his legions shattered in an unsuccessful attempt to carry the desert fortress of Hatra, the Romans retained but a shadowy authority over the vast regions which had been lying at their feet the year before. The emperor, however, was not to be baffled in his purpose by these unforeseen strokes of adversity, and had determined to renew the campaign in the following spring. But while meditating on these warlike schemes for the future the hand of death was upon him; on the journey from Antioch to Rome, where a triumph awaited him, his martial spirit passed away (Aug. 8, 117).

Before setting out for the capital Trajan left his relative Hadrian in command of the legions at Antioch. Whether Trajan in the closing moments of his life adopted Hadrian or not is a matter of some uncertainty. The distinctions which were conferred one after another upon Hadrian from the time of his entry into public life, culminating in his appointment to the most important military position in the empire, point almost conclusively to the supposition that the aged emperor intended Hadrian to succeed him. But whatever may have been the circumstances which elevated Hadrian to the imperial dignity, his accession (A.D. 117-138) was a fortunate event for the commonwealth. He was in every way capable of being entrusted with the destinies of the vast and intricate organization of which he had become the chief. Hadrian was a man of great versatility and breadth of view. He had an insatiable desire for light on all conceivable subjects, and delighted to range over the whole field of knowledge, speculation, and superstition. With the reputation of being the very reverse of austere in his private life, he still appreciated the severe philosophy of the Stoics, and was at the same time at home among the soothsayers and magic men who crowded around him in the East. Hadrian took a keen, and yet amused, interest in the multitude of faiths which in his day were contending with one another for supremacy, but he gave a complete adhesion to none of them, and was always more anxious to understand than to believe their doctrines. In public life Hadrian displayed many of the highest qualities of a ruler. He did more than any of his predecessors to organize the imperial system, and tempered its inherent absolutism by surrounding the head of the executive with a trained body of competent officials for the different departments of public business. Hadrian lived very little in Rome; most of his time was spent in visiting the various provinces of the empire, and in making himself accurately acquainted with the real condition of the inhabitants. The happiness of the people was the supreme object of Hadrian's policy; justice and moderation was the spirit in which that object was pursued.

In the East the new emperor reverted to the principles of Augustus. He abandoned Trajan's schemes of aggrandizement, concluded peace with the Parthians, and the line of the Euphrates continued to be the eastern limit of the empire. Although Hadrian was a good soldier, he had no desire to play the part of a conqueror, and his inexhaustible activity was devoted to works of reform and peace. The pacific temper of Hadrian's administration produced a favourable impression upon many of the Jews, and the putting of Lucius Quietus to death soon after his accession was looked upon by some of them as a punishment for the harsh manner in which this commander had suppressed the rebellion in Palestine and Mesopotamia. Hadrian is the only emperor who is spoken of in the Sibylline Oracles of this period in a sincere tone of admiration. Great hopes are built upon him by the pious Jew of Alexandria who gives utterance to his expectations through the medium of the Sibyl. Hadrian is described by this writer in an oracular manner as the man with a silver helmet who bears the name of a sea. He is apostrophized in lofty terms as an eminent, an excellent, a brilliant sovereign who knows all things. He is a second Cyrus, and the priests are exhorted to appear before him in their white linen garments in order that the Temple of God may be restored.

The hopes of the Sibyl were probably based upon Hadrian's well-known love for restoring the decayed magnificence of the past. Whenever the emperor in the course of his wanderings came upon the desolate remains of former greatness it was difficult for him to resist the temptation to restore them. His immense constructions were to be seen in every province of the empire, and many of the dilapidated towns of Syria were for a time called back to life through his instrumentality. On Roman coins of this period Hadrian is represented as raising Judaea and her children from the dust, and it is possible that these coins were intended to commemorate some decree of his for the restoration of Jerusalem. Since its destruction by Titus the Holy City had remained in ruins and the sanctuary of Israel had become a haunt for beasts of prey. Hadrian had seen the desolation created by his predecessor, and was induced by a variety of reasons to rebuild the ill-fated town (circa 130). In addition to gratifying his antiquarian tastes and reviving an ancient seat of civilization, Hadrian, who never liked his soldiers to be idle, found the restoration of Jerusalem an excellent means of occupying the legion which had been stationed there since the time of Vespasian. But the new city was not intended to be a future centre of Judaism. It was, on the contrary, to be a Roman town, and to offer a home for the veterans of the neighbouring camp after their period of service had expired. So distinctly was this the case that the hallowed name of Jerusalem was discarded for the new constructions which were to spring up on the hills of Zion: the sacred spot was to have all traces of its past obliterated; it was henceforth to be spoken of as Aella Capitolina, a name given it in honour of the emperor and the supreme divinity of Rome. Jerusalem was to be a heathen city; within its walls Venus was to have her shrine, and a temple to Jupiter was to stand on the ruins that had been consecrated to the worship of Israel's God.

At the time the emperor was planning the transformation of Jerusalem into a heathen city, the jurists of Rome advised him to forbid the practice of circumcision. This prohibition, like the edict against mutilation, was unquestionably issued in the interest of morals and had no ulterior purpose, but the Jews not unnaturally regarded it as an attack upon their faith. The impracticability of enforcing this edict would have made it endurable, and the issuing of it might not have led to serious results. But the desecration of the Holy City was more than the Jews could bear, and the outcome of this portion of Hadrian's policy was one of the most sanguinary and protracted revolts in the annals of the Roman Empire. Ju-

Head of Hadrian, Found Near the Tombs of the Kings

daea was the centre of hostilities, but the insurrectionary movement was supported by the Jewish race throughout the world.

A mysterious personage named. Bar-Kokheba or Ben-Kosiba, placed himself at the head of the insurgents (A.D. 132-5). It is certain that Bar-Kokheba was a man of great valour and military ability, but the information which has come down to us concerning him makes it impossible to say whether he was a fanatic or an imposter. Notwithstanding the fact that Bar-Kokheba led the Jewish host, Rabbi Akiba was the soul of the revolt. At this period Akiba was holding a pre-eminent position as a doctor of the Law. Among the Jews of Palestine, as well as among their co-religionists abroad, his name was held in the highest veneration. He was the originator of new methods of interpretation; he had the reputation of being a second Ezra, and it became a saying among the doctors that the power of Moses was weak till he was interpreted by Rabbi Akiba. Akiba was a man of the people as well as a scribe; his heart was full of charity and affection for the multitude; his interest in their welfare was so deep and genuine that he ultimately came to be called "the Hand of the Poor." A portion of Akiba's life had been spent in visiting the Jewish communities in the Roman and Parthian Empires, and in his contact with the heathen he had learnt that some of their customs were worthy of respect. Considering the age in which he lived and the almost universal belief in such arts as magic and astrology, Akiba's mind was singularly free from vulgar superstitions, and it was a saying of his that Israel stood under no planet. But in spite of all these admirable qualities of mind and heart this eminent rabbi's belief in the immediate coming of the Messiah made him one of the most disastrous teachers the Jews had ever seen. These Messianic ideas created an alarming ferment among the credulous population. One of the wiser doctors of the time, apprehending their dire results, tried to cast ridicule upon them by saying, "Grass shall grow from thy jaws, O Akiba, before the Messiah appears." But the hopes of the infatuated rabbi were of a nature which neither reason nor mockery could affect, and when Bar-Kokheba appeared upon the scene Akiba immediately pointed him out as the long-predicted Messianic king. The rebel chief was the star (kokab) that should come forth out of Jacob; hence his name Bar-Kokheba, "the Son of the Star." Akiba's devotion reached such a pitch that he abandoned his life-long meditation on the Law and accepted the humble position of Bar-Kokheba's armour-bearer.

The recognition of Bar-Kokheba as the Messiah by so distinguished and revered a rabbi was in the nature of a consecration. It surrounded him with a halo of sanctity, and he was looked upon by multitudes with passionate enthusiasm as the long-expected deliverer of Israel from the yoke of Rome. Before the Romans were roused to the serious character of Bar-Kokheba's rebellion it had assumed very formidable proportions. All the towns in Judaea which had no Roman garrison declared for the insurgent chief, and a strongly fortified place called Bethar, some distance southwest of Jerusalem, became the headquarters of the Jews. In the closing years of their national life the use of Roman money had sorely perplexed the conscience of the Jews, and one of the first acts of Bar-Kokheba was to re-stamp die imperial coinage. Some of his coins are intended to commemorate the deliverance of Israel, and on this money of the revolt, as it was called, may still be seen the impression of two trumpets for the purpose of giving symbolical expression to the fact that Israel was being summoned together for a holy war. Success at first crowned the Jewish cause; the Roman forces in Palestine were too small to hold the field; even Publicius Marcellus, at that time legate of Syria, was not strong enough to cope with the insurrection. When Hadrian became aware of the alarming condition of affairs in Judaea reinforcements were sent to the scene of hostilities under the command of Sextus Julius Severus, the most distinguished soldier of his age. Severus was recalled from Britain to conduct the campaign. Adopting the tactics of his predecessor Vespasian, he declined a general engagement with the infuriated masses opposed to him. Severus, who was ably seconded by experienced lieutenants, divided his army into a number of separate corps and attacked the Jews in detail. One after another of the Jewish strongholds was captured, the defenders were decimated and the country laid in ruins. The fortress of Bethar with its wonderful subterranean passages was held by Bar-Kokheba with the tenacity of despair. But the Romans, aided by the horrors of thirst and famine, eventually obtained the mastery, and

Fighting with Wild Beasts

the rebel leader perished amid the ruins of his cause.

It is perhaps well that we possess so few details respecting the course of this revolt and the manner in which it was suppressed. According to the scattered intimations of ancient writers it was a war of extermination. The devastation and massacre which marked its progress and crowned its close were of much greater magnitude than the terrible scenes enacted in the days of Vespasian and Titus. Without taking account of the vast numbers that perished by famine and disease, it is credibly reported that over half a million men fell fighting in the field. The miserable survivors whose lives were spared glutted the slave markets of the East. Some of the fugitives from Roman vengeance concealed themselves in caves and subterranean passages; many of them were impelled by hunger to devour the bodies of the dead, and those were considered fortunate who escaped into the wilderness. It would almost seem to have been the object of the Roman administration to make Palestine intolerable to the children of Abraham, and the desolate aspect of Judaea at the present day is a silent witness of the awful severity with which this final rising was suppressed. As a consequence of the insurrection the name of Judaea became so hateful to the Roman authorities that it was generally discarded, and the province was henceforth known as Syria Palaestina. The Jews were forbidden on pain of death to set foot in Jerusalem; they were even denied the melancholy satisfaction of gazing afar off upon its ruins. In the third century this edict fell into disuse, and was not again put in operation till the reign of the emperor Constantine. But this general prohibition did not apply to one day in the year the anniversary of the capture of Jerusalem by Titus. On that day of bitter memory the Jews could obtain permission to weep over the site of the Temple and to anoint the stone where it was believed the Holy of Holies had stood.

The revolt under Hadrian was the last supreme effort of the Jews to separate themselves from the confederation of nations held together by Roman arms. Under succeeding emperors the facilities afforded by the caves of Palestine for leading a lawless life sometimes produced temporary disturbances, but these movements, although professedly patriotic, were often mere outbreaks of brigandage, and never assumed a serious aspect. The military power of the people had been completely destroyed. But if their power had perished their animosity became, if possible, more bitter and profound. So long, however, as peace was not broken the Romans paid comparatively little heed to Jewish rancour, and on the whole continued to allow the race a considerable measure of religious and political toleration. Hadrian's mistaken edict forbidding circumcision was abrogated by his successor, Antoninus Pius, and the Jews had henceforth perfect liberty to perform this rite upon their own children. As before the war, they were free from service in the legions, and at least from the reign of Severus, they were excused the performance of such municipal duties as ran counter to their religious prejudices. In fact, it had never been a part of Roman policy to treat the Jews with greater harshness than the rest of the provincials; their position in this respect was even a favoured one, and the calamities which fell upon them under Roman domination were almost entirely of their own choosing. However much we may honour the motives and heroism of a Bar-Kokheba or a Simon Bar-Giora, it was neither in the interests of Jewish liberty nor for the general welfare of mankind that such leaders should prevail. Their success would have immediately involved the Jews in anarchy, and the era of religious persecution they would undoubtedly have inaugurated against the non-Jewish population must, sooner or later, have compelled the nations to do the repressive work which was unwillingly undertaken by the emperors Vespasian, Trajan, and Hadrian.

The Sanhedrin, or Supreme National Council

It was one of the fixed principles of Roman policy to interfere as little as possible with the internal organization of the various peoples who fell under the sway of Rome, and when Judaea, after the deposition of Archelaus (A.D. 6), was placed in charge of a procurator, the Sanhedrin of Jerusalem acquired a wider range of authority within the new province than it had possessed since the Maccabees assumed the title of king. It is not possible to say with certainty when this supreme council first came into existence. According to Jewish tradition its origin dates back to the time of Moses, but there is no evidence to show that Moses organized a permanent assembly with functions similar to those of the Sanhedrin. Nor is this institution to be confounded with the elders of the people or the court of justice at Jerusalem referred to in the Old Testament. The first distinct mention of it in Jewish literature occurs in the reign of Antiochus the Great (B.C. 223-187), and the first faint traces of its existence do not go further back than the Persian period. In the time of Antiochus it is not called a Sanhedrin, but a Senate (Gerousia); it is an aristocratic body, the High Priest as the most prominent member of the community is at its head; and as the Greek kings who succeeded Alexander the Great generally left local affairs in the hands of the vassal states, the Jewish Senate would be in possession of very extensive powers. Under the Maccabees the Senate still continued to hold a place in Jewish life, but the autocratic tendencies developed by some of these princes must have led to a curtailment of its authority. Pompey did not interfere with the Sanhedrin when he abolished the Maccabaean monarchy (B.C. 63), but his successor Gabinius (B.C. 57-55) deemed it prudent to divide its authority with two other local bodies which he established in Judaea. The arrangements of Gabinius were soon afterwards annulled by Julius Caesar when he effected a settlement of Eastern affairs after the fall of Pompey (B.C. 47); the Sanhedrin of Jerusalem again received its ancient powers and its jurisdiction once more extended over the whole Jewish portion of Palestine. Although Herod the Great, at the commencement of whose career the High Council is first expressly called a Sanhedrin, mercilessly decimated its members on his accession to the throne, it is not likely that he altogether terminated its existence. It seems more probable that he purged this institution of all elements which were openly hostile to himself, and filled up the vacancies thus created with representatives of that section of the Pharisees who acquiesced in his rule. The division of Herod's kingdom into three parts (B.C. 4) had the effect of limiting the direct jurisdiction of the Sanhedrin to the province of Judaea; no alteration in this respect took place on the advent of the procurators; the scope of its authority continued to remain unchanged till the outbreak of the Jewish war (A.D. 66), at the end of which the Sanhedrin finally disappeared.

According to a Jewish tradition of comparatively late origin, the Sanhedrin was merely a college of scribes, at the head of which stood a Nasi, or president, and an Ab-beth-din, or vice-president. An assembly of this description no doubt came into existence after the destruction of the Jewish state, but it is not to be identified with the Sanhedrin mentioned in the writings of Josephus and the New Testament. In these authorities the Sanhedrin, besides being an ecclesiastical court, possesses legislative, administrative, and judicial powers as well, and it is the High Priest, the representative of the nation both in civil and ecclesiastical affairs who is its president. When Jesus is brought to trial at Jerusalem it is the High Priest Caiaphas who is head of the Sanhedrin which condemns Him; and when St. Paul is afterwards charged before the same council, it is the High Priest Ananias who performs the functions of presiding judge. In the few places where Josephus mentions a sitting of the Sanhedrin he is entirely in agreement with the writings. of the New Testament, and these contemporary witnesses are surely to be preferred to the dubious traditions of the Mischna. At the head then was the high priest; the other members belonged to the priestly aristocracy, and the most eminent representatives of the scribes, together with the elders, the men of years and experience who always filled a prominent place in Jewish affairs. It is not possible to say with certainty of how many members the Sanhedrin was composed, but it is highly probable that Jewish tradition is correct when it assigns the number as amounting to seventy-one. It appears that new members were admitted by the laying-on of hands, but no record remains of the qualifications necessary to obtain a seat in their council of the nation. Although the priestly aristocracy was the official element in the Sanhedrin and transacted its business and played the leading part before the public, the real masters of the situation were the scribes, and they unquestionably exercised the greatest influence within the council itself. The secret of this influence lay in the fact that the scribes almost entirely belonged to the popular party, and the priests, who were mostly Sadducees, were obliged to shape the policy of the Sanhedrin in accordance with the views of those among its members who possessed the ear of the multitude.

So few historic traces are left which bear on the activity of the Sanhedrin, that it is difficult to define with accuracy the exact scope of its authority. It is clear, however, that its action was limited, on the one hand, by the large powers entrusted to the procurator, and, on the other, it did not extend to cases which lay within the competence of the eleven local councils which existed in the province of Judaea at the commencement of the Christian era. Its direct authority did not extend beyond Judaea itself, but within the boundaries of this province, in all likelihood it possessed very much the same judicial and administrative power as was confided to the provincial councils of the neighbouring Greek provinces. The Sanhedrin had practically no power over the lives and property of the Roman citizens who had settled temporarily or permanently in Judaea. They were subject to the jurisdiction of the procurator alone, and had the privilege of appealing from him to the emperor. If, however, a Roman profaned the Temple he immediately came within the jurisdiction of Jewish law, and the Sanhedrin had a right to summon him to appear before its tribunal. To be permitted to judge a Roman at all was an immense concession to Jewish religious feeling, but the Caesars appear to have made another almost equally great when they permitted Jews in different parts of the empire to be handed over for trial to the Sanhedrin at Jerusalem even if the offence had not been committed in Judaea, and was purely a question of religious belief. That this was the case is plainly shown by the nature of the commission which St. Paul received from the high priests when he went from Jerusalem to take proceedings against the Christians who lived in Damascus. Even cases which the Sanhedrin was not competent to decide, and which had to be referred to the procurator, were, as a rule, decided by him in accordance with the maxims of Jewish law. He, as well as the tribune of the troops in Jerusalem, had the

Portion of Cornice, Temple Kades, Galilee.

power of calling the Sanhedrin together. But the procurator's sanction was not requisite to legalize a sitting of the Sanhedrin, or to give validity to its sentences, except when they were of a capital nature. It is chiefly in its capacity as a court of justice that the Sanhedrin is mentioned in the New Testament. Jesus and Stephen were both condemned by it as guilty of blasphemy; Paul was charged before it as a transgressor of the Law; Peter and John as false prophets and fomenters of sedition. It was the supreme interpreter of the laws and traditions of the Jewish people, that is to say, of a code of regulations which embraced the entire civil and religious life of Judaism, and its decisions were regarded as obligatory on every member of the Jewish race throughout the world.

Besides the Sanhedrin at Jerusalem there also existed in those parts of Palestine where the Jews preponderated in Judaea, Galilee, and Peraea a number of local councils which possessed criminal and legislative jurisdiction within their respective districts. Most towns and villages had one of these local councils in their midst. The smallest of them consisted of seven members, and in larger towns the number of members amounted to twenty-three.

It was only in those cases where the local Sanhedrin could not arrive at a decision, or was doubtful as to the interpretation of the Law, that the issue had to be decided by the High Council of Jerusalem. In all other respects the local Sanhedrin appears to have possessed very much the same powers as the one in the Holy City, and to have pronounced sentences involving fines, imprisonment, and death. The sittings of these local bodies usually took place in the synagogue, which was transformed for the time being into a court of justice, and in order to constitute a legal sitting it was necessary for at least three members to be present. The hearing of causes took place on Mondays and Thursdays; two witnesses were required to procure a conviction, and sentences of corporal punishment were inflicted on the spot. It is these local councils which Jesus has in His mind when He says, "Beware of men; for they will deliver you to the councils, and scourge you in their synagogues; "and it is with reference to the power the local council has of sending men to prison that He says, "Agree with thine adversary quickly, whiles thou art in the way with him; lest at any time the adversary deliver thee to the judge, and the judge deliver thee to the officer, and thou be cast into prison. Verily I say unto thee, Thou shalt by no means come out thence, till thou hast paid the uttermost farthing."

The Temple

The Temple on Mount Zion, with its imposing ordinances of worship and its array of hereditary priests, was an institution of much greater antiquity than the Sanhedrin, and was regarded in Roman times by every faithful Jew as the only sanctuary where an acceptable sacrifice could be offered to the God of his fathers. It had its origin at a period when the Hebrew tribes, which had settled in the land of Canaan, were compelled by, the pressure of surrounding peoples to adopt a more centralized form of rule, and to subject themselves to a single head. The creation of a monarchy in the days of Saul and David was intended to tighten the bonds of national unity which had hitherto been comparatively weak. In the early career of humanity unity in religion was the basis of effective national unity, and the erection of the Temple after David's death was designed to strengthen the feeling of religious solidarity among the Israelites. The new edifice rose in stately grandeur on one of the hills of the capital, to serve as a common centre of worship for the whole people and to keep alive the conviction that they were one. But for several centuries after its institution the Temple at Jerusalem had to tolerate the rivalry of the numerous High Places which had existed among the Israelites as places of sacrifice from ancient times.

Still, from the hour of its completion, the Temple continued to grow in influence and importance. The development of religious ideas produced by the prophets tended to depress the old sanctuaries in popular estimation and to exalt the sanctity of the Temple. But in spite of these favouring circumstances, and in spite of Josiah's attempt to abolish the High Places, it was not till the return from Babylon that they completely disappeared, and that the Temple came to be regarded as the sole sanctuary of the Jewish race. Old Israel ceased to exist with the Captivity; it was not a nation, but a religious community which returned to Palestine after the Exile; and the Temple which this community rebuilt, and around the sacred precincts of which it settled, became the only orthodox seat of sacrificial worship, and continued to maintain this position till the final downfall of the Jewish state.

The popularity of the Temple in the first century of the Christian era may be inferred from the immense multitude of Jews which used to flock to it from all parts of the Roman and Parthian Empires. Josephus very probably exaggerates when he says that three millions of people were to be found assembled in Jerusalem on the occasion of certain festivals. It is, however, undoubtedly true that the worshippers who frequented the sanctuary were vast in number, and were not confined to the Jews of Palestine alone. In apostolic times Parthians and Medes and Elamites and the dwellers in Mesopotamia, in Judaea and Cappadocia, in Pontus and Asia, in Phrygia and Pamphylia, in Egypt and the parts of Libya about Cyrene, and sojourners from Rome both Jews and proselytes, Cretes and Arabians, were among the multitude who worshipped at the Temple, and whose pious offerings made it one of the richest sanctuaries in the East. Whatever commotions might be disturbing the peace of Judaea, pious bands of pilgrims were always ready to leave their homes for Zion's holy hill, and Jerusalem was filled with worshippers when the legions of Titus closed around it. It may be permissible to speak of the synagogue as a rival to the Temple, for the synagogue, as time went on, succeeded more and more in satisfying the religious aspirations of the Jews. But the synagogue was an unconscious rival, and the rabbi who taught in it was as ardent in upholding the necessity for offering sacrifice in the Temple as the priest who ministered at the altar. Not only did the rabbi uphold the privileges of the Temple while it was in existence, but for centuries after its destruction he looked back on. its departed glories with regret, and was firmly persuaded it would be restored again with all its ancient ceremonial at the commencement of the Messianic age.

The worship at the Temple was conducted by a hereditary priesthood, which in the days of Jesus is said to have numbered about twenty thousand men. As it was impossible for such a large body to minister in holy things at the same time, the priesthood was divided into twenty-four families or classes, which were again subdivided into smaller groups, and each of these divisions was presided over by a leading priest who was called the head. All the members of the priesthood were in theory on .a footing of equality, for all of them were equally members of a sacred caste which traced its descent from the family of Aaron. As a matter of fact, however, as much social disparity existed amongst the priesthood as amongst the rest of the community. High above the ordinary priests stood those well-known families from which the high priests as a rule were drawn. As members of the Sanhedrin, and as officials entrusted by the Romans with important civil and judicial functions, these high-priestly families exercised an authority which placed them in a very different position from the ordinary priest, who only emerged from his obscurity on those occasions when he had to minister in the Temple. As is very frequently the case, difference of position created divergence of interest; the high-priestly families and the higher Temple officials sided in the main with the established order of things, and did not scruple to oppress and rob their poorer brethren, when the opportunity presented itself. The inferior ranks of the priesthood were, on the other hand, in sympathy with the popular movement against Rome, for the rapacity of the Temple nobility had so impoverished them that, apart altogether from religious convictions, they had everything to hope and nothing to lose from change.

Although the Jewish priesthood was in its latter days divided upon political questions, it always continued to remain at one as to the conditions which had to be complied with before a new member was admitted within its ranks. Unlike the prophets and the scribes, the priests were a hereditary caste, and the candidate who claimed admission into it had to show that he possessed a genealogy which was above suspicion, and which proved that he belonged to the family of Aaron. When the Sanhedrin was satisfied on this important point, the candidate became a member of the priestly class, and had a right to a share in the temporalities of the priesthood. But before he was permitted to exercise any priestly functions, he had to prove that he was free from certain bodily infirmities which are specified in the Law. If he failed to satisfy this second test, he was, according to the Talmud, clothed in black garments and had to go his way; but, if he was found to be without physical blemish, the ceremony of ordination was proceeded with. This ceremony was of a very elaborate character, and lasted seven days. At the end of this time the new priest was arrayed in white clothing, and went into the sanctuary to assist his brethren in the service.

In the ordinances of worship the priests were assisted by a subordinate class of officials known as the Levites. The Levites were divided into the same number of classes, and possessed an organization similar to the organization of the priests. According to the Sinaitic legislation which was in full force during Roman times, the Levites were not the direct descendants of Aaron, and were not considered as priests. They stood in a kind of servile position to the priesthood, and as the priests were regarded as the servants of Jehovah so the Levites were regarded as the servants of the priests. They were not permitted to officiate at the altar or to enter the inner sanctuary; their duties were of an inferior character, and mainly consisted in slaughtering the animals offered for sacrifice, and in acting as choristers and doorkeepers, and watchers over the fabric of the Temple.

At the head of this great sacerdotal corporation stood the High Priest, the prince of the Temple, who united in his own person the highest civil and ecclesiastical dignities. He was not merely the chief dignitary of the Jewish Church; he was, at the same time, the chief representative of the nation in all its secular affairs.

Stele from Herod's Temple, Jerusalem, in the Museum Tschinili-Kirschk, Constantinople.

The Herodian family and the procurators had been thrust upon the community by the force of outward circumstances, and possessed no internal relation to the national life. The position of the high priest, on the other hand, was the direct result of the hierocratic form of society which had existed among the Jews since the return from exile, and it was in virtue of his spiritual dignity that he became the head of the people in the secular acceptation of the term. Although no political attributes are ascribed to him in the Law, the position which he occupied as the supreme pontiff of the Jewish Church compelled him to assume them; he was the natural intermediary between the Jews and their foreign masters; he conducted all political affairs which remained in Jewish hands, and the quasi-regal forms which took place at his investiture are a kind of symbol of the authority which he was afterwards to exercise.

In consequence of the multiplicity of secular duties which the high priest had to discharge, it was only occasionally that he took an official part in the services of the Temple. In those services a unique position was assigned to him. He alone was permitted to offer sacrifice whenever he chose, the other priests had to do so only in the order of their course; he alone could enter the Holy of Holies to burn incense on the Day of Atonement, and it was through him alone that on this great day the congregation of Israel came into the immediate presence of Jehovah.

The most important personage connected with the sanctuary after the high priest was the Captain of the Temple, who was responsible for the safety of the sacred edifice as well as for the sums of money and other treasures which it contained. Like many of the heathen temples of antiquity the Temple at Jerusalem was a kind of treasure-house as well as a place of sacrifice. Although it had been plundered on several occasions, it was still considered by the people to enjoy the privilege of inviolability; it was regarded as the securest place for their savings, and the property of the widow and the orphan was often deposited within its walls. In the forecourt a number of safes were kept, into which the money placed under the charge of the Temple authorities was laid, and also the treasure which belonged exclusively to the Temple itself. To assist him in the important duty of protecting the sacred building with all its precious contents, the Captain of the Temple had a body of Levites under his command. All the gateways to the Temple were carefully guarded by these officials both night and day, and during the time the sanctuary was open to the people they had to see that no one defiled it or intruded into those portions which were forbidden them.

In the Roman period the priesthood was a richly endowed class, and derived its revenue from a variety of sources, the chief of which consisted in what was practically a number of imposts on the produce of the soil and the animals bred by the Jewish husbandman. The first-fruits of the ground were in all cases the property of the priests, they had also a claim on all the choicest products of the harvest, and although the quantity required was not definitely fixed by law, the husbandman was expected to give at least a fiftieth of the whole to the servants of Jehovah at Jerusalem. After these dues had been paid the claims of the Levites had to be satisfied, and these claims assumed truly formidable proportions, amounting to no less than a tenth of the entire harvest. The Levites, however, had in their turn to pay back a tenth of what they received from the peasantry to the priesthood. When it is remembered how unwillingly the Jews paid the tribute which the Romans had laid upon them, it might be supposed that they would show a similar reluctance to bear the enormous burden which had been imposed upon them by the priests. But this was very far from being the case, as is manifest from the scrupulous way in which they used to tithe the very smallest produce such as mint, anise, and cumin. In addition to a large share of the raw produce, a certain portion of all the bread which was baked in Jewish households formed a part of the priest's income; it amounted in the case of bakers to a forty-eighth, and in the case of private persons to a twenty-fourth of the whole. As has just been said, the taxes on the property of the husbandman extended to the domestic animals which he reared, and included not only clean animals such as the ox, the sheep, and the goat, but also such animals as the horse, the camel, and the ass, which were regarded as unclean. The firstborn male of all of these beasts was the property of the priests, but if the animals belonged to the unclean category, they could be bought back by the original owner for a fifth of their value; if, however, they were clean animals they had to be handed over to the priests. So widely did this law respecting the firstborn extend that even human beings were not exempted from its operation, and the first male child born of Jewish parents was supposed to be the property of the priesthood till he had been redeemed by the payment of five shekels, a sum equal to about thirteen shillings of English money.

These various imposts formed the main portion of the sacerdotal revenues, and constituted the ordinary sources from which they were derived; but during the time the priests were exercising their ministry at Jerusalem their regular income was augmented by the share they received of the sacrifices offered in the Temple by the worshippers. The only sacrifice of which the carcass was entirely consumed upon the altar was the burnt-offering, and even of this sacrifice the priests always retained the skin, a most important item when the immense number of animals sacrificed is taken into consideration. Of all the other offerings such as the meal-offering, the sin-offering, and the guilt-offering, the priest as a rule received nearly the whole; he obtained a portion of the peace-offering, and the proceeds of certain kinds of votive offerings also fell into his hands. It will thus be seen that the priesthood by reason of its wealth alone was a most important element in the Jewish state, and it would doubtless have been more important still if the high-priestly aristocracy had not driven the mass of the ordinary priests and Levites into the ranks of the discontented by defrauding them of their just proportion of the sacerdotal revenues.

The duties appertaining to the great body of. the priesthood were limited in their range, and mainly consisted in the offering of sacrifices at the Temple. On the three great festivals of the Jewish calendar, the Passover Pentecost, and the Feast of Tabernacles, the multitudes which came to worship at Jerusalem were so enormous that the entire priesthood was required to assist in the sacred ministrations. But on ordinary occasions this was not the case, and each of the twenty-four classes into which the sacerdotal body was divided officiated at the altar for a week at a time. As each class contained a larger number of priests than was necessary for the proper performance of the usual daily services, it was subdivided in such a manner that every priest exercised his sacred calling once at least before his week of duty came to a termination. Great precautions were taken to ensure the legal purity of the officiating priests. During the period of their ministrations they had to be in a state of Levitical cleanness; the use of wine was forbidden them; after taking a daily bath they had to wash their hands and feet in the brazen laver of the Temple before they were permitted to appear at the altar of sacrifice arrayed in the white garments of their office.

The sacred structure in which the priests performed their sacerdotal duties, and where the multitudes assembled to witness the solemnities of public worship was built in the form of a terrace with the Temple at its summit. The Temple was a roofed edifice of moderate size, and was divided into two unequal portions. The first of these was known as the Holy Place, while the other which lay beyond it was called the Holy of Holies. The Holy of Holies was separated from the Holy Place by a large curtain; it was completely empty, and was only entered once a year on the Day of Atonement by the high priest. The Holy Place was about twice the dimensions of this inner sanctuary, and contained the golden Altar of Incense which was used morning and evening for the incense offering; it also contained the Golden Candlestick, which had always to be kept alight; and the golden Altar of Shewbread, where the twelve loaves which had to be replaced every Sabbath day were laid. Outside the Temple proper lay the Temple courts, roofless enclosures amounting to four in number. The largest of these and the furthest removed from the Temple was the Court of the Gentiles, so called because men of all nations were permitted to enter it. Five gates opened into this vast court. It was here the money-changers had their stalls, and that the vendors of beasts for sacrifice disposed of them to the people. This was the court where the rabbis disputed, and where Jesus and His disciples used to teach. It was in fact a market, a money-changers bureau, a place for public discussion, and a general meeting-point for Jews from all parts of the world.

On the terrace above this court stood the Court of the Israelites, which was composed of two parts—one court for both sexes and another for men alone. Only Jews had the privilege of entering those courts, and notices were put up at the approaches to them forbidding Gentiles to proceed further on pain of death. A peculiarity connected with these courts consisted in the fact that the women's court was available for men as well, but the women on the other hand were not permitted to enter the

BLOCK PLAN OF HERODS TEMPLE .

Levels above Sea and existing remains shewn thus———
Restoration thus :—

Tadi

Sore$

Nitzotz

Moked

Court of Priests

Nicanor

Court of Women

Amphitheas

Sore$

court set specially apart for the men. Some steps above the Court of the Israelites and in close proximity to the Temple stood the Court of the Priests,

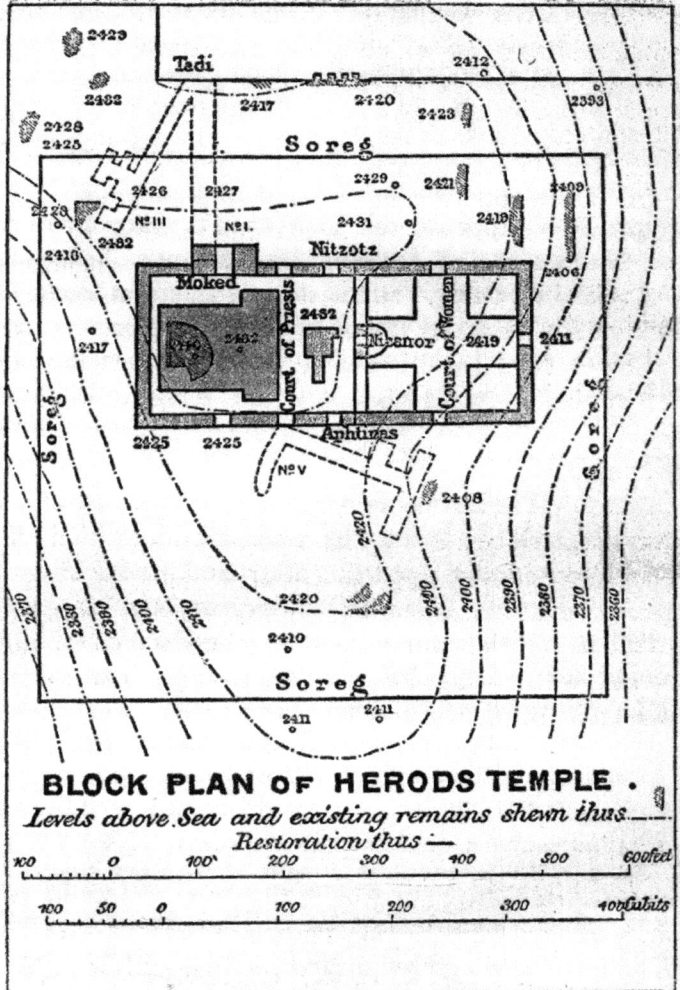

106

which was set apart for the priests alone. Close to this court and in front of the Temple stood the great Altar of Sacrifice. It was a large square structure made of unhewn stones, on which a fire was constantly kept burning, and where public and private sacrifice was daily offered to the God of Israel.

The sacrifice of animals upon the altar at Jerusalem was the ordinary means adopted by the Israelites to gratify or appease the Deity. To many Jews of the Roman period sacrifice had assumed a highly symbolical meaning, but it is probable that some of them still adhered to the primitive conceptions of the divinity which the literal acceptation of this religious rite implied. It may be said that there were three kinds of sacrifices in use among the Jews—the Burnt-offering, the Peace-offering, and the Sin and Trespass-offering. The Burnt-offering was the most customary form of sacrifice; it was the only offering which was entirely consumed upon the altar, and in its highest significance was intended to express the complete devotion of the worshipper to the decrees of the Divine will. The Peace-offering—only the fat of which was burnt, the carcass being used by the offerer as a festive meal—was a sacrifice offered either for the purpose of procuring a temporal blessing from Jehovah, or as an expression of gratitude for one which had already been received. The fat of the Sin-offering was also consumed upon the altar, but the flesh was given to the priests. This was an offering which proceeded from the feeling that union with God had been destroyed by some conscious or unconscious act of sin, and was offered with the object of appeasing the Divine displeasure, and restoring harmonious relations between the offending Israelite and the Most High.

Many of these offerings were of a private character, and only concerned the person who brought them to the altar, but the daily burnt-offering was a public sacrifice for the whole community, and constituted the regular daily service of the Temple. This offering consisted in the sacrifice morning and evening of a lamb without blemish. The morning service began at break of day, and the evening about three o'clock in the afternoon. Certain psalms were appointed for every day of the week, and sacred music, both. vocal and instrumental, was employed to increase the dignity and solemnity of the service. As soon as the sacrifice had been killed and was laid upon the altar, the song of the Lord began. "And all the congregation worshipped, and the singers sang, and the trumpeters sounded: and all this continued until the burnt-offering was finished." But the ritual of the daily service was quite eclipsed by the splendid ceremonial which took place on high festivals, and especially on the great Day of Atonement, when the high priest officiated in person, and formed the centre of religious interest. It was on this day that the high priest entered the Holy of Holies to expiate the sins of the people; and when he appeared again before the curtain which shut him off from human sight, he seemed to the expectant multitudes...

> "As the morning star rising from a cloud,
>   as the moon when it is full;

As the sun shining on the temple of the Most High,
as the rainbow giving light on a bright cloud;
When he put on his robe of honour,
and was clothed with the perfection of glory,
When he went up to the Holy Altar
he ennobled the court of the sanctuary;
As he stood by the hearth of the altar,
he took the consecrated portions out of the priest's hands.

Encompassed with his brethren round about
like a cedar of Lebanon,
All the sons of Aaron in their apparel,
like palm trees compassed him round about,
Holding in their hands the offering for the Lord
before all the congregation of Israel.
And finishing the service at the altar,
that he might adorn the offering of the Most High Almighty,
He stretched out his hand to the cup,
and made the libation with the blood of the grape;
He poured it out at the foot of the altar,
as a sweet-smelling savour to the most High King of All.

Then shouted the sons of Aaron,
and sounded the brazen trumpets;
And made a great noise to be heard,
to recommend the nation to the Most High.
Then all the people together hasted,
and fell down to the earth upon their faces
To worship their Lord,
the Almighty, the God most high.

The singers also sang His praises with their voices,
in the great house was there made sweet melody.
The people besought the Most High,
and addressed their prayers to the God of mercy,
Till the solemnity of the Lord was ended,
and they had finished His service.
Then he went down and lifted up his hands
over the whole congregation of the children of Israel,
To give them with his lips the blessing of the Lord,
and to exalt His name.
And the people bowed themselves down a second time,
to receive a blessing from the Most High."

The Synagogue

An institution of less antiquity and pretension than the Temple, but one which was destined to outlive it, and to play an important part not only in the history of the Jewish religion, but also in the formation of the Christian Church, was the Synagogue. Both in the Talmud and the New Testament it means a meeting-house for religious purposes, a description which explains with tolerable accuracy the object of the numerous places of worship which existed in every town and village of Palestine in the time of Christ. The two main elements which contributed towards the formation of the synagogue were the centralization of the whole Jewish sacrificial system at one place the Temple of Jerusalem—and the determination of the scribes to impress the Law in indelible characters on the heart and mind of every one who called himself a Jew. The effect of making the Temple the only sanctuary in which it was permissible to offer an acceptable sacrifice operated in two ways it elevated the character of the old popular religion at the expense of its vitality, and in the second place it destroyed the ancient seats of sacrifice, and deprived the people who lived at a distance from Jerusalem of the religious privileges which they had formerly enjoyed. In these circumstances it became imperative, while maintaining the exclusive prerogatives which the Temple had acquired, to devise some religious institution to supply the place of what had been lost. But to inaugurate such a change after the Exile might have proved an impossible task if the germs of the synagogue had not already sprung up among the captives during their enforced sojourn in Babylonia. In the dark days of the Exile it had become a custom with the deported Jews to meet together at stated times to console and comfort one another, and to fortify themselves in the faith of their fathers by the reading and expounding of the Law. This custom did not openly conflict with the pretensions set up on behalf of the Temple, it was accordingly continued after the Return, and so palpably met the requirements of Jewish religious life, that it ultimately developed into the synagogue, and became an established institution, with its roots firmly fixed in the affections of the people. For the diffusion of the Law among the whole community the synagogue was admirably adapted, and it is questionable if the Law would have survived the rude shocks which were awaiting it, had the synagogue not existed and held its precepts before the popular mind. No wonder that the scribes, the men whose whole lives were absorbed in the teaching of the Law, did their utmost to exalt the synagogue. It was an unsurpassed instrument for the propagation of their ideas; they accordingly invested it with Divine sanctions, and ascribed its origin to Moses himself.

As far as it is possible to judge from the ruins of old synagogues which still exist in the northern parts of Galilee, these places of worship were of very simple construction, and like Jewish buildings in general, they could lay no claim to architectural distinction. The site for a synagogue was, as a rule, selected because of its proximity to the seashore or to a running stream; and this choice was made for the purpose of enabling the worshippers the more easily to perform the ablutions prescribed for those about to enter a house of prayer. The synagogue was generally rectangular in form, with a portal constructed in accordance with the Greek style of the period, and an exuberance of spiral ornamentation essentially Jewish in character. The interior of the sacred building was of equal simplicity with the exterior. The chest in which the rolls of the Law and the other holy writings were kept was the most notable piece of furniture. It is probable that in the time of Christ there was a reading-desk for the use of the person who was chosen to read the Scriptures, and it is also likely that the reading-desk stood upon a raised platform to allow the reader for the day to be more easily seen and heard by the assembly. Around the reading-desk seats were arranged for the people, the women and the men, as is gen-

Ruins of a Synagogue, Irrid, Galilee.

erally believed, sitting apart in two different portions of the building. The front benches appear to have been intended for the old men, and the places further back for the younger ones.

In New Testament times the doctors of the Law and the wealthier members of the community loved the privilege of sitting in the foremost seats. In imitation of the Temple, a lamp was kept burning in the synagogue; and trumpets to announce the days of fasting and the advent of the new year also formed an indispensable part of its equipment.

In all those districts of Palestine where a purely Jewish population preponderated, and where the people in consequence were presumably under the sway of Jewish law, the local Senate or Council of Elders possessed both civil and ecclesiastical authority, and played an important part in managing the affairs of the synagogue. The exercise of ecclesiastical discipline was in the hands of the elders; and it lay with them to decide who should be admitted to the services of the synagogue, or who should be expelled and excommunicated. In the time of Jesus this power was in full operation, and decrees of expulsion were unquestionably put into force against His followers. Expulsion from the synagogue does not appear to have been at this period accompanied by the infliction of civil penalties, although the rabbis regarded everyone who was banned as richly deserving them.

It is also probable that the elders enjoyed the right of appointing the permanent officials of the synagogue. The most important of these was the Archisynagogus, or, as he is called in the English version of the New Testament, the Ruler of the Synagogue. He is not to be confounded with the Archon or head of the civil community, although the same person sometimes held both offices at once. In general, the Ruler of the Synagogue was chosen from among the elders; it is probable that he was frequently a scribe, and his duties consisted in looking after the structural requirements of the sacred edifice, and in superintending the conduct of the appointed services. It devolved upon him to see that order was preserved in the synagogue, and to take care that nothing occurred which seemed to him inconsistent with traditional ideas of reverence and the obligations of the Law. It did not specially appertain to him to take any active part in the performance of the service: it is possible that he may occasionally have done so, but his functions in this matter were, strictly speaking, confined to procuring suitable persons from week to week to offer the accustomed prayers, to read the appointed portion of Scripture, and to preach before the people on the Sabbath day Besides the Ruler of the Synagogue there was also a servant or attendant, who acted as a kind of verger. His duties, as far as can be ascertained, consisted in cleansing the synagogue, in keeping the lamps alight, in opening and shutting the doors before and after service, and in handing the Scripture roll to the reader for the day. It is also supposed that the teaching of the children fell upon him. As those who were condemned to be whipped received this form of punishment in the synagogue, it is very probable that the synagogue attendant was entrusted with the execution of the sentence. Alms were also collected in the synagogue, but it is questionable if any particular official was delegated to perform this duty in the time of Jesus.

Every synagogue was open for Divine service at least three times a week on Mondays and Thursdays as well as on the Sabbath, and it is probable that the larger synagogues were opened daily at the three accustomed hours of prayer. On the first day of the month, and on the recurrence of the religious festivals and holy days, there were always services in the synagogue. The services on week-days and on Sabbath afternoons were of a comparatively simple character, and principally consisted in the repetition of certain prayers and the reading of passages from the Book of the Law. Sabbath morning was the time when the most important service took place. It was opened with prayers, and while these were being repeated by the person who for the day had been entrusted with this duty, the whole congregation stood up and turned their faces towards the Holy of Holies at Jerusalem. This was the attitude in which all prayers were said. A fixed portion of Scripture, taken from the books of Deuteronomy and Numbers, and which constituted a kind of Creed, was then recited by the reader, after which he repeated a few more prayers, and this part of the service, which was called the Schema, came to an end. The reading of what may be called the Lesson for the day was then commenced. It consisted of a certain number of verses from the Pentateuch, which had been divided into a hundred and fifty-four portions for the purposes of the synagogue, and these divisions were supposed to be read from beginning to end every three years. The reading of the lesson was a very elaborate proceeding, for which no less than seven men were appointed by the Ruler of the Synagogue. Each of these men read at least three verses of the lesson, and these were immediately translated verse by verse from the Hebrew of the original by an interpreter into Aramaic, the language in common use among the population of Palestine in the time of Christ. It is still a matter of doubt whether the office of interpreter was a voluntary duty, undertaken by someone acquainted with both languages, or whether it was placed in the hands of a special and permanent official. This part of the service was both begun and ended with an expression of thanks to the God of Israel.

As the prophetical books were not invested with quite the same attributes of sanctity as the Law, they were not read till the lesson from the Law was finished. No fixed order of lessons for these books was in existence in the days of Christ, and the reader was apparently allowed a certain liberty of choice as to the passages he should select for the edification of the people. The aid of the interpreter was also required at this part of the service, but the same care was not exercised in translating the original text, and after three verses or even more had been read, the translator generally contented himself by giving a kind of paraphrase of their contents. The passages read from Scripture formed the basis or text for a practical discourse to the congregation, and there can be no doubt that the Christian sermon had its origin in the teaching and exhortations which prevailed in the synagogue. Most of these discourses opened with an explanation of the text, which often received a highly strained or allegorical interpretation, and was made to give a sacred sanction to some doctrine or practice which commended itself to the scribes, and which they wished to popularize. For it was the scribes who generally taught in the synagogues; they were the men who had made the Law the study of their lives, and the hold which they in consequence obtained over the masses invested them with an authority which compelled attention and respect. To teach in the synagogues was not, however, an exclusive privilege of the scribes. It was an office which might be undertaken by anyone who felt himself competent to perform it, and this is the reason why Jesus was able, according to St. Luke, to begin His ministry in the synagogues, and to make them of such utility in spreading the doctrines of the kingdom of God. It was customary for the people to listen in silence to the exhortations of the preacher, but when he said anything to displease them, murmurs of discontent ran through the assembly; questions were put to him, and in certain cases he was requested to hold his peace. The service ended with a benediction, and if a priest were present it was his privilege to pronounce it.

It was mainly owing to the admirable provision which the synagogue had made for the religious needs of the people, that Judaism was enabled to survive the overthrow of its central sanctuary, and to exist independently of a hereditary priesthood and a sacrificial system. These institutions had existed for centuries, and were associated in the mind of every Jew with the essentials of his faith, but when he was irremediably deprived of them, the synagogue was fully competent to supply the want, and to offer him the means of maintaining his religious individuality unimpaired. It was a more flexible institution than the Temple; it was better adapted to encounter the vicissitudes to which the Jewish race was constantly exposed; it was not rooted to the soil of Palestine, but was capable of being transplanted without injury to any quarter of the globe.

The Jewish colonists, who helped to people the great cities of antiquity, were not obliged to leave their religious observances behind, when they sought a home beyond the confines of their native land. Wherever a few of them could meet together to read the Law and the prophets, and to hear the wonderful record of Jehovah's dealings with their fathers, there a synagogue at once came into existence, to nourish their religious aspirations, and to strengthen their devotion to the faith. According to Philo and Josephus the purpose of the synagogue was to promote the moral and religious edification of the community, and the teaching to which the congregation listened every Sabbath day was in the main directed towards this great end. It sometimes happened that the exhortations in the synagogue descended into minute and petty details, respecting ceremonial and other external observances to the neglect of the weightier matters of the Law; but this was a blemish which only affected one portion of the service, and did not always occur. It was impossible to frequent the synagogue without becoming thoroughly familiar with the lofty moral elements contained in the Law; and the great ideals of righteousness, mercy, and humility enunciated in the impassioned language of the prophets must have stirred the popular imagination, and sunk deep into the national character and life. It was the synagogue which achieved this immense result, and tended to make some of the highest standards of human excellence the common property of the Jewish race.

The Law and Tradition

In the preceding chapter it has been seen that the most important part of public worship consisted in the reading and exposition of Holy Scripture, and that the synagogue was quite as much a school of instruction as a house of prayer. The books on which this instruction was based, and which constituted the contents of Holy Scripture in the time of Christ were essentially the same as those which now form the Old Testament canon of the Christian Church. In fact, they are quoted by the apostles, and were adopted by the

Church as canonical writings on the authority of the Synagogue. These sacred books were divided by the rabbis into three classes—the Law, the Prophets, and the Writings, or Hagiographa. The Law, in the stricter meaning of the word, was contained in the Pentateuch; the Prophets included, besides what are known as the prophetical books, most of those documents which give an account of the pre-exilian history of the Israelites. The Writings were the last works to obtain admission within the sacred volume; the canonicity of some of them was long a matter of contention among the doctors of the Law, and it was not till the opening centuries of the Christian era that these disputes were settled, and that the canon in its present form was finally accepted by all the rabbis.

The principle which regulated the admission of books into the sacred canon was not primarily based on their antiquity or their authorship, but on the nature of their contents. Before all things it was imperative that the document which laid claim to the august title of Holy Scripture should contain nothing which was at variance or out of harmony with writings already recognized as coming from God. In the case of such works as the Song of Solomon, and the Book of Ecclesiastes, it was not

Ancient Case Containing the Samaritan Pentateuch

around the question of date or of authorship that the dispute among the rabbis was keenest; these were matters of secondary importance in comparison with the supposed meaning and substance, and it was only after this point had been settled in their favour that they were permitted to rank as portions of the sacred record. Admission to the canon did not, however, immediately place a book upon the same level of authority as its older predecessors in

114

that collection. Although all the books were believed to owe their origin to God, this did not prevent different degrees of inspiration from being recognized amongst them. In this respect the first place was unquestionably assigned to the Torah, or Law. In the centuries immediately preceding the Christian era, it is regarded as the supreme arbiter in matters of faith; it is believed to possess everlasting force; it is an incorruptible light, and it is better to die than violate its commands which are in reality the injunctions of God. To love the Law was the most sacred of human duties, and to be permitted by the foreign rulers of Palestine to practise it was looked upon as a boon of incalculable worth. In fact, it was better to rise in rebellion and fight with the courage of despair than to allow the Law to be trodden under foot. As time went on this tendency to exalt the Divine attributes of the Law continued to develop, until it attained its highest pitch in the oldest portions of the Talmud. To the rabbis of the first and second centuries after Christ the Law was a complete revelation of God's will, and with the Book of Joshua, which formed the concluding part of the original document, it would have remained the only revelation if Israel had not fallen into sin. It was the one thing absolutely indispensable to Israel. Nothing is expressed in the other books of Scripture which is not already implied in the Law, and no prophet has uttered anything which is not already revealed in the Law. Moses wrote it, but only at the dictation of God. Even the words in the last verses of Deuteronomy, in which the law-giver's death is recorded, were dictated to him beforehand by God, and it was the part of a liar and a despiser of God's Word to assert that a single verse of the Law had been written by Moses alone.

The pre-eminence accorded to the Law was not, however, intended to have the effect of reducing the other portions of Holy Scripture to a position of insignificance. No one but a renegade from Israel would deny their authority. In the language of the rabbis, to touch them defiles the hands, which means to say that they are only to be handled with becoming reverence. In quoting them precisely the same formula is used as in making a quotation from the Law, and the New Testament as well as the rabbis sometimes speak of them as forming a part of the Law itself. St. Paul, for instance, in making a quotation from the Book of Isaiah, introduces it with the words, "In the Law it is written," and in the Fourth Gospel a passage from the Psalms is introduced in exactly the same manner. To regard these books as parts of the Law, although it appeared to exalt their authority, had in reality a disastrous effect upon their true meaning, and in many cases transformed them from books of history, or of edification, into a mere collection of precepts and injunctions.

But in spite of this theoretical distinction which existed between the Law, on the one hand, and the Prophets and Hagiographa on the other, the uniting of the two collections within the same canon had the effect for all practical purposes, of placing them on the same footing as regards authority, and both Philo and Josephus look upon the whole of the Old Testament as equally divine. According to Philo it did not contain a single superfluous word, and not only every individual word, but every syllable of every word had its origin in

God. Josephus holds substantially the same opinions. To him the whole of Scripture is divine; all its parts agree together; nothing has ever been added to or taken away from it, and it was better to die than utter a word against the doctrines it contained. The New Testament has expressions which are quite at variance with this abject worship of the letter, but it continues to regard the Old Testament as proceeding from God, or from the Spirit of God. In the First Gospel the Messianic dignity of Jesus is proved by adducing passages from the prophets in its support—a method which would not have been adopted unless the evangelist had believed in the Divine origin of his authorities. The Fourth Gospel expressly says that the Scripture cannot be broken, and it is the contents of the Jewish canon which are there referred to Passages from the Prophets and Psalms are frequently quoted as the words of God, and wherever such phrases as the Scriptures saith, or the Spirit saith occur they are equivalent to the expression God saith. Even St. Paul, in spite of his emancipation from the letter adopts the same methods of interpretation as the rabbis, and is in substantial agreement with their views respecting the origin of Holy Writ. In fact, there was a universal consensus of Jewish opinion in the time of Christ that the whole of the Old Testament was divine.

As the Scripture was on all sides admitted to have come from God, to know it was to know the will of God, and accordingly the study of the Law became the supreme duty of man. In the conflict of duties the study of the Law always took precedence. It occupied a higher rank than the duty of parents to children, or of children to parents, and it is related of a certain man that he sold his daughter in order that he might have the means to study the Law. Married men forsook their families to devote themselves to the Law; others renounced marriage altogether, and said, "Let the world be built up by other men, my soul cleaveth to the Law." It sometimes happened that rabbis sold or gave up all they possessed for the purpose of dedicating their lives to the study of the Law. Rabbi Jochanan was journeying from Tiberias to Sepphoris, and Rabbi Chija, the son of Abba, went with him. When they came to a field, Rabbi Jochanan said, "This field was mine, and I sold it so as to give myself up to the Law." Then they came to a vineyard, and he said, "This vineyard was mine, and I sold it so as to give myself up to the Law." Rabbi Chija, the son of Abba, then began to weep, and said to him, "I weep because thou hast kept nothing for thine old age." "But," he replied, "My son, Chija, my son Chija, is it then a small matter in thine eyes, that I have sold something which was made in six days, and have obtained in exchange that which was given in forty days and forty nights. The whole world was made in six days only, for it is written, ` In six days the Lord made heaven and earth; but the Law was given in forty days, for it is written, ` And he was with Jehovah forty days and forty nights."

On the other hand, not to know the Law was to be accursed, and a bastard who had this knowledge was superior to a high priest who had it not. To be ignorant of the Scriptures was to place oneself beyond the pale of human compassion. Chastisement shall befall the man who gives his bread to one who has no knowledge of the Law. The study of the Law was a duty incumbent upon rich and poor alike, and it behoved a father to teach his child the Law as soon as he could speak. He who did not devote himself to this highest of all studies should make amends for his neglect by marrying his daughter to a scribe, and supporting him out of his substance. As a reward for supporting the schools and scholars of the Law, the childless were blessed with children, and it was the duty of the people to maintain those who made this study the occupation of their lives. On the other hand, the students of the Law are required to be satisfied with a hard and humble life, to eat bread with salt, to drink sparingly, and to sleep upon the ground.

Side by side with the written Law, which in its wider meaning was understood to comprise the whole of sacred Scriptures, there also existed, as may be seen from the New Testament, an oral

Inscription Found at Amoas—"One God."

or unwritten Law. The contents of this unwritten Law were called by the rabbis the words of tradition, and in the time of Christ these words were considered to possess the same authority as the written Law itself. Both were equally looked upon and spoken of as revelation. The oral Law, no less than the written, was derived from God, and was communicated by Him to Moses on Mount Sinai. Whilst Moses was alive he repeated and explained it in the Tabernacle of the wilderness; he also communicated it to Aaron, who in turn imparted it to his sons, these again made it known to the elders, and the elders to the masses of the people. As the Sanhedrin was the authoritative exponent of tradition at the opening of the Christian era, it was believed that Moses had created this institution for the express purpose of guarding and preserving the unwritten Law. Not only did he institute the Sanhedrin, but he was the first head of it as well, and before his death he committed the care of the oral Law to Joshua, who was supposed to have succeeded him in the presidency of this councils In after time the Judges and prophets formed the connecting link in the long chain of tradition as it passed downwards to posterity; then came the men of the great synagogue, the last of whom, Simon the Just, bequeathed the hallowed treasures of tradition to the scribe Antigonus of Socho. By him it was handed down to the heads of the Sanhedrin, till it reached the famous doctors Hillel and Schammai, who flourished in the time of Christ. It was then imparted to Gamaliel, the celebrated teacher of St. Paul, and it continued after the fall of the Jewish state to be handed on from generation to generation, till it was finally committed to writing and deposited in the pages of the Talmud. So runs the historic fiction which in-

117

vested tradition with Divine sanctions, and made it such a mighty power in Jewish life.

But the channel through which tradition flowed till it was committed to writing did not, according to the rabbis, succeed in preserving its contents intact. It sometimes happened that portions of the oral Law were lost. The grief which ensued on the death of Moses caused a vast number of traditions to be forgotten, and in many other instances besides, its precepts were believed to have experienced a similar fate. But these losses were only temporary, for, according to the rabbinic theory, the whole of the oral Law was implicitly contained in the written Law, and it was always capable of being restored by a searching study of the written text. This study was the great occupation of the rabbis. It is hardly necessary to say that it was not conducted on historical and philological principles; these methods are of very recent origin, and not only the Jews, but the whole ancient world were strangers to such instruments of research. Nor was it conducted in a multitude of cases with the object of getting at the original meaning of the writer. The lofty simplicity of the sacred text was often too obvious in its signification to satisfy the student of tradition. The rabbis' labours on the written Word were generally undertaken with a view to recover traditions that had been lost, or to find out some hidden precept of Divine wisdom which had not hitherto been brought to light. In order to achieve this object allegorical interpretations were constantly resorted to, as well as all sorts of ingenious and arbitrary combinations of unconnected texts. With such fanciful methods of interpretation it was easy to educe any doctrine from the pages of Scripture, and it was a customary practice with the scribes to put forward their dogmatic assumptions as the restored fragments of a lost tradition, or to urge some new precept as if it were an old one which had in the past been overlooked.

As the contents of Scripture fell into two parts the Legal on the one hand, and the Historical and Prophetical on the other so also did the contents of tradition. And as the Law enjoyed a certain pre-eminence over the rest of sacred literature, so also did those portions of tradition which handled the same subjects as the Law. All traditions of this nature were called the Halacha, or Law of Custom, while all traditions bearing upon the historical and prophetical books were called the Haggada, or edifying comment.

The laws of custom, like the corresponding laws in the Pentateuch, dealt principally with the great sacrificial system which was seated at Jerusalem, and with all the ramifications of that system in the religious life of the people. These laws entered with great fullness of detail into such subjects as the revenues of the priests and Levites, and the sums which they should receive from the people. Feasts and fast days were also the object of minute regulations; the Sabbath, the Passover, the Day of Atonement, the Feast of Tabernacles, all came within the sweep of traditional Law; what should be done on these days and what should not be done, what sacrifices should be offered and what form of ceremonial should be observed in offering them, were matters which were regulated with the utmost detail and precision.

118

A multitude of regulations also existed respecting the purification of unclean persons and things, many laws were also devoted to vows and their proper observance, and a host of binding customs surrounded the subjects of marriage, betrothal, and divorce. Matters of a purely secular character were also within the sphere of tradition, and laws were laid down to regulate such purely civil transactions as buying and selling, and the administration of the criminal law. Upon a great variety of subjects the written Law had to be supplemented by the Law of tradition. The oral Law had to answer all questions on which the written Law was silent. It had to adapt some parts of the written Law to altered social conditions; it had sometimes to modify the rigour of written precepts, and to bring them by a process of interpretation into harmony with the feelings of the age; it had to adjust the written Law to the practical necessities of the times; it had to define the scope of the written Word, and to show in what circumstances it should be applied; and it had also to solve all difficulties and obscurities in the written text. So vast was the field in which tradition worked that its operations never reached an end, and new traditions and interpretations were constantly being added to the immense mass which had already accumulated.

It is difficult to say when these laws of custom first arose. In all probability they did not assume any considerable proportions till the official promulgation of the written Law after the return from Babylon. Such ordinances of the scribes as were in the nature of a commentary on the Pentateuch must have arisen in the centuries subsequent to the Captivity, and the same may also be said of many customs which were traced back to Moses, or which rested on immemorial antiquity. At the same time, it is possible and indeed probable that some of these laws of custom did actually belong, in a modified form, to a remote past, for many of them existed independently of Scripture, and were simply linked to it afterwards by the exegetical processes of the scribes. In theory, all traditions which had the reputation of belonging to the time of Moses, were considered to possess a more sacred character than those of later origin; but in practice, all traditional laws stood upon the same footing as regards authority when once they had been approved by the majority of the scribes.

From traditions which had the legal regulations of the Pentateuch as their basis, and which had assumed a binding force, we may now pass to the consideration of those traditions which were ostensibly grounded on the historical and prophetical books of Scripture, and which only possessed the weight attaching to pious and accredited opinions. Such traditions principally consisted of tales, legends, homilies, and embellishments of the written Word. In contra-distinction from the Halacha, or binding rule, they were known as the Haggada, or saying. The historical and prophetical books lent themselves most readily to the genius of the Haggada, but this form of tradition also entered with wings of fancy into the domain of Law, and wove around its abstract precepts the glow and colour of Oriental imagination. It was, in fact, a free and imaginative exposition of the whole contents of Sacred Writ. Just as the precepts of the Halacha grew up in great part to gratify a pious anxiety to fulfill every jot and tittle of the Law, so did the contents of the Haggada arise to satisfy pious curiosity respecting such matters as the heavenly world and its inhabitants, the past history of Israel and its future destiny among the peoples of the world. So keen was the desire for further knowledge on such subjects that the Haggadist was allowed free scope for the exercise of his imagination; he was not trammeled in his work like the Halachist, by rules of interpretation, and his fancy was allowed to play almost at will around the written text. The aim of the Halacha was practice; the aim of the Haggada was edification. It was the mystic, the imaginative, the transcendental side of the religious life which was nourished by the Haggadist, and in evolving his pious creations he was permitted to expand and transform the sacred narratives into almost any shape he pleased. The written text was toned down and accommodated to the prevalent ideas of the time, briefly told incidents were expanded and encircled with fanciful details which were sometimes of foreign growth, and every event which attracted pious attention was decorated with a garland of legendary lore. The beliefs and hopes of the age are accurately reflected in these legends, they are the form in which all new ideas took shape; they soon came to be regarded as actual history, and were believed in quite as firmly as the written text itself.

At the commencement of the Christian era the lore of the Haggada had attained such large proportions that it is not difficult to construct a complete system of theology out of its contents. It is replete with information concerning God's attributes, and the secret counsels of His will. It unveils the mysteries of the heavenly world, and is acquainted with the nature and functions of the spiritual beings who dwell in it. It knows the names of a multitude of the angels, and the kind of work which has been allotted to them in the Divine economy. It has many mysteries to unfold respecting what took place at the creation of the world, and is full of details as to the primeval state of man. The temptation of Eve, the fall and all its consequences, are minutely set forth in the Haggada. It has a great deal to tell of the evil spirits which haunt the world; it knows their powers and modes of action, how they enter and how they may be exorcised from the hearts of men. A host of traditions were in circulation on the subject of the Messiah and the Messianic age. This was a favourite theme with the populace, and the Haggadists dwelt minutely on the transcendent events which were to take place when the Messianic kingdom was proclaimed. Sin and death, the resurrection, and the great judgment, the new heavens and the new earth, were all illuminated by tradition. In fact, tradition was able to furnish an answer to every question which occupied the heart and mind of the Jewish race.

On questions of a purely historical character tradition was equally at home. In the domain of chronology it was able to tell the dates of all the manifold events which had happened from the creation of the world till the entry of the Israelites into land of Canaan. According to its computations the whole of these events lay within a period of two thousand four hundred and fifty years. It was known to tradition that all the beasts, as well as the serpent, were able to speak when they were first created, and tradition also knew the reason why the faculty of speech was taken from them. The Law had existed as a statute in heaven long before it was proclaimed on earth. The angels were subject to its decrees, and these heavenly beings remonstrated with the Deity when He announced His intention of making so divine a thing known to the sons of men. It was through the angels that man derived his knowledge of the story of the creation, and it was also at their hands that Moses received the Law on Sinai. It is said in the Old Testament that Joseph's wife was the daughter of an Egyptian, and tradition solves all difficulties as to her belief by the assurance that she was converted by an angel to the faith of Israel.

On the whole subject of the patriarchs tradition has much to relate which is not to be found in canonical history. The exact number of Adam's sons is known, and also where they obtained their wives. The sons of Seth were great astrologers according to tradition, and Noah was a distinguished writer on medicine. It was known how he procured all the different kinds of animals which were lodged in the ark, and on what peak of Ararat the ark rested when the waters of the flood began to subside. This patriarch was said to have been the possessor of a library, which he bequeathed to his son Shem. Shem was also celebrated for his knowledge of the medical art, and so was Solomon. But Enoch surpassed them both in his acquaintance with Divine mysteries. Both the past and the future lay before him like an open book, and he predicted the whole course of human history till the Day of Judgment. A great many traditions surrounded the life of Abraham, and in one of them we are informed that it was the study of astrology which taught him there was only one supreme God. Like the rest of the patriarchs Moses had a great reputation for learning. He was skilled in all the wisdom of the Egyptians, and was able to overcome Pharaoh's magicians, Jannes and Jambres, when they set themselves up in opposition to him. It is only through the medium of tradition that the names of these magicians came down to aftertimes. And it is in the same way that succeeding generations came to learn that the rock which Moses struck for water in the wilderness followed the children of Israel till they reached the Promised Land. It was commonly believed that Moses did not die after the ordinary manner of men, but that he was suddenly and mysteriously hidden by a cloud from the eyes of Joshua and Eleazar, as they were accompanying him up Mount Abaris; and it was also believed, on the authority of tradition, that a tremendous struggle took place between Satan and the archangel Michael for possession of his body. It would be easy to multiply the number of these traditions. Philo, Josephus, the Midrasch, and the pseudonymous literature of both Jews and Christians abound in examples; but the instances which have just been adduced are sufficient to show with what freedom and latitude the Haggadists worked upon the written text, and what were the results which they obtained.

The Teachers of the Law

Although the Law was regarded as binding upon every member of the Jewish people, its precepts were of such a character that it was impossible for the ordinary Israelite without assistance either to know or to follow them. In the first place, they were written in a language which he had ceased to speak; for soon after the return from Babylon Hebrew fell more and more into disuse, and Aramaic, a cognate dialect, assumed its place. But even if it had been written in a tongue which the people fully understood, it would have been difficult for them to remember the six hundred and thirteen different commandments contained in the Pentateuch alone, not to mention the multitude of traditions which had accumulated around these commandments. And this difficulty would have risen to an impossibility when the Jewish husbandman—for it was to this class that the great bulk of the people belonged attempted to put his knowledge into practice. As a matter of fact, some of the

Ruins of a Temple, Kades.

Pentateuchal laws had never been put into operation, and only possessed a theoretical value; others had become inapplicable to the altered social state of the community, and others were so worded that it was no easy thing to know when and how to apply them. Besides, the written Law was not intended, as the Jews in the time of Christ had been taught to believe, to cover the whole field of civil, social, and religious life. To give it the appearance of doing so required the exercise of a degree of exegetical skill which the mass of the people could not possibly possess or perhaps acquire.

As a result of these circumstances the people had to fall back upon the assistance of a class of men who made the study of the Law the supreme business of their lives. In the Old Testament these men are known under the name of Sopherim, in the New Testament they are designated as men of learning (grammateis—scribes), or as men learned in the Law (nomikoi—lawyers), or as teachers of the Law (nomodidaskaloi). According to the Jewish habit of throwing every institution back into a remote antiquity, the scribes were said to have come into existence in the time of Moses; they sprang up in reality during the Babylonian exile, and their rise was chiefly owing to this disaster to the national fortunes. The Jews had then perished as a nation, the ties of a common fatherland were for the time dissolved, and the only things which united the deported community were the bonds of a common faith and the hallowed memories of the past. It accordingly became a sacred duty as well as a consolation to preserve and strengthen these bonds; otherwise the Jews would have lost their distinctive characteristics, and been swallowed up among the populations who surrounded and so enormously outnumbered them. To prevent this crowning calamity, the ancient records of the race, its traditions, its laws, its customs were sedulously collected and disseminated among the exiles. Copies of these records were required for the edification of the weekly assemblies which afterwards developed into the synagogue. A class of copyists sprang into existence, and these copyists are the scribes.

The return from Babylon and the establishment of the Law as an obligatory code increased the numbers and importance of the scribes. The growth of the synagogue into a national institution added to the demand for copies of the sacred book; as the belief in its Divine origin grew in intensity, the functions of the scribes became correspondingly enlarged, and they naturally developed into canonists and guardians of the text as well as copyists of the Law. It has also to be observed that the language in which the Law was written ceased to be a living tongue soon after the Exile, and the scribes had to undertake the task of interpreting its contents to the people. This duty involved the assumption of the widest powers and responsibilities, and at the opening of the Christian era we find the scribes exercising the three-fold office of jurists, judges, and popular instructors.

It was in their capacity of interpreters that the scribes were drawn into assuming the functions of jurists and legislators. These duties devolved upon them in this wise. It had been solemnly laid down that every act in life, from the cradle to the grave, should be done according to the Law. Now the written Law in many instances does not go beyond general principles. Some of its precepts are ambiguous, and in process of time others had become almost impossible of fulfillment. But most important of all is the circumstance that in a multitude of cases it laid down no positive regulations whatsoever. In other words, it was not a complete code of Law. Still the theory remained that this incomplete code must supply an answer to every question which might arise in all the manifold and complicated relations of human life. How was this theory to be maintained in face of the fact that the written Law was inadequate and incomplete? Only in one way, namely, the creation of such elastic rules of interpretation as would permit the scribes to construct a code of law, at once more comprehensive in its character and more capable of adaptation to the changing requirements of a living society. And this was what actually did take place. A set of exegetical rules was elaborated by the scribes which allowed them the widest latitude in interpreting the written Law. By means of these rules a new code was practically evolved out of the existing one, and this new code actually derived its authority from the laws which it was in many cases meant to supersede. This new code is called the law of tradition because it was represented as being nothing more than an ancient and authoritative interpretation of the written law an interpretation which dated back to the time of Moses himself. It was in reality no such thing, but simply the work of the scribes. This work was framed in the spirit of the Mosaic code, but it became, in process of time, much more elaborate and comprehensive in its character. It was also more flexible, because it was not stereotyped in written documents. For, although the scribes attempted to hand down the precepts of tradition intact from one generation to another, it is certain that circumstances were more powerful than the rules of the school, and that the laws of tradition were modified as time went on to meet the practical needs of the community.

The whole body of the scribes co-operated in the task of law-making, but as the more eminent among them resided at Jerusalem, most of the alterations and amendments in the law had their origin in the Holy City. It was a habit of the scribes to meet together for the ventilation and discussion of legal questions. These questions were often the subject of prolonged debate, and it was not until a certain degree of unanimity had been arrived at among the doctors that any projected change in the law had a chance of being effected. After the destruction of Jerusalem and the final downfall of the Jewish state, the scribes formally became the lawgivers of Judaism. But before this catastrophe, and in the days of Christ, the decisions of the scribes required to be confirmed by the Sanhedrin, and it was not until they had received this confirmation that they attained the force of law and became binding on the whole community. Still, public opinion was so strongly on the side of the scribes that the members of the Sanhedrin did not venture to oppose anything on which the scribes were agreed. When the scribes arrived at the conclusion that a certain interpretation of the Law was the one to be accepted, it was adopted and acted upon by the Sanhedrists.

Very little is said in the New Testament as to the judicial functions of the scribes. Some of their number are stated to have been members of the Sanhedrin, and in that capacity they must at times have performed the functions of judges, for the Sanhedrin was the supreme judicial tribunal of the community. It is also probable that they sometimes acted as judges in the provincial districts. But at this period it was not necessary for a judge to be a scribe and there is every reason to believe that in most cases he was not. As, however, the law was in great measure the work of the scribes, it is extremely probable that they exercised a powerful if indirect influence on the decisions of the judges. No doubt the tendency of the times lay in the direction of placing judicial power in the hands of the scribes; for we find soon after the fall of Jerusalem, that the scribes had become the administrators of justice as the earthly representatives of the will of God.

Another most important function of the scribes consisted in teaching the Law to their disciples in the school, and to the general public in the synagogue. The places in which the more eminent of the scribes taught their disciples were called Houses of Assembly or Houses for the study of the Law, or simply Houses of the Rabbis. It is probable that these schools were in existence in all the more important towns of Palestine in the time of Christ. The halls and rooms of the

Capitals Dome of the Rock, Jerusalem

outer forecourt of the Temple also appear to have been used by the scribes as schools of instruction, and the old rabbinical saying, "Let thy house be a house of assembly," apparently leads to the inference that private houses were sometimes employed for a similar purpose. Besides being places of instruction for their pupils, these schools were also utilized by the scribes for holding discussions with each other on disputed points of Law; discourses were sometimes delivered in them on Sundays and feast days for the edification of the people at large. The chief object of these schools, however, was to teach those who would, in most cases, afterwards become rabbis themselves. A doorkeeper guarded the entrance to them, and a small charge was made for admission. The internal arrangements were of a very simple character. The teacher appears to have sat on a slightly raised platform, while his scholars sat around him on the ground.

The mode of teaching mainly consisted in making the pupils learn the law of tradition by heart. As it was considered derogatory to the pentateuchal code to commit the laws of tradition to writing, to commit them to memory was the only way of preserving them. Although these laws were framed in the most concise manner possible, with the express purpose of being easily retained in the mind, it was found necessary for the scribe to go over them again and again, and in consequence of this frequent repetition, to teach and to repeat came to mean exactly the same thing. The monotony of such a process was varied by allowing the scholar to put questions to his master, and to carry on an argument with him on the various points of law which came up for considerations In these discussions the scribes were accustomed to display a remarkable capacity for entering into minute refinements and distinctions to prove any dictum or interpretation which they particularly wished to establish. He who had the most retentive memory for the precepts of tradition was accounted the best scholar, and he who had the reputation of teaching only what he had received was believed to be the best scribe.

As has already been stated, to teach in the synagogue was not the exclusive privilege of the scribes. But it can hardly be doubted that in the time of Christ they were the men most frequently selected to address the congregation. Being the authorized exponents of the Law, an importance must have attached itself to their words which the utterances of a layman did not possess. Before addressing the public on religious matters in the synagogue, the scribe in the centuries immediately succeeding the Christian era, and very probably in the days of Christ Himself, was expected to have thoroughly prepared himself for his sacred task. And not only was he supposed to be a man of knowledge and education, he was expected to be a man of sincere piety as well. Any scribe who is not inwardly what he is outwardly is no scribe. A scribe's life must be in harmony with his words. Accordingly, it was said of Ben Asai, a rabbi of the first century, "Thou preachest finely, but thou dost not fulfill finely." A scribe was also required to weigh well every word he uttered, lest his hearers should drink of poisoned waters, and cause the name of God to be dishonoured. In his principles he was to be as hard as iron, but in the expression of them it is said that the scribe whose discourse is not as pleasant to his audience as fine honey in the mouth had better hold his peace.

The preaching of the scribes was enlivened by the introduction of parables, allegories, ironical allusions, and pithy sayings which were likely to stick in the memory. "Do you know a woman," said Rabbi Judah, when he saw his congregation going to sleep, "who has given birth to six hundred thousand men?" All roused themselves to hear the answer. "Jochebed," said he, "is the name of the woman; she gave birth to Moses, who was worth all Israel." A rabbi of, the first century, Jochanan ben Sakai, in urging the necessity of immediate repentance, used the following parable:—A certain king invited his servants to a feast, but gave them no time to make ready. Then some of the guests said within themselves, "A king can in an hour prepare a meal and invite us to it." They immediately put on their finest and best garments and waited at the door of the palace. These were the wise. The others thought that there was yet time, and went in soiled raiments. Suddenly the king called them to the banquet; all had to appear before him. Those who had on the clean garments were received with joy, and they ate and drank at the feast; but with the others, the careless ones, who came in soiled attire, the king was angry, and they had to stand aside and look on. A scribe chose as a text the following verse from the Book of Ecclesiastes: "As he came forth of his mother's womb, naked shall he go again as he came, and shall take nothing for his labour, which he may carry away in his hand." He illustrated the passage in this manner. A certain fox stood before a vineyard, which was encompassed by a wall. The grapes tempted him, and he tried to find out an opening in the wall by which he could enter the vineyard. He found one, but it was too small to let him go through. He then made a resolution to fast three days, so as to make his body lean enough to go through the hole. His plan succeeded, and he entered the vineyard. Here he feasted on the grapes to his heart's content, and his body once more grew fat and strong. But a time came when he wanted to leave the vineyard. He again sought the hole in the wall, but when he tried to go out he could not. He was accordingly obliged to starve his body with fasting so as to escape. And when at last he got outside he was as lean as when he entered. Then he turned his eyes to the vineyard and its fruits, and said, "O vineyard, vineyard, how lovely art thou, and how good are thy fruits! but what do I bring away with me from thee? As I entered so must I return." Such, says the scribe, is the life of man: "Naked did he come forth, and naked shall he return."

Besides being illustrated by parable and fable, a text was frequently made the subject of allegorical interpretation, as in the following instance:—Rabbi Jochanan ben Sakai preaching from the words, "Let thy garments be always white, and let thy head lack no ointment," said, "If in this passage we think of white garments in a literal sense, and of real oil, how many white garments and how much oil do the heathen have? But here, by white garments, the garment of virtue is to be understood, the fulfillment of God's commandments, good works." These examples will sufficiently explain the popular teaching of the scribes as it was practiced in the time of Christ.

Before a scribe could properly exercise the high duties of his office he had at least in the centuries which immediately followed the rise of Christianity, and probably in the time of Christ's public ministry as well to go through some form of ordination, but no satisfactory record remains of the manner in which this sacred act was effected. The power of admitting a scribe among the recognized doctors of the Law appears to have been originally vested in the rabbi by whom he had been taught. Such is the teaching of the Jerusalem Talmud which says, "At first every doctor ordained his own scholars; for example, Rabbi Jochanan ben Sakai ordained Rabbi Eliezer and Rabbi Joshua; Rabbi Joshua ordained Rabbi Akiba, and Rabbi Akiba ordained Rabbi Mair and Rabbi Simon." A scribe who was publicly acknowledged as such by his teacher had to make himself thoroughly conversant with the contents of the sacred code, and with all those studies which were believed to throw light upon its interpretation. Whatever the teacher himself knew would unquestionably be imparted to his scholars, and the pages of the Talmud show that the rabbis did not confine their attention exclusively to the ethical or practical contents of the Law. Their field of view was much more comprehensive, and among many other things embraced the study of such subjects as mathematics, botany, medicine, and astronomy. Nor were the languages of Greece and Rome neglected by the scribes. Gamaliel and many of his immediate successors were ardent Hellenists. By some of the rabbis Greek was described as a faultless tongue, and as the only language into which the Law could be properly translated. So warm was the admiration for Greek that the translation of the Septuagint was considered to be the result of Divine inspiration and in its accomplishment was seen the fulfillment of the prophecy that Japhet should dwell in the tents of Shem. Parents were exhorted to teach their daughters Greek, and it was apostrophized as the most beautiful language among the sons of men. In three things said the rabbis of the first century Greece stands superior to Rome, in laws, in language, and in literature. Rabbi Juda went so far as to say that Greek or Hebrew was the only language which should be spoken by the people of Palestine. All these sayings go far towards establishing the conclusion that in the time of Christ Greek formed no unimportant part in the education of a scribe.

One of the principles professed by the scribes was that the sacred duties entrusted to them should be performed without fee or reward. It was considered derogatory to the rabbinical office to look upon it as the means for obtaining a livelihood. "The study of the Law," said Rabbi Zadok, "is not to be used as a spade to dig with." Hillel also said that, "Whosoever makes use of the crown (of the Law for mercenary purposes) perishes." It was accordingly a rule with the rabbis to combine the study of the Law with the exercise of some useful calling. This custom is exemplified in the case of St. Paul, who was a weaver; Hillel was a hewer of wood, Rabbi Joshua ben Chanania was a needle maker, Rabbi Juda ben Ilai was a cooper, and among the other rabbis of the first century whose names are mentioned in the Talmud, some were perfumers, and some bakers, and some tailors. "Great is labour," said a rabbi, as he passed along with his burden, "it honours the Lord." "Do any kind of work," said Rabbi Akiba to his disciples, "even to the skinning of carcases on the highways, and say not as an excuse, I am a priest."

Though honouring labour the rabbis were at the same time warned against pursuing civil occupations to the detriment of the Law. On this question Hillel is stated to have put forth the dictum, "that the man who gives himself up too exclusively to business shall not become wise."

In this respect Hillel is in harmony with Jesus the son of Sirach, who says of the scribes, "The wisdom of a learned man cometh by opportunity of leisure, and he that hath little business shall become wise. How can he get wisdom that holdeth the plough and that glorieth in the goad, that driveth oxen and is occupied in their labours, and whose talk is of bullocks. . . . But he that giveth his mind to the Law of the Most High and is occupied in the meditation thereof, will seek out the wisdom of all the ancient, and be occupied in prophecies. He will keep the sayings of the renowned men; and where subtle parables are he will be there also." It may safely be inferred from the words of Hillel and Ben Sirach that in many cases the scribe did not actively pursue the calling in which he had been instructed. It is also evident from the New Testament that among many of the scribes the principle of taking no reward for their services, if preserved in name, was violated in reality. The stigma of being covetous and devourers of widows' houses is fatal to the lofty pretension of disinterestedness which the rabbis laid claim to, when fulfilling their duties as teachers and administrators of the Law.

In outward demeanour a scribe was expected to conduct himself with a circumspection and decorum which should place his character above the breath of suspicion. Six things were said to be unbecoming in a scribe to walk about perfumed in public places, to appear in torn shoes, to go alone at night, to hold much converse with women in the public streets, to be the last to enter the house of instruction, and to pass his time in the society of the unlearned. A scribe was forbidden to take part in any meal which was not in accordance with the Law, and he was not to allow his daughter to marry any man who was ignorant of the Law. Where he

ΜΗΘΕΝΑ ΑΛΛΟΓΕΝΗ ΕΙΣΠΟ
ΡΕΥΕΣΘΑΙ ΕΝΤΟΣ ΤΟΥ ΠΕ
ΡΙ ΤΟ ΙΕΡΟΝ ΤΡΥΦΑΚΤΟΥ ΚΑΙ
ΠΕΡΙΒΟΛΟΥ ΟΣΔ'ΑΝ ΛΗ
ΦΘΗ ΕΑΥΤΩΙ ΑΙΤΙΟΣ ΕΣ
ΤΑΙ ΔΙΑ ΤΟ ΕΞΑΚΟΛΟΥ
ΘΕΙΝ ΘΑΝΑΤΟΝ.

Inscription on Stele from Herod's Temple.

should live, what kind of bed he should sleep on, what sort of table he should use, the cut of his garments and even the manner of his walk, were all subject to precise regulations.

Great deference was paid by the people to the scribes. Of this fact we are not without evidence in the New Testament, where it is said that they loved to receive the salutations of the people in the market-places and were accommodated with seats of honour at feasts and in the synagogues. According to Rabbi Akiba, honour was to be paid to the scribe as well as to God. He was to be preferred before father and mother, and before prophets, priests, and kings. It was not permissible to address him without using the title rabbi. Most men accounted it a great privilege to see a famous rabbi, and it was no uncommon thing for zealous Israelites to go through a period of fasting, in the hope of being considered worthy of so high an honour. In the language of the Talmud the rabbis were the lamps and the shield-bearers of Israel, the princes of the people, the leaders of the nation and the fathers of the world. A rabbi was to be treated with the same reverence as God Himself. He was not as other men, and he stood in such close relationship to the Creator that he was able to defy the laws of nature and accomplish miracles. The angry glance of a rabbi was sufficient to bring on misery and death. Instances abound in which the rabbis reformed the wicked, healed the diseased, and raised the dead to life. How natural that a class which was believed to possess such lofty attributes, should enjoy the reverence of the multitude.

The immense influence wielded by the scribes in the time of Christ was productive of many evil consequences both upon their own character and the religious life of the community. It led them to assume an exclusive right to the privilege of sitting in Moses' seat, or in other words of formulating the religious beliefs and duties of the Jewish people. So much was this the case, that to resist their pretensions, or to regard the truths of religion from another point of view than theirs, was to play the part of an apostate and blasphemer who did not deserve to live. Many of them displayed a puerile craving for notoriety which showed itself even in the details of their dress. The long flowing garments in which they used to appear in public, and the amulets or phylacteries with which they ornamented the forehead, were obviously designed to attract attention and bring their personality before the multitude. Whether at table, or in the streets, or in the synagogue the same spirit of ostentation manifested itself; and, what is worse, pride, intolerance, and hypocrisy, were often conspicuous elements in their character. In religious matters the dominant tendency of the scribes was to ignore ethical motives and ideals, and to transform religion into the observance of a multitude of external acts and ceremonies. It is needless to enlarge upon this defect in the work of the scribes, for the Gospels abound in instances which prove that they were in the habit of sacrificing the substance of religion for the form, and of losing sight of the central principles of morality in the boundless expanses of casuistry.

It would, however, be manifestly unjust to set down the whole body of the scribes as mere hypocrites and formalists. Even the New Testament which paints them in no favourable light, contains instances to the contrary, and these instances are supplemented by information from other sources. The life of Hillel alone and he must be looked upon as a type of many less famous scribes is a sufficient refutation of the notion that all the scribes were men of unreal lives. Hillel was a contemporary of Herod the Great, and although much mythical imagery has gathered around his name, enough is known of him to make it tolerably clear that he was one of those humble, pure, and humane spirits who save the honour of the human race. According to tradition, Hillel was a descendant of the house of David, and at the age of forty came from Babylon to Jerusalem to dedicate himself to the study of the Law.

130

After the death of his teachers, he, along with his rival Schammai, attained to great eminence among the scribes. Besides an unrivalled knowledge of the Law, and the traditions which first established his fame, he possessed a wonderfully patient, meek, and gentle character, and his heart overflowed with a mild and attractive wisdom. Some of his sayings rise to a high standard of moral elevation, and reveal a very lofty conception of religious duty. "Be of the disciples of Aaron the peaceful," said he, "loving peace and pursuing peace, loving the creatures and bringing them nigh to the Law." And again, "What thou wouldest not have done to thee do not to others; this is the whole Law, all the rest is but the interpretation." Though Hillel is the most striking personality among the scribes after they became a thoroughly constituted class, other rabbis are credited with utterances which are in no wise inferior to his. One of Hillel's predecessors, Antigonus of Sochoh, is reported to have said, "Be not as slaves that minister to the lord with a view to receive a recompense, but be as slaves that minister to the lord without a view to receive a recompense, and let the fear of God be upon you." "Do God's will," said another rabbi, "as if it were thy will, that He may do thy will as if it were His will. Annul thy will before His will, that He may annul the will of others before thy will." "Tithe not overmuch," said Gamaliel; "Practice, not study, is the chief thing," said Simon his son. Such maxims as these, as well as many others which might be added to them, conclusively prove that some of the most eminent of the scribes had a higher conception of religion than the mere observance of its external forms. Yet those very men were unable to dissociate the religious life from the national and ceremonial accidents of Judaism. It was reserved for Christianity to show that religion in its highest aspects is not national but human, that all forms and ceremonies are at most but its temporary envelope, and that its essence consists in an inward disposition of the heart.

The Pharisees and Sadducees

The great difficulty which has to be confronted in all attempts at gaining an accurate conception of the two Jewish parties which came into prominence in the time of the Maccabees, and existed together in a state of silent or pronounced hostility till the downfall of Jerusalem, consists in the dearth and untrustworthiness of the information we possess respecting them. The canonical books of the Old Testament posterior to the Exile make no mention of either Pharisees or Sadducees; the New Testament only refers to them in so far as they took up an attitude of opposition to the rise and progress of Christianity. Equally scanty are the materials contained in the apocryphal and non-canonical literature, both Jewish and Christian; and although the Mischna and the Targums are full to overflowing of the Pharisaic spirit, they shed very little historical light on the growth of the two parties, and their true relations to one another. What these documents do pretend to tell is disfigured by the conceptions of a later age, and for all historical purposes is almost as untrustworthy as the statements on the same subject of patristic writers like Origen, Epiphanius, and Jerome. Josephus, himself a Pharisee, is by far the weightiest authority on the two parties. But his assertions require to be controlled by a knowledge of the lines of development on which Jewish life proceeded, and also by a recognition of the fact that he was writing for Greek and Roman readers. This latter circumstance led him to present a distorted view of the divisions among his countrymen, and to find a fictitious parallel to the Sadducees and Pharisees in the philosophic schools of the ancient world.

Long before the names Pharisee and Sadducee appear in the pages of history the divergent tendencies which these two parties represented were in existence within the Jewish community. It has, in

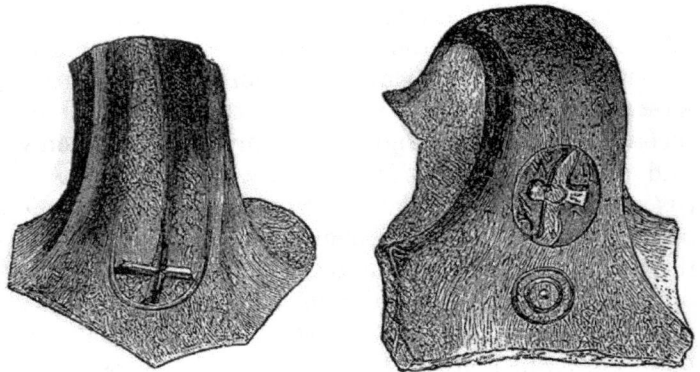

Phoenician Pottery. Ancient Marks on The Handles of Vases

fact, been contended that the foundation of their differences goes back into pre-exilian times, and that the priests and prophets of the old Israelitish monarchy are the true precursors of the Sadducees and Pharisees. But the complete transformation which Jewish society underwent after the return from Babylon, not to mention other serious difficulties, is an almost insuperable obstacle to the acceptance of such a theory. On this question it is safer to regard the post-exilian period as an essentially new epoch in Jewish history, and to look for some of the causes which ultimately produced the Pharisees and Sadducees in the nature and structure of the new theocracy.

The central thought on which the theocracy was reared consisted of two parts the utter uprooting of idolatrous practices; and the establishment of the worship of Israel's God in accordance with the precepts of the Law. The class which worked most strenuously for the realization of this thought was unquestionably the scribes. It was principally through their efforts that Judaism had been kept alive in the disastrous days of the Exile. It was they who had collected and preserved the sacred literature of the race. It was they who came into practical contact with the people when expounding the doctrines of the Law; and their experience in Babylon had no doubt taught them that the only way to make the Jews a people of the Law was to separate them and isolate them as completely as possible from all contact with surrounding nations. In this effort they were not thoroughly supported by the Jewish notables. These men were, for the most part, members of the high-priestly families who had survived the wreck of the old Jewish state, and when the community was reorganized in the time of Ezra and Nehemiah, they at once assumed the most prominent position within it, and formed a sort of petty aristocracy. Secular power as well as priestly privileges was in the hands of these notables soon after the establishment of the new order of things; and although their civil functions were very restricted, the exercise of these functions brought them into contact both with the high officials of the Persian monarchy and with the heads of the neighbouring populations. These notables were not deliberately opposed .to the ideal which the scribes had set before themselves. Up to a certain point they must have supported the scribes in upholding a high standard of reverence for the teachings of the Law, for the Law not only exalted their prerogatives and made their incomes a matter of religious obligation, but also elevated the high priest into the supreme medium of communication between God and man. It was their intercourse with foreign peoples which made them antagonistic to the separatist doctrines of the scribes, and they did not consider that a state of national isolation was necessary to the complete enforcement of the pentateuchal code. Two tendencies were accordingly face to face in the Persian period; the scribes, the theorists, the men of study, were at the head of the current which wished, in the interests of monotheism and the Law, to preserve the Jews of Palestine from all contact with the outer world. The high priests, the men of affairs and of action, were less afraid of the evils which might flow from intercourse with the stranger, and were more disposed to live on a friendly footing with the nations among which their lot was cast:.

In the Persian period (B.C. 586—332) these opposing tendencies produced a certain amount of friction within the community, but it was neither so constant nor so pronounced as to involve the formation of distinct and consolidated parties. But the overthrow of the Persian Empire by Alexander the Great and the opening up of Palestine as well as the rest of Western Asia to Greek colonists and Greek ideas had the effect of accentuating the divergencies between the scribes and the notables, and eventually resulted in the formation of two parties within the theocracy—the Hellenists and the Assidaeans, or pious ones (B.C. 332-167). The Hellenists were essentially the same men who had in the past been resisting the separatist ideas of the scribes, and the Assidaeans constituted a class within the circle of the scribes, which pushed exclusive principles to their utmost limits, and made the rigorous practice of the Law the sole aim and object of existence. The Hellenists were composed of the priestly aristocracy and the official classes, and the genius and civilization of Greece swept them in a short time within its folds. What the scribes had dreaded at length came to pass. Contact with the stranger was proving fatal to Judaism in the persons of its highest representatives. The priestly aristocracy was carried away by the fascinations of Greek life; they became ashamed of their Jewish names, and not only adopted the habits and customs of the Greeks, but their faith was in many cases shattered by Greek philosophy. The extreme section of the Hellenists was partially responsible for the Maccabaean revolt; it was at their instigation that Antiochus Epiphanes decreed the abolition of Judaism, and set up a heathen form of worship in the Temple of Jerusalem. The Assidaean; were utterly indifferent to politics, but this crowning act of apostasy involved the very existence of their faith and compelled them as the servants of God to take the field. As soon as the Syrians saw the mistake they had committed they restored religious liberty to the Jews, and the Assidaeans immediately withdrew from the contest. But the insurrection aroused a spirit of patriotism among the great body of the people, and the Maccabees were supported in the conflict for complete independence not only by the masses, but also by the more moderate among the scribes and Hellenists as well. The Assidaeans and the apostate Hellenists disappeared from the scene; but when national independence was at last secured, the old antagonistic tendencies which had been at work in the community for so many years began to assert themselves afresh, and were for the future represented by the Pharisees and Sadducees.

One of the results of the Maccabaean insurrection was to infuse a certain spirit of patriotism into all classes of the community, and to heighten the respect of the whole people for the Law. But within the limits of loyalty to the Law and the new constitution there was ample room for very serious diversity of opinion. This diversity, although it did not assume the same extreme forms as had been the case with the Assidaeans and Hellenists, continued to run in the same channels as formerly, and was represented by a similar class of men, the Sadducees being the successors of the Hellenists and the Pharisees of the Assidaeans. The Sadducees, like their predecessors, were the Jewish aristocracy. They were partly the courtiers, the soldiers, the diplomatists, and other superior officials who had risen into prominence in the Maccabaean war, and partly the old high-priestly families who had fallen into the background in the early stages of the revolt, but who came once more to the front under Simon Maccabaeus. It is highly probable that the Sadducees owe their party name to the old high-priestly aristocracy. From the time of David till the establishment of Maccabaean supremacy the high priesthood had almost always been in the hands of the family of Zadok. But at the close of the Greek period the doings of the Zadokites made them highly unpopular, and in the Maccabaean period a widespread dislike of their religious indifference, and of their Greek mode of life existed in the public mind. The same Greek tendencies however soon reappeared among the Maccabees and the high officials who surrounded them. The party of the scribes profoundly disapproved of these tendencies, and stigmatized the men who adopted them as Zadokites or Sadducees. Such at least is the most probable explanation of the origin of the word.

Just as the Sadducees inherited the characteristics of the Hellenists, so did the Pharisees inherit the essential ideas of the Assidaeans, and become for the future the representatives of the main current of post-exilian Judaism. It is, in fact, very difficult to point out any substantial difference between the Pharisees and their predecessors. On all religious questions they were entirely at one, and the only point on which any distinction can be said to have existed between them consisted in the fact that the Pharisees were not quite so indifferent to the existence of Judaea as an independent state as had been the case with the Assidaeans. The connection between the Pharisees and the scribes was also remarkably close. Nearly all the scribes were Pharisees, and many of the Pharisees were scribes. The similarity did not, however, proceed so far as to make the two identical, and the difference between them may be best described by saying that the Pharisees were a party, while the scribes were in most respects a class. What makes it certain that the scribes and Pharisees are not to be confounded together is the existence of scribes who were manifestly not Pharisees. These scribes either took up a position of neutrality with respect to the rival parties, or were adherents of the Sadducees; for it is very improbable that the Sadducees had no one to represent them among the doctors of the Law. The relation between the Pharisees and scribes was practically the same as that which exists between teachers and taught. The Pharisees were the men who endeavoured to reduce the teachings and theories of the scribes to practice, and all those scribes who in addition to the written law also believed in the binding authority of tradition were Pharisees as well as scribes.

Portion of Codex Vaticanus.

The attitude of superiority and disdain which the Pharisees assumed towards the great body of the people must have been fatal to the formation of any close bonds of sympathy between them. It is true the people generally supported the Pharisees in their conflict with the Sadducees, but it would be a mistake to infer from this circumstance that the Pharisees were at the head of a popular movement. There is every reason to believe that the people listened to them with respect, though they did not always follow their advice, and that they admired the scrupulous, if ostentatious, manner in which the Pharisees fulfilled the innumerable and burdensome precepts of the Law. But in the main they appear to have looked on the Pharisees rather as a body of holy men, than as national leaders who were drawing their strength and inspiration from the great fountains of popular feeling, and whose hearts were beating in unison with the desires and aspirations of the whole community. Out of the entire population of Palestine the Pharisees only amounted to six thousand men, and these numbers conclusively prove that the Pharisaic party had no attractions for the great bulk of the population. The principles professed by the Pharisees were adverse to their popularity as a party, and compelled them to hold aloof from the multitude. To them the ordinary Jew was an unclean being, and they avoided him as if he were no better than a heathen. It was from the circle of the Pharisees that the contemptuous words proceeded, "This people who knoweth not the Law is cursed." The Pharisees separated themselves from all who failed to come up to their standard of legal purity, and as this was the case with the great majority of the community, it followed that. there was as little intercourse as possible between them and the vast body of the people. It was an article in the Pharisaic creed that the Jewish heathen (Amhaarez), who in their eyes were almost synonymous with the masses, would not participate in the resurrection of the dead, and it was regarded as better for their daughters to fall into the lion's mouth than to marry them. That a class of men holding such ideas as these should be popular is hardly conceivable, and the history of the party shows that they never attained a permanent hold upon the people's heart.

The first actual rupture between the Pharisees and the Sadducees took place towards the end of the reign of John Hyrcanus (B.C. 135-106). It took the shape on the part of the Pharisees of an objection to the competence of the Maccabaean princes for the office of high priest. The Pharisees did not dispute the right of the Maccabees to wear the crown, but they contended that the office of high priest was of a different character, and that it could only be filled by the legitimate representatives of a high-priestly family. The contention of the Pharisees was perfectly justified from a strictly legal point of view. It was notorious that the Maccabees, not being of high-priestly descent, had no legal title to the high priesthood; but it is probable that the Pharisees would have allowed this irregularity to remain in abeyance if the political conduct of the Maccabees had been more in accordance with the Pharisaic policy of isolating Judaea from the rest of the world. The Maccabees were too well aware of the precarious nature of Jewish independence, and of the unstable state of international politics, to commit themselves to such a perilous line of action. On the contrary, John Hyrcanus allowed the ideas and aims of the Pharisees to remain in the background, and devoted the energies of his long reign to augmenting the glory of the country. In this course he was supported by the Sadducees. But the palpably secular aspect which the Jewish state assumed under this prince—its worldly diplomacy, its battles and conquests, its intimate relations with heathen peoples, its love and tolerance of foreign customs 1—repelled the Pharisees, and deeply wounded their religious susceptibilities. To them it was unbearable that the most sacred rites of public worship should be performed by men whose lives were spent in the council chamber or on the battlefield, and they set themselves to compel the Maccabees to renounce the high priesthood and to rest contented with the crown. The Sadducees stoutly resisted the assaults of their opponents on the privileges of the dynasty, and the struggle grew in intensity between the two parties till it finally culminated in civil war. Hyrcanus, during his reign, was able to ward off this crowning misfortune, but the Pharisees broke out into revolt in the reign of Alexander Jannaeus (B.C. 105-79), and for many years the unhappy country became a prey to anarchy, bloodshed, and massacre. After many vicissitudes the victory ultimately remained with the Sadducees, and Jannaeus showed little mercy to his adversaries; but in the succeeding reign of Alexandra Salome (B.C. 79-69) the Pharisees acquired the upper hand, and avenged themselves on their opponents for their miseries under Jannaeus. On the death of Alexandra, the Sadducees, led by her younger son Aristobulus, again asserted their supremacy, and the renewed rivalries of the two factions once more led to civil war. Both sides called in foreign help the Pharisees the Nabataeans, and the Sadducees the Romans with the usual result that all power over the nation was taken from both. Rome, the mistress of so many peoples, now added Judaea to the number of her conquests and the political character of the conflict between the two parties practically came to an end (B.C. 63).

Under Herod the Great the Sadducees had very little influence over the national fortunes, and the opposition which the Pharisees had so long shown towards their political tendencies to a great extent died away. Herod was not the kind of man to share his power with any Jewish party, and during his reign the Sadducees had to be contented with the exercise of their priestly privileges in the Temple. The high priesthood was in the hands of the Sadducees, and Herod did his best to minimize its influence by conferring it upon obscure creatures of his own, whom he set up and deposed at will. Of the two parties, however, he appears to have preferred the Sadducees. An evidence of this preference is seen in the constitution which the Sanhedrin assumed in Herod's reign. Before his accession to the throne most of the members of this body were Pharisees, but after his death the Sadducees formed the majority. It cannot be doubted that Herod, who kept a watchful eye upon everything which was done in the country, was the instigator of this change. The reason of the king's preference for the Sadducees consisted in the fact that they were at once less hostile to his supremacy, and more disposed to support his Hellenic tendencies than their opponents. When Judaea was placed under the control of a Roman procurator, the Sadducees acquired a slight addition to their somewhat shadowy authority. In return they became for the most part the docile and devoted instruments of Caesarism. As they had lost all hold upon the affections of the people, it was Rome only which maintained them in a position of eminence, and it was to Rome that their gratitude was paid. When the revolt of the Jews under Vespasian deprived the Sadducees of Roman support, they suffered severely at the hands of their countrymen, and the destruction of the Jewish state which soon after ensued put a final termination to the party.

The fate which befell the Pharisees was somewhat different. The mantle of their old opponents had fallen upon Herod, and in his efforts to permeate the population with Hellenistic modes of life, the hostility which the Pharisees had in the past vented on the Sadducees was now transferred to him. Even those Pharisees who counseled submission to Herod evidently regarded his rule in the light of a Divine chastisement which it became a pious duty to tolerate till the vengeance of heaven was appeased. As a body the Pharisees not only refused to regard him as their legitimate ruler, but many among them were eager to intrigue against him whenever an opportunity presented itself. To Romanize Palestine was the keystone of Herod's policy; it was essentially the same process as to Hellenize it; and in resisting the measures of the king, the Pharisees were simply resisting another and more radical form of Sadducaism. It is true that the rebuilding of the Temple and the effective manner in which Herod was able to protect Jews resident abroad helped his popularity. At the same time, it must not be forgotten that in rebuilding the Temple the king was as much influenced by a Roman fashion of the time for huge architectural constructions as by a desire to conciliate the Pharisees. Intervals of apparent harmony between Herod and the Pharisees occurred at certain periods of his long reign, but the normal attitude of both parties towards each other was one of ill-concealed hostility and distrust. The execution of some zealous Pharisees for pulling down the imperial eagle which the king had placed over the gate of the Temple is merely one instance of the strained relations which frequently existed between them.

Chamber Above Aqueduct, Jerusalem

Herod's death, the banishment of his son Archelaus, and the incorporation of Judaea into the administrative structure of the empire brought the Pharisees into immediate conflict with Rome. The object of Roman policy was to obliterate as far as practicable the national peculiarities of the provincials. Such a purpose was diametrically opposed to the whole spirit of Pharisaism, which aimed at perpetuating and accentuating Jewish peculiarities so as to construct an impregnable barrier of religious custom between themselves and the rest of mankind. The Roman system was a direct assault upon this principle, and the Pharisees had to begin again with Rome the same battle as they had formerly fought with the Sadducees and Herod. The teaching of the Pharisees on the subject of Roman supremacy was understood by the masses and by many of their own followers as an incitement to rebellion. The rise of the Zealots was the direct result of it, and Sadduk, one of the originators of this new party, was himself a Pharisee. The Zealots were simply the fighting wing of the Pharisaic party, for they held no principle which distinguished them from the body out of which they had sprung, except a profound belief that the yoke of Rome must be shaken off by force of arms. In the hopeless effort to withdraw themselves from the immense imperial machine which held the ancient world in its grasp, the Zealot section of the Pharisees was practically exterminated. With the fall of Judaea as an organized community, the other section gave up the attempt to realize their aims by political action. They henceforth devoted themselves to codifying the vast accumulation of unwritten law which had grown up in the course of centuries. It was on the precepts of this code, which they now committed to writing, that they relied as a means for keeping the Jews apart from the rest of the world, and up to the present day they have not relied on it in vain.

From the political differences which separated the Sadducees and Pharisees, we shall now pass to an examination of the controversies which arose among them on the question of Judaism itself. The first and most important point on which the two parties were divided was the standard of faith. According to the doctrines of the Pharisees the oral, as well as the written Law, was the ultimate rule by which every faithful Jew should regulate his belief and life. The theory that the Law was intended to be applicable to the whole course of human existence, down even to its smallest details, compelled the Pharisees to supplement the silence of the written Law, or its meagre and general statements, by the traditions of the elders. And in order to gain acceptance for these traditions, and to place them on an equality with the written Law, they were obliged to refer their origin to Moses, who was asserted to have received them from God. The Sadducees, on the other hand, maintained that the oral Law possessed no binding force whatever, and that the only rule of faith for the descendants of Abraham was the written canonical code, or, in other terms, the laws which are contained in the Pentateuch. Some of the Fathers of the Church are of opinion that the Sadducees not only rejected oral tradition, but that they rejected the prophetical books of the Old Testament as well. It is impossible to offer a direct refutation of this opinion, but at the same time there is nothing to support it in the literature which was contemporaneous with the activity of the two parties. And as the Jews themselves very soon forgot the distinctive characteristics of the Sadducees, it is not likely that they would be better remembered by Christian writers. On the whole, it is more probable that the Sadducees accepted all those books of the Hebrew Bible which were admitted into the canon, but refused to be bound by anything outside of them.

What were the grounds on which the Sadducees refused to acknowledge the authority of oral tradition? In the first place, because the written Law alone was the old orthodox standard of Judaism, and an aristocracy has always been inclined to hold fast by the established customs and institutions of the country. Other considerations besides the sanction of antiquity also affected their judgment. The traditions of the elders were, in many cases, opposed to the view of life which was entertained by the Sadducees. A rigorism and an austerity were enjoined in them which must have been obnoxious to men whose career lay in the profession of arms; and the laws restricting intercourse with the foreigner were not likely to be popular with statesmen who knew that the continued independence of Judaea rested, to a large extent, on the skillful management of external affairs. Not only were the Sadducees opposed to the principle and the contents of tradition in themselves, they were also hostile to them because of the additional power which tradition placed in the hands of their opponents. A knowledge of the laws of tradition was mainly confined to Pharisaic circles. It was accordingly to the Pharisees that the people were obliged to have recourse on all perplexing points of faith and practice. Such a state of things the Sadducees could not regard with indifference. Whatever increased the influence of the Pharisees diminished their own, and to admit the law of tradition as of Divine obligation would have meant the handing over to the Pharisees of the supreme direction of affairs.

The fundamental difference which existed between the Pharisees and Sadducees concerning the acceptance or rejection of oral tradition as an absolute standard of belief necessarily led to controversy on other subjects connected with the Law. In certain purely civil matters the Pharisees were at variance with their opponents, as, for example, on the law of inheritance and the laws relating to damage. The penal code was also a subject of dispute. By the use of traditional interpretations, the Pharisees strove in the main to mitigate the severity of the more rigorous statutes of the Pentateuch. The Sadducees, on the other hand, faithful to their principle of adhering to the written Law only, were determined to apply these statutes in a literal sense. Differences likewise existed between the two parties as to the proper time and manner of celebrating some of the principal Jewish festivals, such as the day of Pentecost and the Feast of Tabernacles. Puerile evasions were resorted to by the Pharisees to overcome the limits attached by the Law to a sabbath day's journey; the Sadducees would have none of it, and stuck to the original signification of the statute. In burning the ashes of the red heifer, the Sadducees,

140

contrary to their general tendencies, but probably in the interests of the priesthood, required of the officiating priest the highest possible degree of legal purity. On this point the Pharisees were comparatively indifferent, but were in their turn full of zeal for the scrupulous purification of the vessels used in the service of the sanctuary—a zeal which caused the Sadducees to remark mockingly that the Pharisees would cleanse the sun. The attitude of the disputants in these controversies shows that the general bent of the Sadducees was towards an obstinate adherence to the strict letter of the Law, while the Pharisees aimed more at modifying it to suit the altering requirements of the times. This, however, was not always the case. In many instances no question of principle was involved on either side, and the chief outcome of these disputes was to be found in a luxuriant display of scholastic subtleties.

In the domain of religious dogma a profound diversity of opinion separated the two Jewish parties. The most important difference between them arose on the doctrine of the resurrection. According to Josephus, the Pharisees believed that "souls are of immortal vigour, and that there will be rewards or punishments under the earth to those who in this life have devoted themselves to virtue or to vice; the latter will be shut up in an everlasting prison, the former will have the power of coming back to life." From this passage of Josephus it is evident that the prophet Daniel is giving expression to the Pharisaic conception of the resurrection when he says, "And many of them that sleep in the dust of the earth shall awake, some to everlasting life, and some to shame and everlasting contempt. And they that be wise shall shine as the brightness of the firmament, and they that turn many to righteousness as the stars forever and forever." On the other hand, both the New Testament and Josephus are at one in asserting that the Sadducees denied the doctrine of the resurrection. In fact, Josephus says that the Sadducees did not believe in a future life at all. "The souls die with the bodies," and there are neither rewards nor punishments in the underworld. In this respect the Sadducees were in harmony with the old Hebrew view concerning the state of the dead; for the dim, sad, and shadowy existence of the departed in Scheol was not worthy the name of immortality. The Sadducees contended that the Law was silent on the resurrection, and their position may be summed up in the celebrated maxim of Antigonus of Sochoh, "Be not as slaves that minister to the lord with a view to receive recompense; but be as slaves that minister to the lord without a view to receive recompense, and let the fear of Heaven be upon you."

Belief in the existence of angels and evil spirits—a subject closely related to the doctrine of the resurrection—was also a matter of dispute between the Pharisees and Sadducees. In the centuries posterior to the Exile, a belief in this doctrine steadily developed into a general conviction among the Jewish masses. It was adopted and upheld by the Pharisees, but the Sadducees opposed it. Traces of this doctrine are to be found both in the historical and prophetical books of the Old Testament, but it occupied a very insignificant and subordinate place in old Hebrew theology, and no doubt the reason why the Sadducees rejected it is to be found in the immense proportions which the belief assumed in Maccabaean and New Testament times.

On the perplexing problems of Divine Providence and the freedom of the will, there was likewise a conflict of opinion between the Pharisees and Sadducees. How far the differences between them extended it is very difficult to say. Josephus is our chief witness, but his testimony is so completely Greek in form, and, in some particulars, so alien to Jewish habits of thoughts that it cannot be accepted without modifications. The Pharisees, he relates, say that "certain things, but not all, are the work of Fate; and that other things are in our own power to be or not to be. The Sadducees, on the other hand, take away Fate, holding that it is a thing of nought, and that human affairs do not depend upon it; but they place all things in our own power, so that we are the authors of our own good, and receive evils through our own inconsideration." The Jews knew nothing of Fate as it is here described by Josephus, but if by Fate we are to understand Divine Providence, and then make a comparison of these and other statements of the historian with the Old Testament and the Psalms of Solomon, it will be found that the differences of the two Jewish parties on these mysterious matters were not of a fundamental character. The Old Testament was the standard of faith with the Sadducees, and one of its fundamental ideas is the influence of Providence on human affairs. It cannot be supposed that the Sadducees departed from the teaching of their own creed in one of its most essential particulars, and the contention of Josephus therefore loses the greater part of its meaning. On the other hand, the Pharisees did not deny free will. On this point the Pharisaic doctrine of works is in complete harmony with Josephus and the Psalms of Solomon. "Our actions depend upon our own will," says this Psalmist, "and the power of the soul to work righteousness or iniquity is in our own hands."

Both parties adhered to the doctrines of Providence and of free will; the true nature of the dispute between them was evidently one of degree and not of kind. The Pharisees, while admitting the existence of free will, laid greatest stress on the action of Providence; the Sadducees, on the other hand, did not deny the overruling power of Providence, but their bent of mind led them, at the same time, to give unbounded scope to the supremacy of the will. Just as the Psalms of Solomon represent the views of the Pharisees on these insoluble mysteries, so does the Book of Ecclesiasticus, in the following passage, give expression to the sentiments of the Sadducees: "When at the beginning He (God) created man, He left him to the counsel of his own will. If thou wilt thou canst keep His commandments, and to continue faithful depends on thy good pleasure. He hath set fire and water before thee, thou canst stretch forth thy hand unto whither thou wilt."

The Essenes

At the time the Pharisees and Sadducees were in conflict with one another as to the correct interpretation of the Law, a body of Jewish devotees were endeavouring to realize its precepts in their daily life. This body became known as the Essenes. In contrast to the Pharisees and Sadducees the Essenes were not a party, but a religious order, founded upon communistic principles, and subject to ascetic rules of life. Finding it impossible to reduce their distinctive ideas to practice in the heart of the community, the Essenes withdrew themselves from the civil and political life of Palestine, and in the time of Christ they were to be found, to the number of about four thousand, living for the most part in monasteries, under a monastic code of discipline.

The Essenes are first referred to during the Maccabaean war (circa B.C. 150). But some writers have attempted to find the germs out of which the order was ultimately developed at an early period in Jewish history. The Rechabites, mentioned as early as the ninth

Ain Feshkah, Dead Sea.

century before Christ, and who apparently continued to exist as an independent religious community up to the final destruction of Jerusalem, have been pointed to as the precursors of Essenism. The Rechabites were nomadic in their habits, the Essenes were agriculturists, but in some other respects there was a certain resemblance between them. Both communities were ascetic, and both inhabited the same desert oasis on the western shores of the Dead Sea. But in spite of these similarities, it is not easy to establish a clear link of continuity between the two organizations; and while admitting the hypothesis that the Essenes may have sprung from the Rechabites, it is, on the whole, a safer historic method to regard the return from Babylon as a fresh starting-point in Jewish life, and to look for the origin of the Essenes in the tendencies of post-exilian Judaism.

The most marked and characteristic of these postexilian tendencies consisted in an ever-increasing desire to live up to the highest possible standard of legal purity. The Pharisees, as has already been seen, exhibited strong manifestations of this tendency, but it was reserved for the Essenes to carry it to the extremest lengths. With them the dread of catching uncleanness assumed such extravagant proportions as to render almost all social intercourse impossible between them and their fellow men. Defilement might be produced in such a variety of ways by mingling with the multitude, that the Essenes were constrained to separate themselves entirely from the body politic, and to adopt a form of life and discipline which would enable them to gratify their aspirations after a mode of existence more thoroughly in accordance with the most stringent requirements of the Law. It is hardly likely, however, that the Essenes at the beginning, adopted the practical measures involved in the principles which they professed. The probability is, that the absolute need of withdrawing themselves from the main stream of national life forced itself upon them by degrees, whilst they were vainly attempting to reach their religious aims in the midst of the community. Step by step the Essenes retreated from the social and civic life around them. In the earliest references to them they are represented as occupying posts of influence and honour at the Temple and the royal court. But residence at Jerusalem was incompatible with due observance of the highest legal obligations, and the Essenes took another step and retired to the towns and villages of Palestine. But even there it was impossible to avoid the chances of contamination from the unclean world, and many sought a last refuge from the rest of humanity in the desert solitudes of Engadi, on the shores of the Dead Sea. Here, probably in the time of Christ, the greater part of the Essenes lived in peaceful seclusion, subsisting entirely on the daily labour of their hands, and constituting an idyllic little world of their own.

How the Essenes came to be called by that name has long been a source of perplexity to scholars, and its meaning still remains shrouded in obscurity. Many ingenious attempts have been made to explain its origin, but none of them has met with a consensus of opinion sufficiently weighty and unanimous to justify its acceptance. The word has been variously interpreted to mean, the healers, the watchers, the doers, the baptists, the silent, the pious; and recently an old conjecture has been revived to the effect that the Essenes derived their name from a place called Essa, on the western side of the Dead Sea, a spot where the community used to live. The last-mentioned explanation has the merit of being a very obvious one, and is not to be lightly cast aside. Still it is equally reasonable to suppose that the Essenes, like the Pharisees and Sadducees, received their name from the most distinctive characteristic which they displayed. In the eyes of the world the most marked feature of Essenism was the strenuous piety of its adherents. The Syriac for "pious "bore a close resemblance to the word Essene, and as Syriac was the language in ordinary use among the Palestinian Jews in the time of Christ, it is very probable that the widespread reputation of the order for piety caused them to be known as the Essenes or pious ones. Even this explanation of the name is not altogether free from difficulties, but it has been accepted by many competent and distinguished scholars, and among probable meanings it appears the most probable.

The same morbid craving for purity which drove the Essenes into the wilderness, reappeared in the internal organization of the community. There were four different degrees of membership, and for a member of a higher stage to come into contact with one in a lower, resulted in his being immediately defiled. The three years' probation which every candidate for admission into the order had to pass through was also instituted with a view to preserve the utmost possible purity within the society. As soon as any one signified his wish to join the community, he received a hatchet, a girdle, and a white garment, and to test his constancy he had for one year to submit himself to the same mode of life as was adopted by the Essenes. At the end of the first year's probation the novice was advanced a step; he was cleansed with the water of purification, and admitted to the common worship of the society. For two more years he remained in this stage. If the candidate at the close of that period was considered to have acquitted himself satisfactorily, he was admitted to the hallowed midday meal, and initiated into all the mysteries of Essenism.

But before this final act of initiation was effected, the novice had once for all to take a tremendous oath. By this oath he solemnly bound himself to obey all those who exercised authority in the society, and to act with justice and modesty if at any time he were elected to a similar position of power. The conditions of the oath also pledged him to conceal nothing from his fellow members, and never to reveal the Essene doctrine to the outer world. He also promised under the oath to preserve the names of the angels, and the sacred books of the order; also to hand down to future adherents all Essene teaching in its undiluted purity. Besides these regulations affecting the welfare of the order which the newly-admitted Essene solemnly swore to keep, the oath of initiation included matters of a purely moral and religious nature. The Essene, in all the affairs of life, was bound by his oath to be a constant lover of truth and reprover of falsehood; he was not to pollute his hands with dishonest gain; he was to abstain from inflicting injury upon any one, and to detest those who did; but, above all, he was to show piety towards God and justice towards men.

The leadership of the community and the management of its affairs were entrusted to a small body of men elected by the members from among themselves. These officials were called directors or administrators, and strict obedience to their commands was one of the regulations of the society. The powers of the directors were very extensive, but they were not permitted to expel Essene offenders from the order. For this purpose a tribunal, composed of at least a hundred men, had to be convened. A decree of expulsion was in many cases equivalent to a sentence of death. So strong was the hold which the practices of the community had obtained upon all who joined it, that even Essenes who had been cast out of the order by the supreme council were in many instances content to perish rather than partake of food prepared by other than Essene hands. Sometimes when a poor wretch who had been expelled was reduced to the last extremities, the order would take compassion upon him and receive him back. But as a rule, when a sentence of expulsion had once been passed, it was looked upon as irrevocable.

The principles of the Essene organization were absolutely communistic; no one had any private possessions, and the property of the order was the common property of all. "They despise riches," says Josephus, "and the community of goods among them is wonderful; and no one can be found among them who possesses more than another. For it is a law among them that those who enter the order give up their property to the community, so that neither abject poverty nor excessive wealth is anywhere to be seen. The property of each is added to the property of all, and one common stock exists for all as brethren." The communistic life of the Essenes put a stop to buying, selling, barter, competition, and all the ordinary customs of trade: it meant, in fact, the abolition of trade. "They neither buy nor sell anything to one another," Josephus continues, "but each one gives to the other what he needs, and receives in turn what he requires. And though offering no equivalent at all, they may have without hindrance whatever they require.

Agriculture was the chief occupation of the Essene communities. The members of the order did not waste their lives in idle and fruitless contemplation, but always awoke before sunrise to begin the labours of the day. The first words of the Essenes in the morning were addressed to God, and not until their devotions were over did the brethren enter into conversation with one another. Their daily duties were laid down for them by the administrators of the community, and work was continued with the utmost diligence from early morning till eleven o'clock. At that hour preparations were made for the midday meal, the most solemn function of the day. Then every Essene, on returning from the fields, took off his rough working garments, and after taking a purifying bath of cold water, arrayed himself in white apparel, and entered the dining-hall of the order with the same solemnity as if it were the house of God. Here a simple meal, consisting of only one dish, was placed before every member of the order, and both before and after the repast grace was said by the presiding priest. When all had left the table, the white garments were laid aside, and the work of the day resumed till evening. Strangers were permitted to sit down with the Essenes at their evening meal, which appears to have been more of a social character than the one at midday.

The frugal simplicity of their daily fare is an example of the austere and simple habits which marked the whole life of the Essenes. It is related of them that they wore their clothing till it was completely worthless. It is not certain that they abstained from the use of flesh and wine, but they undoubtedly discarded the use of ointment, and believed that a rough exterior possessed a kind of virtue in itself. On days of penitence and fasting, and on the great Day of Atonement, the Jews did not anoint themselves; the Essenes elevated these exceptions into a rule, and allowed simplicity of life to degenerate into mere asceticism. Except on the solitary occasion of their admission into the order, the Essenes never emphasized their assertions by an oath. He who cannot be believed, say they, without calling God to witness, is already condemned. They had a curious rule which forbade them to spit except in certain directions. On the Sabbath day it was forbidden to discharge the excretions of the body, and on other days this natural function involved uncleanness, and had a certain stigma attached to it. The Sabbath was much more strictly observed by the Essenes than by any other section of the Jews. No fires were to be lighted on that day; all food had to be prepared the day before, and the day was kept as one of complete cessation from all kinds of work.

On the subject of marriage the majority of the Essenes held decidedly ascetic views. Like all Orientals, they formed a very low estimate of women, believing them to be at once faithless to their husbands, and the enemies of domestic peace. Even those who did not adopt the celibate views of the majority looked upon marriage as a kind of necessary evil which had to be endured for the sake of perpetuating the race. This was regarded by the non-celibate Essenes as the highest and only object of the married state, and when they entered into the bonds of wedlock it was only with those women who were considered likely to have posterity. To prevent the order from dying out it was a practice among the Essenes to adopt children and educate them in the principles of the community. It is difficult to say from what quarter the Essenes derived their antipathy to marriage. It is possibly a plant of foreign growth which found its way among them, but it may just as easily have arisen out of certain Jewish customs relating to purity. To regard marriage as a hindrance to piety was undoubtedly to go beyond a truly Jewish view of life. At the same time, the roots of this view are to be found in Judaism itself.

On most questions of a theological character the Essenes did not differ materially from the Pharisees. In their synagogues the service was probably

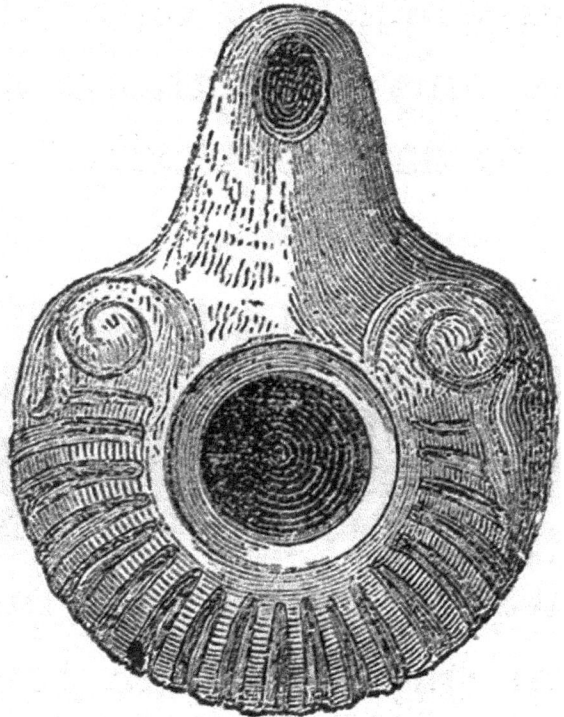

Night Lamp

conducted after the manner of the Jews. The Sabbath day was observed with extraordinary rigour, and Moses was so highly honoured among them as a legislator that it was accounted worthy of death to blaspheme his name. In fact, Moses occupied among the Essenes a position only inferior to God Himself. Unfortunately a good deal of obscurity surrounds the point as to what books were in use among the Essenes. The reverence paid to the memory of Moses places it beyond doubt that the canonical books of the Old Testament were just as sacred to the Essenes as to the scribes and Pharisees. But it is not at all clear that these were the only books considered as sacred by the community. Josephus expresses himself with unusual vagueness on this matter, but it is probable that his reference to the holy books of the society is meant to include other writings besides the canonical Scriptures. Some have even ventured to name such productions as the Book of Noah and the Book of Jubilees as of Essene origin, but so far entirely without reason. If the Essenes did possess sacred books of their own, in all likelihood they have perished.

The Essenes in popular estimation were believed to possess a wonderful knowledge of God's future intentions with regard to men. This knowledge was looked upon as the outcome of their profound study of Holy Writ, and of the intimate relationship which their ascetic practices enabled them to maintain with God. Several remarkable instances are mentioned by Josephus of Essene predictions. Judas the Essene he relates foretold in the days of Maccabaean supremacy, that Antigonus, a brother of King Aristobulus, should suddenly meet his death at Stratons Tower. This prediction was literally fulfilled. Later on, Menahem another Essene prophesied of Herod while yet a boy, that he should one day obtain the crown. He afterwards predicted that the new king should reign over the people for many years. Both of these predictions came to pass. Besides being adepts at prophecy, the Essenes were likewise credited with a kindred gift—an admirable skill in the interpretation of dreams. Among the Jews, dreams are sometimes spoken of as mere phantasms and delusions of the mind in a state of sleep; as a rule, however, they were regarded as silent intimations of the Divine will, and one of the methods by which God revealed His purposes to men.

How successful the Essenes were in unraveling the mysterious meaning of these intimations is attested by the wonderful manner in which Simon, a member of the order, interpreted a dream of Herod's son Archelaus. This prince dreamt that he saw nine full ears of corn devoured by oxen. The meaning of the dream was a puzzle to the diviners who were called upon to interpret it, just as Pharaoh's dreams baffled the skill of the Egyptian soothsayers. Simon, like another Joseph, told Archelaus that the nine ears of corn denoted nine years, and the oxen which devoured them denoted a mutation of affairs. The interpretation was that Archelaus should reign as many years as there were ears of corn, and after passing through several vicissitudes of fortune should die. Archelaus had already reigned the allotted time, and five days after his dream was interpreted, he was summoned to Rome by the emperor, and banished to Gaul where he ultimately died.

In addition to their reputed powers as prophets and interpreters of dreams., the Essenes were also held in high estimation as medicine men. Among the Jews of the time of Christ most diseases were looked upon either as the work of evil spirits, or as punishments inflicted upon men by the immediate decree of an offended God. The prevalence of such opinions at once precluded any inquiry into the natural causes of disease, and prevented the acquirement of any rational or scientific system of remedy. Of the two beliefs respecting the origin of diseases the older was the one which attributed them to God alone; it was the influence of Persian ideas after the Exile which led the Jews to imagine that diseases were inflicted upon them by the malignity of evil spirits. When God was accounted to be the cause of a disease, the sick man was of opinion that he had done something to arouse the Divine wrath, and that his ailments were the punishment of the offence. In these circumstances the surest and most obvious method of attaining restoration to health lay in appeasing the resentment of God. This was best effected not by the use of medicine, but by resorting to the appointed ordinances of sacrifice and prayer. Medicine, it is true, was not altogether discarded, but it occupied a very secondary place as a means of cure, and to rely upon it alone was to incur the odium of impiety. As a matter of fact the remedies in use among the people, and the roots and medicinal stones which the Essenes collected, were often calculated to do more harm than good, and there is much justification for the irony of the son of Sirach when he says, "He that sinneth before his Maker let him fall into the hand of the physician."

But the main tendency of Jewish thought in the time of Christ was to attribute diseases to the machinations of the powers of evil. At the head of this malignant host stood Satan, the prince of the world, and he was surrounded by a multitude of inferior spirits. Many of these demons were believed to be the souls of the dead who roamed through the air haunting tombs and desert places in a disembodied form. The ghosts of the giants who lived in antediluvian times, the ghosts of the builders of the tower of Babel, and the ghosts of those multitudes who perished at the Flood were all numbered among the evil spirits which brought diseases and death on men. And the spirits of the wicked became demons after death. These demons entered the human body by the nostrils, being presumably inhaled with the breath; they produced dumbness, lameness, madness, blindness, epilepsy, and indeed every ailment of which there was the least doubt about the origin. Once a demon had taken possession of a man the ordinary manner of getting him expelled was by resorting to the mysterious processes of exorcism. The Jews had a wide reputation throughout the Roman Empire as exorcists; the rabbis practiced exorcism in Palestine, and there can be little doubt that the Essenes made use of it as well. The spells and incantations on which the exorcists relied were believed to have been handed down by such men as Noah, David, and Solomon, who in turn were supposed to have learned them from the angels. Several instances are on record of the manner in which exorcism was performed. Tobit's wife, we are told, was vexed by a wicked spirit which had already caused the death of seven men who had previously married her. But Tobit was instructed by the angel Raphael how to exorcise this malignant and jealous demon. Accordingly when he went into the marriage chamber, he prepared a decoction composed of the ashes of a perfume, with the heart and liver of a fish and fumigated his wife with it. When the demon smelt the smoke he fled into Upper Egypt which was then considered as one of the farthest limits of the world. And when the demon got there the angel chained him to prevent his return.

A similar instance of exorcism was once witnessed by Josephus, when a Jewish exorcist expelled a demon in the presence of the emperor Vespasian and his soldiers. In order to prove to demonstration the virtue of his art, the exorcist, Eleazar by name, placed a basin of water at some distance from his patient which the demon was to upset when expelled. He then put a ring with a magical root attached to it to the nose of the sick person. When he had done this the demon at once flew out of the possessed man's nostrils and spilt the basin of water in his flight. Meantime the man fell down, and Eleazar, reciting an incantation said to be composed by Solomon, adjured the demon to return to him no more. From this narrative it will be seen that certain kinds of roots were used for the purposes of exorcism; one of the most celebrated was the root Baaras found in a lonely valley near Machaerus on the eastern shores of the Dead Sea. The plucking of this root was a dangerous operation, and if improperly performed was sure to cause immediate death. One of the methods for procuring it was to remove most of the earth from its roots, to fasten a dog to it and allow him to pull it up. As soon as the dog had done this work he died. It is not expressly stated that this was one of the roots which the Essenes were fond of gathering; but it is very probable that it along with many others was to be found in their medicine chest.

In their zeal for the absolute supremacy of God the Essenes went beyond the Pharisees and totally denied the freedom of the human will. By them everything was ascribed to God; the whole course of man's existence was foreordained by him; the immense power of the Divine majesty left no room whatever for the free initiative of man. The Essene doctrine of a future life also differed, if we may trust Josephus, from the ideas on the same subject which were current among the Pharisees. . The Pharisees believed in a resurrection of the body; the Essenes held that the body perished after death and that the soul only was immortal. Before the body came into being the soul, according to the Essenes, existed as a pure spirit, possessing within itself all the attributes of immortality. There was no indissoluble connection between the soul and the body; the body was no more than a temporary prison-house into which the soul was enticed, and the death and dissolution of the body was a moment of joy and liberation for the soul. At death the souls of the wicked were consigned to eternal torments in a dark and frigid subterranean den; the spirits of the good were transported beyond the ocean to the islands of the blest—a region free from burning heat or storms of rain and snow, and always tempered by a gentle west wind wafted from the sea.

The repudiation of the resurrection of the body represents a serious difference of opinion between the Essenes and the orthodox teachers of the Law, but their attitude towards the Temple was more serious still and constituted a real breach with Judaism. The Essenes neither frequented the Temple for purposes of devotion nor offered sacrifices on its altars. They looked upon their own modes of worship as superior in point of purity to the services which took place at Jerusalem, but this belief did not prevent them from occasionally sending presents to the ancient sanctuary of their race. It has been said that the action of the Essenes in ceasing to sacrifice at the Temple was the result of high priests being appointed who had no hereditary right to the sacred office; it was in the nature of a protest against the performance of high-priestly functions by men who, according to Jewish law, had no authority to do so. On the other hand, however, the action of the Essenes may quite as easily have arisen from a higher conception of what constituted the true nature of sacrifice. Many of the prophets held sacrifice in light esteem; such moral qualities as mercy and such religious graces as repentance were preferred before it. In the light of these truths it is not at all improbable that the Essenes ceased to consider the offering up of sheep and oxen as a proper method of approaching God.

Before concluding this sketch of the Essenes two questions remain to be considered. In the first place, is Essenism, as many believe, a pure product of Judaism? and, in the second, is there any original connection between Christianity and Essenism?

$$I \: b \Lambda O T I \: b T$$
$$IMPANTONINI$$
$$IMPHADRIANI$$
$$IMPTRAIANPARTHOR$$
$$IMPNERYAE$$

Roman Milestone: Names of Antonine Emperors

The answer to the first of these questions depends almost entirely on the trustworthiness of Josephus. If the account of the Essene community furnished by this historian is to be at all relied upon, it must be conceded that foreign elements entered into the composition of Essenism. Those elements are most palpably before us in the Essene doctrines of the soul and immortality. It is quite at variance with purely Jewish ideas to believe, as the Essenes are said to have done, in the pre-existence of the soul, or in a dualism between soul and body, or that the body is a mere temporary prison-house of the spiritual part of man. Now, if there is a word of truth in what Josephus says as to Essene views on these points, we are forced to the conclusion that this society was not purely Jewish in some of its fundamental principles. Admitting for a moment the general veracity of Josephus, we are led to inquire what the foreign influences were which acted upon Essenism, and to a certain extent determined its character. But in entering on this inquiry great divergencies of opinion immediately arise. Some trace these alien influences to the Buddhists of India, others to the religion of the Persians, and others to the current conceptions of Syro-Palestinian heathenism. It is not difficult to adduce plausible arguments in behalf of each and all of these theories. Buddhism presents several striking resemblances to Essenism, and at the time when the Essene community sprang into existence there was a sufficient amount of intercourse going on between the East and the West, to give probability to the supposition that the Essenes had incorporated Buddhist beliefs and practices into their system. It is also equally probable that the Essenes borrowed many of their religious customs from the Persians. The sun-worship of the Parsees, their ablutions, their use of white clothing, and their rejection of bloody sacrifices, all find a counterpart among the Essenes. In their capacity as exorcists, medicine men, and interpreters of dreams, the Essenes occupy the same ground as the heathen population of Syria, and it is not at all unlikely that they derived many of their practices from the people who surrounded them.

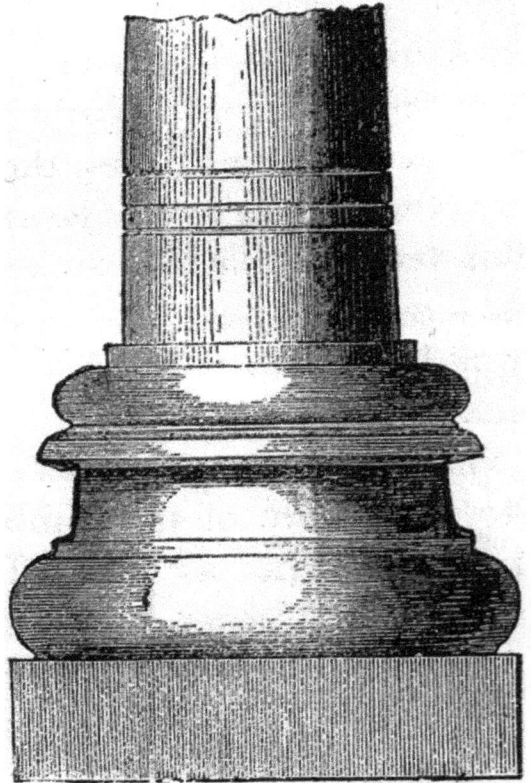

Base of Column, Jerusalem

If, however, Josephus is to be accepted as a witness of any value on Essene doctrine, all these theories as to where it originated must be cast aside, for he says expressly that it resembled the opinions of the Greeks. And as a matter of fact, the Pythagoreans who existed in Greece long before the rise of the Essenes, present so many parallels with them that it is impossible to ascribe these resemblances to mere fortuitous coincidence. Both the Essenes and the Pythagoreans held exactly the same views as to the true ideal of life, and both adopted almost exactly the same practices in order to attain it. The Pythagoreans, like the Essenes, neither offered sacrifice nor confirmed their assertions with an oath. They had the same horror of impurity, they had the same love of ablutions, they held almost the same ideas on the superior sanctity of celibacy, and cherished the same beliefs on the subject of the soul. Add to this the immense sway which Greek thought in general exercised in Palestine from the days of Alexander, and it is hardly possible to resist the conclusion that the extraneous influences which permeated Essenism had their home in Greece.

If, however, all those statements of Josephus in which he brings out the close relationship between Essenism and certain phases of Greek thought are unworthy of credit, there remains the opinion entertained by a number of eminent scholars, that the Essenes are an unadulterated product of Palestinian Judaism. On the supposition that Josephus, in view of his Greek readers, distorted the Essene doctrine of the soul, it is not difficult to deduce all the other beliefs and practices of the order from the Old Testament and the Talmud. The Essene observance of the Sabbath, the honour paid to Moses, the dread of contracting uncleanness, are all purely Jewish. The white garments worn by the order, the common meal, and the tendency towards celibacy, have all a basis in the customs of the Jewish priesthood. In the same way, the bath before meals and the zeal for purity which drove the Essenes from the world are simply exaggerations of the Pharisaic practice of washing the hands before food, and of the Pharisaic spirit of exclusiveness. In fact, it is not necessary to go outside the circle of Jewish ideas to find at least the germs of every Essene belief and practice with the sole exception of the doctrine of immortality. But whether Josephus totally misrepresented the Essene view of this doctrine, or whether there is a substratum of truth in what he says respecting it, has not as yet been satisfactorily solved one way or the other. So long as this question remains open it will be impossible to say whether Essenism is a plant of indigenous growth, or whether a number of its roots are fixed in foreign soil.

It is not so difficult to arrive at a positive conclusion with respect to the alleged original connection between Christianity and Essenism. On certain subjects, such as the rejection of oaths, the blessings of poverty, and the danger of riches, there is a resemblance between the teachings of Jesus and Essene doctrine. But these similarities sink into insignificance, and lose almost all value when compared with the vast gulf which divides Jesus from the Essenes in matters of fundamental importance. The profound antagonism which Jesus manifested towards the Pharisees as to the nature of the Sabbath extended of necessity to the Essenes as well. The difference between Jesus and the Essenes on ceremonial cleanness is a difference of principle. Ceremonial purity was a chief cornerstone of the Essene system, it was a matter of no moment with Jesus. The only form of purity which He taught was purity of heart. The Essenes fled the world, Jesus freely mingled in it; the Essenes could only consort with members of their own order, Jesus stooped down to meet the outcast, the publican, and the sinner. In Essenism there is no trace of the proselytizing spirit so characteristic of Christianity. On the contrary, the Essenes, instead of trying to seek and to save that which was lost, appear to have been satisfied with life in a small monastic community.

As has been truly said, the agreement between Essenism and Christianity is in details of secondary importance, the difference is one of principle.

The People

Under Roman rule, Palestine was inhabited by a mixed population. Judaea was the only province in which the great mass of the people was purely Jewish. Jerusalem and the surrounding district were peopled by the descendants of the Babylonian exiles, and the hatred which was cherished against foreigners in this region resulted in its being left exclusively in the hands of the Jews. Outside Judaea, and throughout the rest of Palestine, the population consisted of Jews, Syrians, and Greeks. The Syrians belonged to the same race as the Jews, and had always retained a footing in the Holy Land; the Greeks entered it as colonists after the conquest of the East by Alexander the Great. In all the towns along the coast of the Mediterranean, with the doubtful exceptions of Jamnia and Joppa, which were partially Judaized by the Maccabaeans, a Gentile population preponderated. At no period of their history had the Jews been able to gain a permanent footing on the seacoast of Palestine, and the settlement of Jewish colonists in the towns of Raphia, Gaza, Anthedon, Ascalon, Azotus, Appolonia, Caesarea, Dora, and Ptolemais, dates from the time of the Greek invasion of the East. Some of these towns were important centres of commerce and industry, and in them the Jew was able to gratify his trading instincts while remaining on the sacred soil of Palestine.

Passing from the seacoast to the interior of Palestine, we find the northern province of Galilee was bounded on the west and north by the Gentile populations belonging to the districts of Ptolemais and Tyre. On the east it was separated by the Jordan and the Sea of Galilee from Gaulanitis, Batanaea, and Trachonitis, the population of which was composed partly of Jews, partly of Syrians, and partly of nomadic hordes. These nomads were hardly within the pale of civilization. They made the almost impregnable caves of the Trachonitis their refuge and home. Sallying forth from their natural fastnesses among the rocks, they preyed upon the surrounding country, and Herod had to settle warlike colonists among them from Babylon and Idumaea, in order to keep them down. After Herod's death the Trachonitis relapsed into its old anarchic state, and one of his successors complained that the people of this region were living the life of wild beasts. The settled population of Gaulanitis and Batanaea was more Gentile than Jewish, and the towns of Caesarea Panias, and Julias, or Bethsaida, were mainly inhabited by the heathen. Caesarea Panias was situated at the sources of the Jordan, and was famous for its celebrated grotto of the Greek god, Pan. It had been a Hellenic town several centuries before the birth of Christ; in it Herod the Great built a temple to Augustus, and his son Philip raised it to a position of some importance among the cities of his tetrarchy. Julias also owed its rise to Philip. It was formerly known as Bethsaida, but Philip in honour of his imperial patron's daughter changed its name to Julias, and it henceforth became a Hellenic town.

On the south, Galilee was separated from Judaea by the province of Samaria. In spite of the intense hatred which existed between the Jews and the people of Samaria the Jews refrained from classing the Samaritans among the heathen. This was owing to the fact that a certain portion of the inhabitants of the province adhered to the Mosaic code; and although they rejected all the other books of the canon, and considered their own sanctuary on Mount Gerizim quite as sacred as the Temple at Jerusalem, the orthodox Jews continued to regard the Samaritans as being to some extent brethren in the faith. Side by side with this heterodox Judaism a great deal of heathenism also existed in Samaria, for the province contained a large Gentile population. Sebaste, the capital of Samaria, was a Gentile town, and it is probable that many of the colonists who came from Babylon to Samaria after the fall of the old Israelitish monarchy only partially adopted the religion of the land. Alexander the Great settled Greek colonists in the province, and from his days till the conquest of Samaria by the Maccabees, Greek civilization must have exercised a powerful influence on the inhabitants. The old city of Samaria was destroyed by the sons of John Hyrcanus (circa 107 B.C.); Herod rebuilt it, and under the new name of Sebaste it became one of the most important towns of Palestine.

It will thus be seen that Galilee was surrounded on all sides by a population which was more Gentile than Jewish, and a strong Gentile element was to be found in the province itself. So much was this the case that it was called Galilee of the Gentiles. The two most important cities of the province, Tiberias and Sepphoris, were practically Hellenic centres. In the country districts and the smaller towns, such as Nazareth, Cana, Dalmanutha, Magdala, it is probable that the Jews were in the majority.

A number of important Hellenic towns, situated with the exception of Scythopolis on the eastern banks of the Jordan, were formed probably by Pompey into an independent confederation, which became known as the Decapolis, or Ten Cities. On the downfall of the Syrian monarchy these cities fell into the hands of the Jews, but most of them contained a Gentile population, and bore Greek names. The towns of the Decapolis were Damascus, Philadelphia, Raphana, Scythopolis, Gadara, Hippus, Dion, Pella, Gerasa, and Canatha, and the citizens were to a great extent composed of Greeks who emigrated into Syria on the establishment of Greek supremacy in this quarter of the world.

Southwest of the Decapolis lay the province of Peraea, a narrow strip of territory running along the eastern banks of the Jordan. Peraea extended from Pella in the north to the fortress of Machaerus on the shores of the Dead Sea; it was bounded on the east by the Decapol is and the territory of the Nabataeans. Very little is known respecting the population of Peraea, but there is every reason to believe that it contained the same mixture of Jews and Gentiles as existed in most of the other parts of Palestine.

In Roman times, the Hellenic towns of Palestine were quite independent of Jerusalem, as well as of each other. They all acknowledged the supremacy of Rome, either in the person of the Herods or of the Roman procurators, and they all contributed so much annually to the Herods or to the imperial exchequer. Beyond these things they were left as much as possible to manage their own affairs in their own way. Every town of any note was the centre of a certain district, which varied in extent after the manner of our English counties. All the internal affairs of the district were under the control of a representative council, consisting in some cases of several hundred members. In name some of these councils possessed more authority than others, but in practice it was possible for all of them to conduct the business of the district with little or no interference from the imperial officials. It was, however, very seldom that they succeeded in doing this owing to the antagonism of rival factions within the communes. In Caesarea the Jews enjoyed equal civic rights with the Gentiles, and the same privileges were probably accorded them in such cities as Tiberias and Sepphoris. In Samaria, in the Decapolis, and in the older Gentile cities along the seacoast, it is hardly likely that the Jews were admitted to all the privileges of citizenship. The management of internal affairs in Jerusalem was entirely in Jewish hands, and a similar state of things no doubt existed in the Jewish portions of Galilee and Peraea.

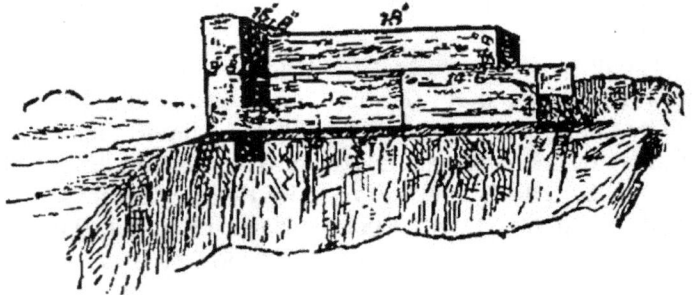

Latin Stone Altar

In the Hellenic cities of Palestine, Greek polytheism did not succeed in extirpating the indigenous forms of faith, and the temples of Semitic gods and goddesses existed side by side with the sanctuaries of Greek divinities. This was more especially the case in the towns along the coast, and the original inhabitants of such places as Gaza, Ascalon, and Azotus, did not desert the shrines of their local deities. But in other departments of life, Greek influence was supreme, and in some parts of Palestine, Greek literature was cultivated with a fair amount of success. One of Cicero's teachers, Antiochus, an eclectic philosopher, was a native of Ascalon. The emperor Tiberius was taught by the Syro-Grecian Theodorus of Gadara; this town also produced Meleager, who may be called the father of the Greek anthology. As a rule the Syro-Grecian was a light and mocking spirit, and excelled as a musician, jockey, juggler, and buffoon. He was a corrupt and degraded creature, and exercised a very pernicious influence on the morality of the empire.

These defects of character, however, did not prevent him from being an excellent and successful trader. He carried on business operations throughout the Roman world; and Syria was justly celebrated for its linen, purple, silk, and glass. Galilee was an important seat of the linen industry, and the linen products of Scythopolis commanded the highest prices in the Roman markets. Ascalon and Gaza were celebrated commercial ports, and Caesarea possessed a harbour which rivaled the ancient quays of Tyre.

It was impossible for the purely Jewish population to escape the multitude of Greek influences by which they were surrounded, and the effects of Greek civilization are to be found in nearly every phase of Jewish life. The Temple of Jerusalem was mainly constructed in the Greek style, and most of the public buildings were built in accordance with Greek architectural designs. Religious feeling prevented Greek painting and sculpture from being tolerated in the Jewish parts of Palestine; but the Book of Daniel refers to Greek musical instruments, and it is not improbable that Greek music was common among the Jews. Roman, Greek, and Phoenician coins were the current money of the realm, and the Gospels are not wanting in allusions to the coinage of Rome. The amusements of the people were largely derived from Greece, and Greek games were celebrated in most of the chief towns of Palestine. Even at Jerusalem there were chariot races, con-

Clay Image Found at Gezer, Samaria

tests with wild beasts, running, wrestling, and boxing, just as if the centre of Judaism had been a purely Greek city. Jericho possessed a theatre, a hippodrome, and an amphitheatre, and in other parts of the Holy Land buildings of a similar description were to be seen. The rabbis, it is true, were hostile to these heathen forms of amusement, but their denunciations were only heeded by a comparatively narrow circle; the Greek games offered an irresistible attraction to the great mass of the populace.

Except among the learned, Hebrew had become extinct as a living tongue, and in the time of Christ the language in general use was Aramaic. But traders and the higher classes also understood Greek, and a vast number of Greek words had found their way into common use. Greek names were very frequently employed for money, weights and measures. It was the same in civil, military, and legal affairs. Many commercial terms were also Greek, and

Greek words had even come to be used for food, clothing, and household furniture. Among the ruling classes it was very usual to call children by Greek names, such as Alexander, Aristobulus, Philip, and so forth. The Greek names, Andrew and Philip, also occur among the disciples of Christ, which would lead us to believe that Greek names for persons were being adopted by all classes of the community. Greek had become the mother tongue of nearly all the Jews who lived in the West, and the vast multitudes of them who came as pilgrims to Jerusalem must have fostered the spread of Hellenism in the Holy City and in other parts of the land as well.

It does not appear, however, that the Jews of Palestine were drawn like their brethren of the Dispersion into the fascinating toils of Greek speculation. In Palestine, the action of Hellenism upon the Jewish population was almost entirely confined to the secular side of life. The Palestinian rabbi regarded Greek philosophy with suspicion; he had no taste for that ingenious harmonizing of Greek and Hebrew thought which was so ardently cultivated by the Jews of Alexandria; he had an inward conviction that Greek wisdom was inimical to the Law, and did his utmost to suppress its growth. The diffusion of Greek ideas among the masses would undoubtedly have destroyed the belief that the Jews held of Jehovah as a tribal God; it would have shattered their faith in the multitudinous ordinances of the Law, and it would have reduced them in their own eyes to a position of simple equality among the other races of mankind. But the tendencies of Greek thought were not as the rabbis imagined in the direction of polytheism. On the contrary, the Greek philosophers were busily engaged in dissolving the old polytheistic conceptions of antiquity. They were slowly feeling their way towards the monotheistic conclusions of the Jews, and would ultimately have arrived at a lofty idea of the Divine attributes, even if Judaism had not existed. Nor was the dissatisfaction with the gods of Olympus confined to the schools of the philosophers; it had penetrated all ranks and conditions of ancient society. So much was this the case that it was a very common occurrence for Gentiles who had ceased to believe in polytheism to embrace the faith of the Jews. "Many of them," says Josephus, "have agreed to submit themselves to our laws." And again: "For a long time back great zeal for our religion has laid hold upon multitudes; nor is there any city of the Greeks, or indeed any city at all, even though barbarian, where the observance of the seventh day, on which we rest from toil, has not made its way, and where the fasts and lamp-lightings and many of our prohibitions as to food are not observed.... As God penetrates the whole world, so the Law has made its way amongst all men." These pious Gentiles are frequently mentioned in the New Testament, and it was from their ranks that a large proportion of the early Christians was drawn.

Unfortunately, the rabbis of Palestine did not grasp the significance of the momentous change which was coming over the religious consciousness of the ancient world. At the very time that Greece was growing weary of her gods, and was feeling after a higher form of faith, at that very time the rabbis

158

were busily inculcating amongst the people of Palestine an intenser hatred of the Gentiles and all their works. According to their teaching, it was an act of disobedience to the Law to hold any intercourse whatever with the Gentiles. It defiled a Jew to sit with them at table or to enter under their roof. It was even asserted that the Gentiles had lost the nature of men and only retained the instincts of the beasts. All knowledge of God was denied them; they were God's enemies, and when they made inquiries of a Jew respecting Divine things it was his duty to answer them with a suppressed curse. According to Jewish ideas, all Gentiles were base born, and all their women were unclean. To marry a Gentile woman was a heinous offence; the children of such an alliance were bastards, and had no part in the inheritance of Israel. It was forbidden to counsel or befriend a Gentile, and the benefits conferred by a Gentile on a Jew were in reality no better than serpents' poison. The growing hatred of the Gentiles is seen in the question which was raised in the time of Christ as to the lawfulness of paying tribute to Rome. When the Jews had to pay tribute to the Greek monarchs no heart-searchings on this matter had arisen among them. These new qualms of conscience were the outcome of a more furious antipathy to the Gentile world.

A bitter feeling of resentment was aroused throughout the Roman Empire by the irreconcilable attitude of the Jews towards the rest of mankind. Cicero speaks of them as a nation born for servitude, and stigmatizes their religion as a barbarous superstition. Seneca despises them as a wretched and criminal people, and Tacitus says with some truth that the Jews had made themselves notorious by their hatred of the human race. Juvenal falls into many absurd mistakes regarding the tenets of Judaism, but he certainly does not misconceive the tendency of much contemporary rabbinic teaching when he says, that the Jews would point out the way to no one but their own fellow-believers." The practice of denouncing Gentiles as unfit to be associated with, was sufficient in itself to make the Jews detested, and was utterly opposed to the humane sentiments of national brotherhood which were taking root in the ancient world. "The Jews," says Appolonius of Tyana, "have for a long time fallen away, not only from the Romans, but from all mankind; for a people that devises an anti-social life, ...is further apart from us than Susa or Bactria, or the still more distant inhabitants of India." The contempt which the Jews brought upon themselves by their separatist customs is also expressed by Appolonius in a conversation which he is said to have held with Vespasian on the Jewish war. "If," said he, "someone came from the seat of war, and announced that thirty thousand Jews had fallen through you, and in the next battle that fifty thousand had fallen, I took the narrator aside and intentionally asked him what he was thinking of, that he had nothing more important to say than this."'

The Messianic Hope

In a preceding chapter we have seen how bitterly Roman domination was hated by the great mass of the Jewish population of Palestine. Administrative oppression has often been set down as the cause of this state of hatred, but it would be more accurate to say that it arose out of the religious convictions of the Jews. It is no doubt easy to point out several instances of harshness in the attitude of the Roman conquerors, but it is also necessary to remember that the Roman officials in many cases showed an unwonted consideration for the susceptibilities of the vassal state. Till the outbreak of the insurrection, which terminated in the destruction of Jerusalem, the Jews suffered far less from internal disorder under Roman rule than in almost any previous period of their national history, and they enjoyed at the same time a greater share of local liberty than had ever fallen to their lot in the flower of the Maccabaean age.

What lay at the root of their detestation of Roman supremacy was not so much its oppressiveness; it consisted in a religious feeling that it was an intolerable sacrilege for Gentile outcasts to pollute the Holy Land, and exercise lordship over the chosen people of Jehovah. As the hatred of the Romans arose from religious rather than political causes, so did the hope of purging the Holy Land of its heathen desecrators have its roots in religious rather than political soil. The futile attempts which had been made at revolt tended to confirm the belief, that the deliverance of Israel was not to be effected by natural but by supernatural means. The hope of being ultimately rescued from Roman rule was based upon the belief that the Jews were Jehovah's chosen race. He had selected theme as His peculiar people from among all the families of the earth. He had entered into a covenant with them, and had solemnly promised them a glorious future if they held aloof from the abominations of the heathen, and remained steadfastly faithful to Him. It was impossible for God to break His word. What was needed was patience. The Gentile domination was only transitory. It was to be looked upon, said many, as a punishment for the Gentile habits of the Sadducees. But the people had almost expiated the sins of their leaders. The end was at hand; the brilliant promises of God would soon be fulfilled. The stranger would be trodden down; Israel would be consoled, and the Messianic kingdom with its centre at Jerusalem would suddenly burst upon the world.

Many traces of a belief in a near approach of the Messianic reign are to be found in the New Testament documents. Simeon believed that he should not taste of death till he had seen the Lord's anointed. Joseph of Arimathea is mentioned as one of those who was waiting for the kingdom of God. Many were inclined to believe that John the Baptist was the promised Messiah, and the nature of the Messianic belief is clearly set forth in the words of disappointment uttered by Christ's disciples after their Master's crucifixion, "we trusted that it had been He which should have redeemed Israel." Among all sections of the multitude the attitude of expectation had risen to a feverish height. Many like the Zealots had waited till they could wait no longer; they took up arms in the conviction that the Messianic era would be hastened, when God saw His people making heroic efforts to deliver themselves.

It will now be our object to look a little more closely at the full scope of the Messianic expectation. While doing so we shall have to bear in mind that this hope did not exist in the popular imagination as a rigidly defined dogma: It was equally permissible to accord it the most colossal proportions, or to hold it with the relative sobriety of the ancient prophets. Still the prevailing tendency of Judaism was to enlarge the dimensions of its glorious expectations, and to embrace the Messianic belief in its most supernatural and transcendent forms.

The current conceptions of the Messianic age are very well reflected in the popular apocalyptic literature of the first century. All of these writings taught the multitude to believe that the day of deliverance was to be preceded by a period of wickedness, calamities, and portents, of the most astounding kind. Religion, it was believed, should fall into decay. Truth and faith should fail and hope should be deceived. At that time fools should increase and the numbers of the wise be brought low. A sudden thirst for wealth should spring up and be accompanied by deeds of robbery and impurity and every evil work. It was also supposed that the peace of the home would be destroyed. Children were to rise up against their parents and parents against their children. In society there was to be an equally fearful outbreak of anarchy and hate, in which the whole social organism would be overturned. "The mean man shall lord it over the honourable, and the petty shall be exalted over the glorious, and the many shall be delivered to the few, and those who were nothing shall lord it over the powerful, and the poor shall abound over the rich, and the impious shall be exalted above heroes, and the wise shall be silent and fools shall speak."

In addition to all these disorders there was to be a terrible outbreak of war, famine, and pestilence; so much so that the dead would lie unburied and be mangled by birds and beasts of prey. Many even conceived that the whole order of nature was to be thrown into confusion as a sign that the Messianic advent was nigh at hand. Bitter water was to become sweet, earthquakes were to shake the solid frame of things; the stars were to forsake their courses; the order of the two great luminaries was to be reversed the moon was to shine by day and the sun by night. According to other predictions, the sun was to suffer eclipse, and those who were looking up for the consolation of Israel should witness terrific battles taking place between horsemen and footmen in the clouds.

As the Messiah could not possibly appear in the midst of such a chaos, it was currently believed that the prophet Elijah should precede him, in order to repair the ruin and disorder into which all things had fallen. The reason why Elijah was so closely connected in the popular mind with this great task is no doubt to be attributed to the belief that he did not share the fate of mortal men by descending into the grave, but was among the select few who were admitted into the abode of the Most High. His work, according to a Jewish tradition, was to be accomplished in the short space of three days, and at the end of that time the Messiah Himself, immediately preceded by Moses, Enoch, and Jeremiah, was to appear.

Before proceeding to describe the Messiah's work it may be as well at this point to consider what were the prevalent conceptions respecting His nature and attributes. It was believed by many that He pre-existed in a state of heavenly bliss before He entered upon His functions in the world. Some understood this pre-existence to mean nothing more than an ideal existence in the purposes of the Divine will, but others believed that it was a real existence, similar in nature to the life of the angels. In the Similitudes in the Book of Enoch, it is said of Him that He was chosen and hid with God before the world, and shall be before Him unto eternity. His countenance is as the appearance of a man, and full of grace like that of the holy angels. But the pre-existence of the Messiah in a heavenly state was not deemed incompatible with a full belief in His humanity. We all expect, says the Jew Trypho, in Justin Martyr's Dialogues, that the Christ will be born as a man from men. His birth was expected to take place either at Jerusalem or Bethlehem, He was to be a descendant of the house of David, He was to be gifted with power and righteousness and wisdom, but He was to live obscurely among the sons of men, in ignorance of His great destiny, till the time came when He should be anointed by Elijah the prophet.

Immediately the Messiah officially appeared, although no one knew whence He came, He was to be opposed by the hostile forces of the heathen, "an innumerable multitude of men assembled from the four winds of heaven." "And it shall come to pass when all nations have heard His voice, each will leave in its own region the war which they have against one another; and there shall be assembled together an innumerable multitude, as thou didst see wishing to come to take Him by storm." The battle between Messiah and His enemies was to take place around Mount Zion, and Ezra in a vision is made to describe the awful nature of the contest. The Messiah "did not lift His hand nor hold a spear or any implement of war, but...He sent out of His mouth as it were a wave of fire, and from His lips spirits of flame, and from His tongue He emitted sparks of tempest; and all these were mingled together, waves of fire and spirits of flame and a multitude of tempest. And He fell upon the multitude which was ready for the assault, and burned them all, so that suddenly nothing was perceived of the innumerable multitude, save only dust of ashes and an odour of smoke." According to the Apocalypse of Baruch the armies of the heathen were to be headed by a leader corresponding to the Antichrist of the New Testament. After the destruction of his forces the servants of the Messiah were to bring him bound to Mount Zion, where he was to be put to death.

In the Jewish imagination of the first century the overthrow of the heathen was looked upon as an indispensable preliminary to the establishment of the Messianic kingdom. The great kingdoms of the Gentiles which had come into existence before the Messianic age were mere kingdoms of the world, but the rule which the Messiah was to inaugurate should be the reign of God on earth, and the kingdom should be known as the kingdom of God, or, in other words, as the kingdom of heaven. The Messiah as the direct representative of God among men should stand at the head of this new dominion, and regulate it in accordance with the decrees of the Most High. The scope of the old kingdoms of Israel was mainly limited to the Holy Land; the Messianic kingdom was to take a wider sweep, embracing in its mighty circumference the whole extent of the habitable globe. In the language of the most widely-read prophet of the time, it would extend "over all peoples, nations, and languages," and the Book of Enoch expresses the same thought by figuratively saying that the Messianic kingdom shall include "all the beasts of the earth and all the birds of heaven."

Jerusalem was to be the capital of this world-wide dominion. The city as it stood, it was believed by some, would be elevated to a proud position of political grandeur, and purified by the exclusion of the Gentiles. But this conception was to many minds too tame. The old Jerusalem of pre-Messianic times would perish in the flames, and a supernatural city the new Jerusalem should descend upon Mount Zion from the clouds of heaven. Before Adam's fall this heavenly city had existed in the earthly paradise in which God had placed the first parents of mankind. But after the fatal disobedience of man, the holy city was lifted up into heaven, where it was destined to remain, along with many other treasures, till the advent of the Messianic reign. In the meantime, however, some select spirits, such as Abraham and Moses, had been permitted to gaze for a moment on its celestial glories. "I showed it to my servant Abraham by night between the divisions of the victims. And again I also showed it to Moses on Mount Sinai, when I showed him the image of the tabernacle and all its vessels." The buildings in the new Jerusalem were to be adorned in the most brilliant manner with precious stones, and it was to exceed in size and splendour the most magnificent cities of the world.

In the Messianic era, not only the Jews of Palestine, but the whole of the elect people scattered throughout the world would share in the blessings of this glorious time. The ten tribes which had been carried away captive were to be led back to the Holy Land, and all the Israelites dispersed among the nations were to return to their original home. "I will assemble them all out of the midst of the Gentiles." Even those who had died before the advent of the Messiah were not to be forgotten. They were to be raised from their graves, so as to taste of the delights which would then be showered upon mankind.

Opinions were divided as to the position which the Gentiles should occupy in the Messianic kingdom. Many believed that they would be put under the yoke, and that Israel would tread on their neck. But others thought that in those days the whole heathen world would be converted, that all their eyes would be opened to see what was good, and that the immortal God would rule the world according to one Divine law.

In the expectation of the Jews the Messianic era corresponded in many particulars to the golden age of which the poets of antiquity loved to sing. It was to be a period when nature should display a truly miraculous fruitfulness. At that time manna shall again descend from heaven and the air be filled with fragrant odours. Abundance of wheat and wine and olives shall spring from the fruitful earth. Milk, oil, and honey shall always be plenteous in the homes of men. Multitudes of sheep and oxen shall pasture on the luxuriant grass. The vine which is planted in the earth "shall bear fruit in abundance and of every seed that is sown in it shall one measure bear ten thousand and one measure of olives shall produce presses of oil." "In one vine shall be a thousand branches, and one branch shall produce a thousand bunches and one bunch shall produce a thousand grapes." In that golden era the wild beasts shall lose their ferocity and submit themselves to man. The wolf and the lamb shall eat grass together on the mountains, serpents, scorpions, and other noxious reptiles shall lose their fangs, and carnivorous beasts shall change their nature and pasture like oxen in the fields.

The peace which shall then come over the face of nature shall also be manifested among men. Neither war nor the sound of battle shall vex the earth, and kings shall live in harmony with one another till the end of time. "And judgments and accusations and contentions, and vengeance and blood and passions, and envy and hatred, and whatsoever things are like these, shall go away into condemnation when they have been removed. For these are the things that have filled the world with evils, and on account of these things the life of men has been greatly disturbed." Health and length of days shall follow in the train of peace. "Health shall descend like dew, infirmity shall retire, and anxiety and distress and groaning shall pass away from men." "The children of men shall become older from generation to generation, and from day to day till their lifetime approaches a thousand years. And there shall be none old or weary of life, but they shall all be like children and boys, and shall finish all their days in peace and gladness, and shall live without a Satan or any other evil destroyer being present; for all their days shall be days of blessing and healing." "No man shall die prematurely or without having fulfilled the legitimate end of his being among those men who observe the laws, nor shall such fail to reach the age which God has allotted to the race of man. But the human being proceeding upwards from childhood as it were by the different stages of a ladder, and at the appointed periods of time fulfilling the regularly determined boundaries of each age, will eventually arrive at the last of all, that which is near to death or rather to immortality; being really and truly happy in his old age, leaving behind him a house happy in numerous and virtuous children in his own place.

Many of the Jews believed that the Messianic kingdom would endure forever. This belief was based on the utterances of Old Testament prophecy, and was no doubt greatly popularized in the time of Christ by the saying of Daniel, "His dominion is an everlasting dominion which shall not pass away, and His kingdom that which shall not be destroyed." A similar conviction is expressed in the Sibylline Books, the Psalms of Solomon, and the Book of Jubilees. In the last-mentioned work the following promise is made to Jacob respecting the duration of the Messianic kingdom, "To thy seed will I give the whole earth which is under heaven, and they shall rule as they please over all peoples, and accordingly they shall draw the whole earth to themselves and inherit it forever." How widely spread was the idea of the eternal nature of the Messianic reign is fully seen in the Gospel of St. John, where the people say, "We have heard out of the Law that Christ abideth forever." Side by side with these conceptions there also existed another current of thought which limited the Messianic kingdom to a certain number of years. Some believed it would last till this world of corruption came to an end, but did not venture to predict when that end would be. Others were more definite. On the supposition that a thousand years is reckoned by God as one day, many believed that the Messianic kingdom should endure a thousand years. The calculation of others was based on the time spent by Israel in Egypt, and this limited the Messiah's reign to four hundred years, after which it was supposed that he and all men should die. One rabbi said that the kingdom would last forty years, the time assigned to Israel's wanderings in the wilderness, and another, supporting himself by a passage in Isaiah, was equally confident that this glorious epoch would continue seventy years. But when the Messianic reign came to a termination, all agreed that it would be followed by a general resurrection of the dead and the pronouncing of a final judgment upon men.

It was under the inspiration of these astounding visions, and in order, as they imagined to realize them, that the Jews persisted with such blind tenacity in their hopeless conflict with Rome.

The Jews Abroad

While under Roman domination Palestine possessed an importance altogether out of proportion either to the size of its territory, the number of its inhabitants, or even to the fact of its being a great military highway between Asia Minor and Northeastern Africa. It acquired this position of importance in consequence of the large Jewish population which at that time existed in all the great commercial centres of the ancient world. The number of Jews outside Palestine was probably greater than the population of Palestine itself. These emigrants, Jews of the Dispersion as they were called, often rich and influential as well as numerous, were capable of making their power felt in the courts of emperors and kings. All the Jews, scattered up and down the Persian and Roman Empires, continued to retain a profound affection for the Holy Land. Jerusalem was the common centre of the race; the Temple on

Mount Sion was the visible symbol of their common faith; the decrees of the Sanhedrin were recognized as binding upon all, and the Temple tax paid by Jews of all ranks and conditions of life, in all parts of the world, impressed them with the consciousness of their national unity. At this epoch, religious and patriotic feelings were indissolubly blended together; they were also kept alive by pilgrimages to the home of their fathers and the sanctuary of their God. Many disintegrating forces were at work in the first century of our era to break up the unity of the Jewish race. Among the educated in the West, Greek thought had undermined the ancient basis of their faith, and almost the only thing they had in common with the fanatical population of Judaea was an outward adhesion to its external forms. The Jews, both in Palestine and abroad, had ceased to speak the language of their sacred books, and when coming to Jerusalem as pilgrims they were unable to understand each other, and found themselves in a city containing a Babel of tongues. But notwithstanding these discordant and repelling influences, the Jews clung steadfastly to one another, and in face of opposition from the Gentile world they felt and acted as one. It was this intense cohesion of the Jewish race which made Palestine so formidable to the Roman conquerors.

The existence of these powerful Jewish communities in different parts of the world is attributable to various causes. After the breakup of the old Israelitish kingdom, a great number of Jews were forcibly deported from Palestine, and many of them never returned. When Palestine fell into the hands of Alexander the Great and his marshals, this event was followed by emigration from Judaea on an extensive scale. It was part of the policy of these rulers to found new cities, and to bring about the amalgamation of the mixed nationalities over whom they ruled. All the inhabitants of these new cities were accorded equal rights and privileges. The Jews largely availed themselves of these advantages, and in the first century of the present era all the commercial centres of Northern Africa, the East of Europe, and Western Asia were thronged with Jewish traders and merchants. In this way," says Philo, "Jerusalem became the capital, not only of Judaea, but of many other lands, on account of the colonies which it sent out from time to time into the bordering districts of Egypt, Phoenicia, Syria, Coelo-Syria, and into the more distant regions of Pamphylia Cilicia, the greater part of Asia Minor as far as Bithynia, and the remotest corners of Pontus. And in like manner into Europe; into Thessaly, and Boeotia, and Macedonia, and Aetolia, and Attica, and Argos, and Corinth, and into the most fertile and fairest parts of the Peloponnesus. And not only is the continent full of Jewish colonists, but also the most important islands, such as Euboea, Cyprus, and Crete. I say nothing of the countries beyond the Euphrates. All of them, except a very small portion, and Babylon, and all the satrapies which contain fruitful land, have Jewish inhabitants." The incorporation of Palestine into the Roman commonwealth by Pompey had also a powerful effect in increasing the numbers of the Dispersion. Not only did the conqueror carry off many Jewish captives to Rome itself, but the result of his conquest was to open up the vast dominions of the empire to the Jewish trader, and henceforth Jewish colonies began to spring up and multiply in the West of Europe. Thus it came to pass that, partly by forcible deportation, and partly by voluntary emigration, every land and every sea, as the "Sibylline Oracles" say, was filled with Jews.

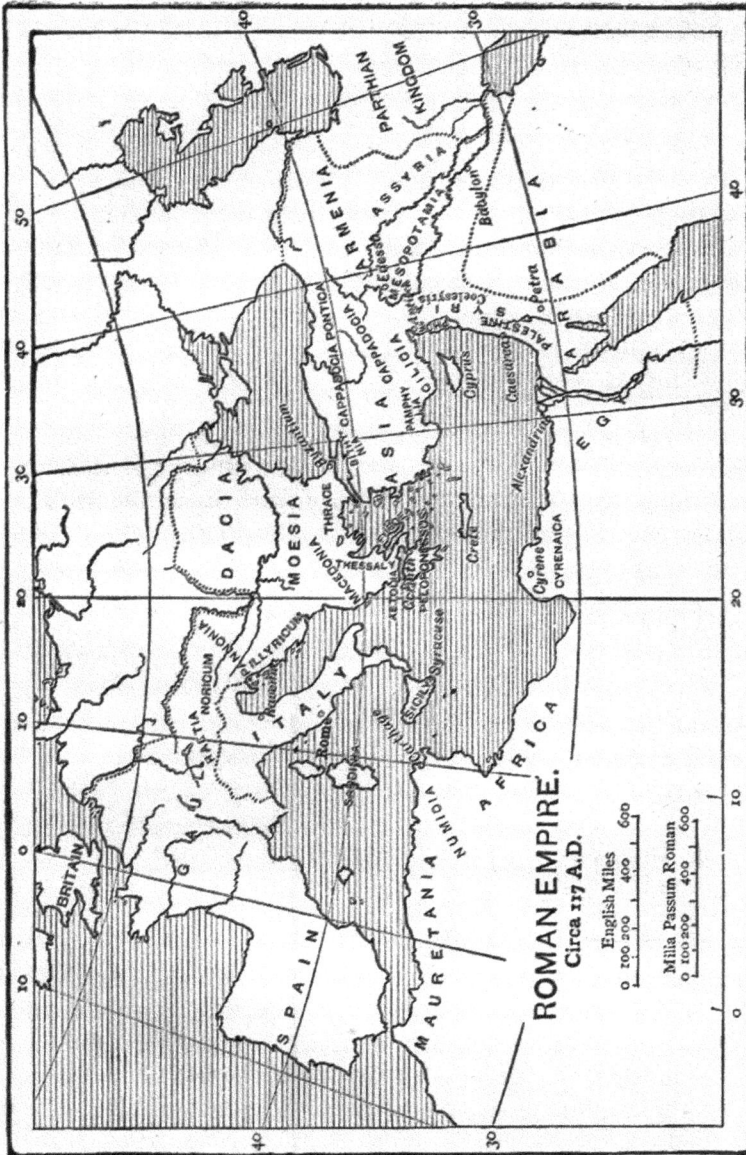

Map of the Roman Empire

We are informed by Josephus that, in Babylonia and Mesopotamia, the Jewish population was not to be counted by thousands, but by millions. There is nothing remarkable in this statement when it is remembered that only members of the tribes of Judah and Benjamin returned to Jerusalem after the days of captivity had come to an end. Most of these Eastern Jews dwelt in and around the fortified cities of Naarda and Nisibis in Mesopotamia. So powerful were they that the Romans deemed it prudent not to provoke their enmity, and they constituted a serious danger to Trajan in his campaign against the Parthians. But the Jews were even more numerous in Syria than in the regions watered by the Tigris and the Euphrates. At the time of the great war with Rome from ten to eighteen thousand Jews were massacred in Damascus alone. An immense Jewish population inhabited Antioch, the Syrian capital, and Jewish colonies were thickly planted in other parts of the country. In Antioch they possessed full civil rights, and the great splendour of their synagogue in that city was an outward token of their material prosperity. The provinces of Asia Minor were also densely populated with Jews, and wherever Christian missionaries went they were certain to find Jewish synagogues and a Jewish community. In Bithynia, Phrygia, Lydia, and Pontus, there were Jewish settlements, and some of the Dispersion had even wandered as far as the Crimea.

In the first century Egypt contained a Jewish community numbering about a million souls. After the fall of the southern kingdom and the destruction of the first temple by Nebuchadnezzar, many Jews fled from Palestine to the valley of the Nile. When the great Macedonian conqueror founded Alexandria, in the fourth century before Christ, large numbers of Jews took up their abode in the new city, which was afterwards to become a rival in greatness to Athens and Rome. Two of the five quarters into which Alexandria was divided were chiefly inhabited by Jews. Here many of them rose to eminence as merchants, magistrates, poets, and philosophers, and the proud position which Alexandria occupied in the ancient world was in no small degree owing to the genius and ability of its Jewish inhabitants. The Jews in Egypt enjoyed equal rights with their Greek fellow-citizens, and continued to possess the favour of the Greek kings of Egypt till these monarchs finally passed away before the power of Rome. Under the new order of things the Jews were permitted to retain their ancient privileges, and Augustus, at the close of his successful struggle with Antony, rewarded them for their devotion to his cause. It has always been the misfortune of the Jews to arouse the hatred of the populations among whom they lived, and this was also the case at Alexandria. In the time of Caligula the animosity which existed between the Jewish and Gentile sections of the Alexandrian populace culminated in tumult and bloodshed. The Jews were driven out of every quarter of the city except one; their buildings and property were destroyed; Flaccus, the Roman viceroy, openly sided with the opponents of the Jews, and cast many of the most eminent Jewish citizens into prison. Caligula made this anarchial state of things still worse by ordering the Jews to erect his statue in their places of worship, and it was not till the accession of Claudius that the Jews regained their privileges and repose. Later on, in the reigns of Vespasian and Trajan, the Jews of Alexandria made common cause with other portions of their co-religionists who had revolted against Roman rule. On each occasion they were unsuccessful, and the insurrections in which they participated were drowned in blood.

Cyrene, another town in the north of Africa, contained many Jews, and there are traces of Jewish settlements all along the southern coasts of the Mediterranean. According to Josephus and the Acts of the Apostles there were Jews in Crete and Cyprus, and St. Paul in his wanderings found Jewish synagogues in all the important cities of Greece. Jewish inscriptions have been discovered in Athens, and Jewish colonists even dwelt in the small islands which are dotted over the Aegean Sea.

As may be imagined, such a migratory people flocked in large numbers to Rome itself No less than five Jewish cemeteries have been discovered on the site of ancient Rome, and some of them date back to the second century of the Christian era. Besides the Jewish captives taken to Rome by Pompey, most of whom were soon liberated on account of their peculiar customs, there must have been numbers who settled in the great capital of their own free-will. Roman Jews listened to the oratory of Cicero, and mourned over the corpse of Caesar. In the reign of Augustus eight thousand Roman Jews accompanied a deputation from Palestine to complain of the government of the country. Under the influence of Sejanus, Tiberius banished them from Rome, sending four thousand to Sardinia to suppress brigandage in that island. Josephus ascribes this action of the emperor to the fact that some Jewish impostors had succeeded in swindling a Roman matron named Fulvia who was favourably disposed towards Judaism. But it is more probable that he used this incident as a pretext for putting a stop to the proselytizing propaganda which the Jews at Rome were then prosecuting with so much success, especially among the female members of the Roman aristocracy. The measures of Tiberius, however, were not permanently successful, and Jews were once more established in their old quarter beyond the Tiber during the reign of the next emperor, Caligula. Claudius, his successor, issued an edict soon after his accession to the throne granting complete toleration to all Jews within his dominions, but he was afterwards compelled, on account of the tumultuous proceedings at their assemblies, to forbid them meeting together in the capital. Under succeeding emperors the Jews of Rome had sometimes to pass through periods of trial and persecution, but as a rule they only shared this fate with other subjects of the empire, and no record remains of any further attempts to drive them from the city.

What position before the law did the Jews occupy in the different provinces of the Roman Empire? In Rome itself some of them had acquired the coveted right of citizenship, and many of the provincial Jews were also Roman citizens. Jews who were Roman citizens are mentioned .as dwelling in Ephesus, Sardes, Delos, and other towns of Asia Minor. Some Jews of Jerusalem also possessed this honour; but it must have been of peculiar value to the Jewish population who lived outside Palestine, and were often exposed to the bitter animosity of the Gentiles. At times when religious and national antipathies ran high it would be difficult for the Jew who was not a Roman citizen to be sure of justice. Armed with this privilege he could if he chose have his case, whether it was civil or criminal, adjudicated upon by Roman judges. He had thus a reasonable assurance that his cause would be removed from the arena of passion and prejudice, and judged entirely upon its merits. A Jew in this favoured position had always the right of appeal to the imperial tribunal at Rome, and even if he were convicted by Roman magistrates of a criminal offence, he was exempted from the ignominious punishments of scourging and crucifixion.

Unless a Jew was a Roman citizen he only enjoyed the privileges accorded to a stranger in the ancient cities of the provinces. At Cyrene and Ephesus and a few towns on the Ionian coast the Jewish communities settled there had managed to obtain equal civil rights from their Macedonian rulers, but it was exceptional for Jews to possess these rights in cities founded before the conquests of Alexander the Great. It was part of the cosmopolitan policy of Alexander and his successors in Syria and Egypt to admit all the inhabitants of the new cities which sprang up after the Greek conquest of the East to equal rights and privileges. In this way the Jews of Alexandria and Antioch stood on a footing of perfect equality with their Greek fellow-citizens, and this state of things remained unaltered after these great capitals had come under the dominion of Rome. Under the delirious reign of Caligula the Alexandrian Jews were for a brief period deprived of their ancient civic status, but it was restored to them by Claudius immediately after his accession to the throne. It is also a remarkable instance of Roman respect for established usages that notwithstanding the rebellious disposition of the Jewish community in different parts of the empire, the Romans continued to allow the Jews to retain their civic privileges in all those cities where they originally possessed them. After the destruction of Jerusalem the inhabitants of Antioch conceived that a favourable moment had arrived for getting the Jews deprived of their ancient privileges. The Roman general was exasperated with the whole nation, nevertheless when the people of Antioch brought forward their petition Titus refused to accede to it.

In addition to their other privileges and immunities under Roman rule the Jews of the Dispersion also enjoyed the right of meeting together—a right which was frequently denied to the Romans themselves after the establishment of the empire. If worship in common at the synagogue was to exist at all it was indispensable that the Jews should have free permission to assemble on the Sabbath day. But this right of association was in many respects an immense concession on the part of Rome, and unless the empire had been extremely powerful it would have been attended with disastrous consequences. The distinction which the modern world draws between spiritual and patriotic interests hardly existed in ancient times. Among the Jews of the first century religion and the sentiment of nationality were indissolubly interfused; it was not a mere religious sect that the Romans were permitting to exist and associate for purposes of devotion; it was likewise the members of a nation which at that particular time cherished exalted visions of one day dominating the world. It is indubitable that these visions of world-wide empire for the Jewish race were frequently fanned by the teachings of the synagogue. Some of the Jewish insurrections which burst out in several parts of the empire with such uncontrollable and sanguinary fury are to be attributed to the abuse by the Jews of the right of association. Nowhere is it recorded that the Romans withdrew this privilege, much as they must have been tempted to do so by the turbulent conduct of the people who enjoyed it. On the contrary, Judaism, in spite of its dangerous tendencies towards the public peace, continued to be treated by the Romans in the words of Tertullian as a "religio licita"; it had a regular and valid legal status, and the favourable treatment which the Jews received in comparison with the Christians is attested by the fact that it was no uncommon thing for the latter in times of persecution to profess the Jewish faith.

The Jews of the Dispersion were also permitted by the Romans to establish tribunals of their own for adjudicating upon all matters pertaining to the welfare of the community. The Mosaic Law, with the innumerable traditions that had grown up around it, embraced every department of life; it was a civil as well as a religious code; all parts of it were equally binding upon the faithful Jew, and certain definite pains and penalties were attached to the transgression of its provisions. Over and above obedience to the law of the land the Jews were also amenable to their own law. The interpretation of this law required a special tribunal, and the Romans not only allowed this tribunal extensive powers, but also supported its decisions with the imperial executive. Some of the scourgings to which St. Paul was subjected were no doubt inflicted on him by order of Jewish tribunals. Being a Jew he was under the jurisdiction of the Jewish courts, and it was only in his capacity as a Roman citizen that he could appeal against their decisions. In all disputes in which only Jews were concerned, and in all matters relating to the internal organization of the sect, the Romans appear to have given the Jewish courts full powers of action. These powers included the right of fining, imprisonment, and scourging, but probably the Romans reserved to themselves among the Dispersion, as well as in Palestine, the authority to pronounce a sentence of death. Where Gentile interests were involved a Jewish tribunal was of course incompetent to act, and in all cases where a Jew became a disturber of the public peace he would be dealt with by the imperial authorities.

Finally, the Jews of the Dispersion were permitted by the Roman authorities to collect the Temple tax and transmit it to Jerusalem. The annual transmission of large sums of money to the Temple treasury was a serious grievance to many of the provincials, who considered that their cities were being impoverished by the loss of gold which the Temple tax entailed. It is certain that the Jews in several cities would not have been allowed to send the proceeds of this tax to the Holy City unless they had been under the tolerant rule of Roman law. As it was, the provincials of Cyrene and Asia Minor required to be warned by imperial decree not to interfere with the Jews in the matter of this tax, and one edict declared that to touch money dedicated to the Temple would be treated as robbery of the Temple itself. The Romans also respected Jewish susceptibilities on the subject of the Sabbath day. On that day a Jew could not be summoned to appear before an ordinary court of justice, and if the public distribution of money or corn happened to fall on the Sabbath, it was decreed by Augustus that the Jews should receive their portion on the following day. On account of the restrictions imposed on them by the Sabbath, the Jews were also exempted from military service in the legions.

Excepting Caligula, whose insistence on the cult of the Caesars was fatal to the fundamental principle of Judaism—the unity of God none of the emperors seriously interfered with the privileges of the Jews. Owing to a misunderstanding respecting the nature of circumcision, which was confounded with certain pernicious practices of mutilation, a law forbidding this rite came into operation in the reign of Hadrian. This law had the purification of morals as its object, and was not in the remotest degree aimed at religious belief, but it was naturally regarded by the Jews as a direct attack upon their faith. Antoninus Pius repealed the law in so far as it affected the children of Jewish parents; it only continued to remain in force against those citizens who were bent on embracing Judaism. In the reign of Severus it was made a penal offence to openly become a Jew, and some of the Christian emperors legislated in the same spirit. But all these measures were dictated by political considerations. The Romans learned from experience that the Jews were indifferent subjects; that they created a community within the community; that they lived in a state of perpetual friction with their non-Jewish fellow-citizens, and were ready to take up arms against the empire itself in defense of ideas and customs which had little or no meaning to the practical Roman mind.

Very little information has come down to us respecting the internal organization of the Jewish communities of the Dispersion. At Antioch there was an archon of the Jews, and at Alexandria the head of the Jewish population was called an ethnarch. It is probable that the Jews possessed the right of nominating the ethnarch, but his nomination would require to be confirmed by the imperial authorities. The duties of this official were both administrative and judicial, and within his own jurisdiction he had many of the prerogatives of an independent prince. After a time Augustus apparently replaced the ethnarch by a council of elders; this council was not appointed by the Jews, but by the emperor himself, and it very probably acquired most of the powers that were formerly vested in the ethnarch. Whether this council, like the Sanhedrin of Jerusalem, was composed of seventy members is unknown. The only trustworthy reference to its numbers is contained in the statement of Philo that thirty-eight elders of the council were scourged when. Flaccus was viceroy of Egypt. At Rome the Jewish community was organized on a different principle from the Alexandrian. It had neither a supreme council nor an ethnarch. It was split up into as many divisions as there were synagogues, and each synagogue was an independent unit managing its own affairs and appointing its own officers. The interests of the synagogue were looked after by a council; at the head of this council was a president; the president was assisted in his duties by a committee of the council called archons, and the members of this committee had to be re-elected once a year. It does not appear that any of these officers were recognized by the State, or possessed any authority other than that which was willingly conceded to them by the Jewish community.

Among the Jews of the Dispersion the visible bond and centre of unity for all classes and sections of the community was the synagogue. The habit which this people had acquired during the Babylonian captivity of meeting together at regular intervals to hear the words of the Law and the exhortations of the prophets was a habit which they ever afterwards retained. Into whatever quarter of the world a little band of Jews might be tempted to wander, it became their invariable custom to meet together on the Sabbath day for purposes of religious instruction and edification. Sometimes when the number of settlers was too small, or the colony was too poor, they would assemble in each other's houses, but as soon as sufficient funds had been collected it was the practice to erect a synagogue. In this way it came to pass that synagogues were to be found in almost every place of any consequence throughout the Roman Empire. Athens, Corinth, Ephesus, Thessalonica, Caesarea, Antioch, all contained synagogues, and there were many synagogues in such cities as Alexandria, Damascus, and Rome. In Rome, and very likely in other places where synagogues were numerous, it was usual for each synagogue to have a distinctive name, and just as Christian churches are known by the name of some patron saint so were many Jewish synagogues in Rome at least known by the name of some distinguished patron or protector of the race.

In what language was the religious service of the synagogue conducted among the Jews of the Roman Empire outside Palestine? On this matter it is impossible to speak with certainty. It may have been that the lessons from the Old Testament and the liturgical portion of the service were first read in Hebrew, and then for the edification of the hearers translated into Greek. Or it may have been and this supposition is more probable that only one or two Hebrew prayers were used, and that all the other parts of the service were performed in Greek. In any case, it is certain that the Greek translation of the Bible was made use of in the synagogues; this is expressly stated by several of the early Christian apologists. This translation was also better known to the Jews of the Dispersion than the original Hebrew; otherwise it is hardly likely St. Paul would have quoted from it in writing to Christian converts, many of whom must at one time have been Jews.

Just as the synagogue was a local centre for a particular community, so was the Temple at Jerusalem a general centre for the whole Jewish race. Here pilgrims coming from all parts of the civilized world were accustomed to meet each other. Philo says they came by tens of thousands by land and sea from the north and from the south, from the east and from the west, and Josephus, in exaggerated language, reckons these pilgrims by the million. Some of them came on behalf of the community among which they lived to pay the temple tribute; others came to witness the solemn sacrifices on the altar, and as an act of devotion to their God. A common meeting-place, such as Jerusalem then was for Jews from all quarters of the world, had unquestionably a unifying effect upon the race, and when each band of pilgrims returned to their home among the Gentiles they would carry back with them a more ardent enthusiasm for their people and their faith.

Samaritan Inscription

The warm affection entertained by the Jews outside the Holy Land for the beliefs and customs of their fathers, did not enable them to escape the powerful influence of Gentile ideas. Surrounded in the cities where they had settled by a heathen population, mixing in some places in the affairs of public life speaking the language of Greece, and educated in its literature and philosophy, the Jews in the Roman Empire would have been more than human if they had not fallen into Gentile ways of thought. Even the Jews of Palestine, with the advantage of comparative isolation from the great world, could not entirely shut out Western influences; it is not surprising therefore that their co-religionists among the Gentiles were, to a great extent, submerged in them. Among the Hellenic Jews, historians, poets, and philosophers arose, whose minds had been formed by the great masterpieces of Greece, and who followed the footsteps of Greek writers, both in their style and modes of thought. These Hellenized Jews pursued a twofold object; they aimed, on the one hand, at so modifying Judaism as to make it more attractive to the Gentiles, while, on the other hand, they presented Gentile beliefs in such a guise to the Jewish mind that they assumed a remarkable affinity with many cherished doctrines of Judaism. The outcome of this harmonizing process was a strange compound which was neither Gentilism nor Judaism; but it served to testify .to the fact that men were then groping for some higher form of faith which would combine the elements of truth contained in both.

These attempts at effecting a fusion between Jewish and Hellenic ideas had begun at least two centuries before the Christian era, and reached their climax in the reign of the early Roman emperors. The fundamental assumption on which the Jews proceeded was that the heathen had derived all their wisdom from the ancient Hebrew records, that all the learning and philosophy of Greece were contained in the Pentateuch and the prophets, and that the pagan divinities were only Jewish patriarchs disguised under foreign names. Accordingly the legend of Hercules was identified with the story of Abraham. Moses was the same person as Musaeus, the teacher of Orpheus; he was worshipped by the Egyptians under the name of Thoth, and by the Greeks under the name of Mercury. He was the founder of Egyptian religion and civilization; to him philosophy owed its origin; and the discovery of hieroglyphics, as well as the invention of shipbuilding, was the product of his genius. Hercules and the sons of Abraham went on expeditions together, and Abraham himself was a descendant of the giants who built the tower of Babel. The Mosaic Law only required to be philosophically interpreted, said the Hellenic Jews, in order to show that it contained every important truth enunciated by the great thinkers of Greece.

The man who brought this process of assimilation to the highest pitch was Philo of Alexandria. Many others had preceded him in the task, but their labours have for the most part come down to us in fragments, and he may be taken as the typical representative of a very prevalent condition of mind among the Hellenic Jews in the early days of the Roman Empire. Little is known of Philo's personal history. He speaks of himself as being an old man at the time he went on an embassy to the Emperor Caligula, in the year 39 A.D. It is, therefore, likely that he was born some few years before the Christian era. He was a native of Alexandria, and was descended from one of the most eminent Jewish families of the city. His education must have been watched over with the greatest care, for he had imbibed all the highest learning of the age. Philosophy was his greatest study. "The encyclical sciences," he says, "attracted me like beautiful slave girls, but I turned from them to the queen—Philosophy." Public life had no charms for him, and he complains when he is forced into the vortex of worldly and political cares. He had the reputation of being a man of lofty and unblemished character, and he passed through life with a noble disregard for its wealth, honours, and ambitions. The same high sentiments animated his wife; when she was once spoken to about the simplicity of her attire, she answered that a husband's virtue was sufficient ornament for a wife.

The manner in which Philo addressed himself to the task of reconciling Judaism and Greek thought consisted in giving an allegorical interpretation to the Mosaic Law. He was not the originator of this method of interpretation; traces of it are to be found in the Old Testament itself; it was practiced by the Greeks; and it had been used by the Jews of Palestine and the Dispersion, long before Philo's time. But no one before Philo had adopted this method on such an extensive scale. According to Philo, the allegorical interpretation of Scripture was justifiable, on the ground that many of the sacred narratives will not bear to be taken literally. He considers it, for instance, absurd that God literally required six days to create the world, or that he literally assumed a material shape when communicating His will to the ancient patriarchs. The form in which these narratives were clothed he regards as a concession to human weakness; the form is only the external husk of Divine truths which lie concealed within. It is the task of the wise man to break open this husk, and to show the world what depths of heavenly wisdom lie unfolded in the simplest statements of Holy Writ. The effect of this process was to deprive the old Hebrew records of their plain original meaning, and to import into them the conceptions of a later age. With Philo, the four rivers which flowed out of the Garden of Eden, become the four cardinal virtues. The personages in the Book of Genesis lose their individuality, and are transformed into mere types of character. Noah is a type of righteousness, Abraham is a symbol of acquired virtue, and Isaac of innate virtue. Adam is a type of pure reason, Eve of sensual perception, and Enoch of repentance. The names of countries assumed a new and profound significance in Philo's hands; Egypt, for example, meant spiritless life; and Chaldea, false knowledge. In the story of Jacob's journey to Padanaram, it is recorded that he lay down to sleep at a certain place because the sun was set. According to Philo, the sun is reason, the place is God, and Jacob is wisdom acquired by discipline; the meaning of the passage being that man first attains Divine knowledge when the sun of human reason has set. The precepts of the Law were allegorized in the same manner. The Law forbids the use of camel's flesh for food, because although this animal chews the cud, it has no divided hoof. To chew the cud, according to Philo, is the symbol of memory; but the disciple of wisdom should not rely on memory unless it is accompanied by the divided hoof, which is a type of the difference between good and evil.

These are only a few practical illustrations of Philo's system of interpretation, but they are sufficient to exhibit the manner in which he went to work. Some of his explanations of the sacred text contain lofty and elevated ideas, and he frequently reaches heights of which the rabbis of Palestine had never dreamed. But neither the acuteness nor sublimity of his interpretations can conceal the fact that they are entirely foreign to the original meaning of the text, and can only be attached to it by a fanciful and elaborate juggling with words. Philo, it is hardly necessary to say, was not conscious that this was the case, he was acting in perfect good faith, and in his wildest flights truly believed that he was merely revealing the deeper significance of the Scripture records. Philo considered himself as a champion of the ancient faith of his people, but the symbolical processes in which he delighted was an infallible sign that its primitive simplicity no longer satisfied him. To place the symbolical meaning of circumcision above the positive injunction to perform the rite was certain finally to cause it to be dispensed with altogether. It was inevitable that people should ultimately cease to pay any heed to the positive commandments of the Mosaic Law, such as keeping the Sabbath, and abstaining from certain kinds of food when they were being constantly told that the highest value of these commandments did not consist in their outward observance, but in their symbolical meaning. The effects of Philo's teaching was in all probability made manifest in one of his own nephews, Tiberius Alexander, who was for a short time the Roman procurator of Judaea, and had abandoned Judaism. In fact, Philo's compromise with Greek ideas was too forced and unnatural a product to afford permanent satisfaction to the ordinary human being. It was popular for a time; it exercised an undoubted influence on large numbers of the Jewish people, but towards the close of the first century its power over Judaism came to an end. Most of the Jews who felt the attractions of Greek modes of thought, were drawn into the early Church, and it was henceforth on Christianity that the writings of Philo exercised their power. And it is a remarkable circumstance that, whilst his ideas were acquiring a commanding position in the Church, his followers were being denounced as heretics in the synagogue.

The rabbis had good reason for distrusting Philo's learned speculations. It has been well said that probably no Jewish writer has done so much as Philo to impair the exclusiveness of Judaism and to break it up. "While literally believing the history of his people, he mainly treated it as a didactic and allegorical poem, intended to inculcate the doctrine that it is by mortification of the senses man acquires an insight into God. For this purpose he regarded the laws of Moses as the best guide; but as it was indisputably possible to attain the end in view without those laws, they lost their absolute value, and had besides their object outside themselves. Philo's God was no longer the old living God of Israel, but an unsubstantial abstraction of the mind, and required a Logos to become a force in the world. Israel was thus bereft of its Palladium, the unity of God." I

Notwithstanding the fatal concessions of Philo and the allegorical school, the Jews continued to be looked upon with contempt by the educated world of Greece and Rome. The claim of the race to an honourable and remote antiquity was treated with ridicule. Instead of being the teachers of Plato and the Greek philosophers, they were nothing but descendants of the dregs of the Egyptian populace. Moses was merely an Egyptian priest attached to the temple of Heliopolis, and when he led his people into Palestine they were simply a despicable rabble, consisting of the blind, the lame, and the leprous. All the fine reasons adduced by such men as Philo for keeping the Sabbath as a day of rest were brushed aside; it was asserted that this day was observed out of a spirit of indolence, and that its origin was to be traced to a sore disease the Jews had contracted in the Wilderness. It was preposterous for the Jews to assert that the gifts of civilization had been made the common property of the world through their instrumentality; what, it was asked, had they done for art, literature, or science? Some even hinted that the Jews offered human sacrifice and worshipped the head of an ass. But the most serious charges against them were accusations of atheism and exclusiveness. All the deities of Greece and Rome were represented in the temples in a plastic form, and it was inconceivable to these two peoples that the Jews should have no visible representation of their object of worship. Matters were made worse by the hostile attitude of the Jews towards the heathen divinities. Heathendom was perfectly prepared to recognize the Jewish God, and to assign him a place in its pantheon, why then, it was said, should not the Jews be equally willing to respect the gods of heathendom? The gods of Rome had proved themselves more powerful in battle than the God of Israel, as was manifest from the Roman conquest of Palestine.

Accordingly, the persistent hatred of the Jews for other gods, coupled with the fact that they had no visible divinity of their own, led many of the ancients to conclude that this people must be atheists. The accusation of exclusiveness had a better foundation than the charge of atheism, and was based upon a nobler sentiment. Rome in her triumphant career of conquest had broken down the barriers of nationality, and the free intercourse of races which ensued had given an accelerated impulse to the growing idea that all men ought to meet together in a fraternal spirit on the wide platform of their common manhood. The Jew repudiated these ideas of human brotherhood. He prided himself upon being a member of a chosen people; he lived within the charmed circle of Divine grace; the heathen were outside of it; they had no share in the inheritance of Abraham's children, and should be shunned as unclean. At a former period of their history this exclusive spirit was justifiable on the part of the Jews, for it was by means of it that they were able to preserve intact the precious heritage of their religious beliefs; but under the Roman Empire the necessity for this attitude of exclusiveness had departed, and it became, as the educated heathen truly observed, a hateful and anti-human feature in the life of the race.

Some of these attacks upon the Jews were openly met by such writers as Philo and Josephus, but tactics of a more covert description were also resorted to. In the first century of the Christian era and the one immediately preceding it, it was a very common device for men who wished to obtain a hearing or to further the interests of a cause, to hide the authorship of their productions and put forward their ideas under the cloak of some distinguished name. Books were put into circulation bearing the names of mythical personages or of people who had never written a line, and their contents were read as proceeding from the persons whose names they bore. The literary productions of yesterday were passed off as writings of the greatest antiquity; verses were forged in the names of Homer, or the Greek tragedians, which were not poetry at all, and some of the most famous philosophers had writings fathered upon them, the contents of which were in direct antagonism to all their genuine works. The immense value of these artifices was quickly appreciated by the Jews. It was difficult for them to gain a hearing in their own name, and so they adopted the expedient of defending themselves and propagating their faith under cover of the illustrious personages of antiquity.

Heathen kings were made to take a profound interest in the Jewish Scriptures; heathen poets were made to bear witness to the sublimity of the Jewish faith, and heathen oracles were made to predict a mighty destiny for the Jewish race.

One of these pious frauds is an account of the translation of the Mosaic Law into Greek. In order to magnify the value of this translation in the eyes of the heathen world a certain unknown Jew, long after the event, concocted a wonderful story of the almost miraculous manner in which the Greek version of this part of the Old Testament came into existence. He clothed his tale in the form of a letter purporting to have been written about the middle of the third century before our era by Aristeas, a high official in the service of Ptolemy Philadelphus the second, king of Egypt. In this fictitious letter Aristeas tells his brother Philocrates how Ptolemy was informed by his librarian that he had no copy of the Jewish Law in his great library at Alexandria. Being apprised of its Divine origin and philosophic importance, the king was most desirous to have a translation of the sacred record. With this end in view he sent two ambassadors, one of whom was Aristeas, to Jerusalem. On his arrival in the Holy City Aristeas, in the name of the king, presented Eleazar the high priest with many valuable gifts, and asked him to send a certain number of skilled interpreters to Egypt to translate the Law. Eleazar complied with the request, and seventy-two scribes were selected, six from each of the twelve tribes of Israel. While at Jerusalem Aristeas came to know the true nature of the Jewish Law. The high priest showed him how it was based upon the principles of justice and moderation; he pointed out its reasonableness, its sanctity, its profound symbolic meaning, and how full of wisdom were its precepts on the folly and wickedness of idolatry. When the interpreters arrived in Egypt they were received with marked distinction by the king. For seven successive days he feasted them at the royal table, and ordered his servants to put before them such meats as the Law allowed. The wisdom of these interpreters on all the deepest problems of life on morals, politics, and philosophy filled the king and his councilors with admiration. The seventy-two scribes finished the translation in seventy-two days. The king was charmed with the treasures of wisdom it contained, and requested his librarian to tell him how it came to pass that the poets and philosophers of Greece made no reference to this wonderful book. The librarian informed him that it was too sacred to be handled lightly, and that the Divine vengeance descended upon all who put it to unworthy uses.

This legend, with its long panegyric on the Mosaic Law, fulfilled its purpose most successfully. It was accepted as the genuine testimony of a heathen statesman, a heathen librarian, and a heathen king, and as such it must have exercised a certain amount of influence on the ancient world. Other utterances of a similar nature were equally fortunate. The name of Orpheus was dragged into the service of the Jews; at the close of his career he is made to renounce all his previous beliefs concerning the heathen deities, and to teach his son that there is only one true God. "Oh, my son, I will show thee where I see his footsteps, and the powerful hand of the mighty God. But himself I cannot see. For wrapped around him is a cloud which hides him from me. . . . Of mortals gifted with speech none has seen God except one—a descendant of the Chaldean race." In like manner the Greek poets Hesiod and Homer are made to sing of the Jewish Sabbath; Aeschylus proclaims the majesty of God, and Euripides His omniscience. Under the name of Sophocles the following verses were spread about among the heathen by Jewish propagandists:

> "One in very truth, God is one,
> Who made the heaven and the far-stretching earth,
> The deep's blue billow, and the might of winds.
> But of us mortals, many erring far
> In heart, as solace for our woes have raised
> Images of Gods,—of stone or else of brass,
> Or figures wrought of gold or ivory;
> And sacrifices and vain festivals
> To these appointing, deem ourselves devout."

But the most important fictitious compositions produced by the Jews outside Palestine was a large collection of Sibylline Oracles. The Sibyl, according to ancient belief, was a priestess of Apollo. She dwelt in caves and by the waters, and her functions among the Romans consisted not so much in revealing the future as in bestowing help and counsel upon mankind in times of unusual calamity. Asia Minor was the original home of the Sibyl. Her votaries sought her in solitude; she moved about from place to place, and this circumstance ultimately gave rise to the belief that there were several Sibyls gifted with oracular powers. One of the causes which led to the great popularity of the Sibylline utterances was the destruction of a number of these oracles in the Capitol at Rome. This took place in the first century before the Christian era (B.C. 83); the Senate sent a commission to Asia Minor in order to find documents to replace them, and from that time forward the Sibylline Oracles acquired an immense power over the popular mind. The private manner in which the Sibyl communicated counsel and warning to men rendered her an admirable instrument in the hands of Jewish propagandists. By them she was transformed from a heathen priestess into a prophetess of the God of Israel. She is made to reveal the past and the future, as it had been told to her by God, and she warns men who now call her false and mad that they will do so no longer when they see her great predictions come to pass. She solemnly exhorts all mortals to abandon idolatry and reverence the one true God. He is eternal and invisible, but He dwells within all men as a common light. Those who persist in bowing down before the demons of Hades, for such are the deities of heathendom, and neglect the infinite and omnipotent Creator of all things shall one day meet with a bitter reward. These makers of idols, these worshippers of birds and beasts and creeping things, shall finally be cast to the flames, and shall day by day be consumed in an eternal fire. But the serv-

180

ants of the true God shall taste the bread of heaven and dwell forever in the green fields of Paradise. At first, says the Sibyl, all men worshipped the one true God; it was only after the building of the Tower of Babel that they fell away into heathenism. These false gods are no gods at all; they are merely the departed spirits of ancient heroes and kings. The rule of the worshippers of these gods has been long and painful, but it is destined to come to an end. Even Rome, the greatest and most powerful of heathen principalities, shall fall. Her dissolution is approaching; terrible calamities will precede her final doom; but after that period of woe is over the Jews, the people of the great God, shall assume the supremacy and lead the nations into the way of life. Happy shall be the man or woman who lives in such a time. Righteous laws shall descend from heaven, and concord, love, and friendship shall fill the human family with delight. The age-long miseries of humanity shall at last disappear, and division and envy and hate and folly will be seen no more. The curse of poverty will be removed, and neither theft nor murder will disturb this blessed era of compassion and peace.

The solemn and consolatory utterances of the Sibyl fell upon fruitful soil. No doubt some of the educated classes could detect a Jewish accent in the words of the heathen oracle, and divine the proselytizing purpose that inspired them. But the masses of the people were not critical, and the promise of a golden age from whatever quarter it came, and under whatever conditions, was sufficient to attract many a baffled and distracted heart. The old divinities of Greece and Rome no longer satisfied the higher religious aspirations of the community, and belief in them was at the same time being shattered by the poets, dramatists, and philosophers of antiquity.

Ancient thought was developing a more and more pronounced monotheistic tendency, and the ethical teaching of the age was in direct antagonism to the immoralities ascribed to many of the gods. In fact, religion in the Roman Empire had fallen into a condition of chaos, and it is not surprising to learn that in the first century of our era, and some time before it, the peoples of the West were looking to the East for light. Many of these Oriental forms of faith had a certain elevation of character in the midst of much extravagance, and offered some sort of satisfaction to the head, the imagination, and the conscience of mankind. Most of them contained monotheistic elements, and the deities of which their pantheon consisted were in many instances reduced to the position of mere attributes of one supreme divinity. The conspicuous position assigned in these religions to priests and women was attractive by its novelty, and the mysterious symbolism frequently involved in the exercise of worship was well calculated to stimulate and gratify the pious imagination. Ascetic natures were appealed to by the practices of fasting, penance, and mortification of the flesh. Habits of chastity were inculcated, and attempts were even made to appease the burdened conscience and to connect religion more intimately with the virtues of life.

Of all the Oriental religions claiming the attention of the West, Judaism in its Hellenic form was the most ethical and profound. As presented to seekers after light in such writings as the "Sibylline Oracles," it was either divested of several of its more repugnant peculiarities, or these ordinances were not made imperative. The merchant Ananias who converted Izates, king of Adiabene, told him that God could be honoured without submitting to the rite of circumcision, and Ananias may be taken as expressing the general spirit of Hellenic Judaism. While the Hellenic Jew obeyed all the injunctions of the Law himself, he did not insist upon them as imperative in the case of heathen converts. In fact, he purposely placed many of them in the background, and in propagating his faith relied chiefly on enunciating the cardinal doctrine of a God of justice and judgment who upheld the moral order of the world, and who would in due time usher in a blessed earthly future for mankind.

Facade of A Christian Church in The Valley of Jehosaphat

The simplicity and directness of these ideas, as well as their intrinsic value, made them a religious force of immense importance in the Roman Empire. People did not stop to scrutinize the fictitious forms in which Judaism was frequently clothed; its substance was to them a consolation and a stay, and with this they were content. Among multitudes of Greeks and Romans contempt for the Jew was superseded by veneration for his faith. The barriers which Jew and Gentile had erected against each other were broken down, and it was no uncommon thing for a Gentile to become a student of the Law, an observer of the Sabbath, a contributor to the Temple tax, and an humble participator in the services of the synagogue. Of course there were cases in which the eclectic spirit of the times led people to adopt Jewish practices who did not adhere to the fundamental beliefs of Judaism; and there were also cases in which Judaism was adopted as a consequence of matrimonial arrangements, or from a desire to escape the burden of military service, or from some other purely external reason. But in the majority of instances Judaism would be accepted for itself alone, and as a result of what it had to offer to the conscience and the heart.

It must, however, be acknowledged that one great stumbling-block stood in its way, namely, the practice of circumcision. It was impossible to overcome the justifiable repugnance of the Greek and Roman world to this barbarous rite. To secure complete incorporation into the community of Israel circumcision, baptism, and, as long as the Temple stood, the offering of sacrifice, were indispensable on the believer's part. It was only after this form of initiation had been submitted to that the convert became what was called a proselyte, and possessed in the eyes of the

Gateway of Small Synagogue

Jew all the essential privileges appertaining to the descendants of Abraham. We may safely infer from the invincible antipathy excited by circumcision that the number of proselytes was comparatively few, and that the great majority of adherents to Judaism belonged to the class of what was known as "devout and God-fearing men."

This class was undoubtedly a large one. Of this fact there is abundant evidence from many quarters. "For a long time back," says Josephus, "great zeal for our religion has laid hold upon multitudes; nor is there any city of the Greeks, or indeed any city at all, even though barbarian, where the observance of the seventh day on which we rest from toil has not made its way, and where the fasts and lamp-lightings, and many of our prohibitions as to food are not observed."

The Roman philosopher Seneca confirms the words of the Jewish historian, and says that Jewish customs were adopted everywhere, adding bitterly that the conquered had given laws to the conquerors. It was among these Gentile adherents of Judaism that Christianity obtained its greatest triumphs. Christian missionaries addressed them in the synagogues. St. Paul preached to them at Antioch, in Pisidia, at Thessalonica, at Athens, and elsewhere; he induced many of them to embrace the Christian faith, and the task must have been a comparatively easy one. The proselyte cannot have felt altogether at home in Judaism. After submitting to every ordinance of the Law he still knew that he was not regarded as standing on a footing of equality with the born Jew. He was not of the seed of Abraham; no ceremonial initiation could bridge over that difficulty, or obviate the permanent disadvantages which it entailed. According to the Jewish system proselytes, as not being members of the chosen race, were condemned to a position of religious inferiority, a position out of which they could not possibly emerge.

It is true that the Hellenic Jews laudably attempted to thrust these facts into the background, but they were too deeply rooted in the vitals of Judaism to admit of being altogether suppressed. Such being the case, the proselyte must frequently have felt that his status was defective and unsatisfactory. It inclined him to listen eagerly to teachers who, retaining what was best in Judaism, added the important announcement that the Christian faith admitted of no distinction between the heathen and the Jew; that it was based upon the principle of equality among the nations; that it was human and not racial, and that every man who embraced it stood upon exactly the same footing, enjoying exactly the same rights and privileges, but no more. Such a doctrine satisfied the deepest needs of the Gentile adherents of Judaism, and soon succeeded in sweeping most of them into the Christian fold.